A

MAN'S GUIDE

TO A

CIVILIZED

DIVORCE

A

MAN'S GUIDE

TO A

CIVILIZED

DIVORCE

**How to Divorce with Grace,
a Little Class,
and a Lot of Common Sense**

SAM MARGULIES, Ph.D., J.D.

RODALE

© 2004 by Sam Margulies, Ph.D., J.D.
Cartoons © by *The New Yorker* Collection from cartoonbank.com. All Rights Reserved.

Printed in the United States of America

Rodale Inc. makes every effort to use acid-free ∞, recycled paper ♻.

Book design by Susan P. Eugster

Library of Congress Cataloging-in-Publication Data

Margulies, Sam.
A man's guide to a civilized divorce : how to divorce with grace, a little class, and a lot of common sense / Sam Margulies.
        p.   cm.
Includes index.
ISBN 1–57954–799–0 hardcover
1. Divorce—United States.   2. Divorced men—United States.
3. Divorce mediation—United States.   I. Title.
HQ834.M284   2004
306.89—dc22   2003025506

Distributed to the book trade by St. Martin's Press

2   4   6   8   10   9   7   5   3   1   hardcover

RODALE
WE **INSPIRE** AND **ENABLE** PEOPLE TO IMPROVE
THEIR LIVES AND THE WORLD AROUND THEM

FOR MORE OF OUR PRODUCTS
WWW.RODALESTORE.COM
(800) 848-4735

Contents

DEDICATION vii

INTRODUCTION ix

ONE: THE DECISION TO DIVORCE 1

TWO: GOOD DIVORCE, BAD DIVORCE 15

THREE: MANAGING THE BEGINNING OF THE DIVORCE 41

FOUR: PROPOSING THE COLLABORATION 67

FIVE: AN OVERVIEW OF DIVORCE LAW 81

SIX: HOW TO GET DIVORCED WITHOUT A LEGAL MESS 105

SEVEN: MEDIATION 131

EIGHT: NEGOTIATING WITH YOUR WIFE 153

NINE: SHOULD I MOVE OUT? 177

TEN: FATHERS AND CHILDREN 199

ELEVEN: BUDGETS AS PLANNING TOOLS
FOR SUPPORT DISCUSSIONS 225

TWELVE: NEGOTIATING SUPPORT 249

THIRTEEN: DIVIDING THE PROPERTY 275

FOURTEEN: NEW RELATIONSHIPS AND DIVORCE 305

INDEX 319

To Julie and Sasha

B. Smaller

"We are so in synch. I was just about to ask <u>you</u> for a divorce."

Introduction

ALTHOUGH DIVORCE CAN BE PAINFUL for both men and women, men often have very different experiences than women and have different problems to solve. My focus is men who have been married awhile and who have children. (For the 28-year-old man who is divorcing after 3 years of marriage with no children, divorce is a disappointment, but not very different from breaking up with a girlfriend of 3 years. The limited property gets divided and they go separate ways to start anew.)

Men often lack a model for getting divorced without a useless war. Most divorce books for men are written by divorce lawyers and contain advice on "how to screw your wife one last time." They feed the worst impulses of divorcing men and help turn the divorce into a battle. The American fascination for the adversarial court system leaves most divorcing people vulnerable to many destructive myths. Most people still believe that most divorces are resolved in courtroom fights and that the way to get divorced is to find the toughest, meanest, most aggressive, sneakiest, and loudest lawyer you can find to beat up the lawyer hired by your mate. Many people still believe that divorce is a war to be won or lost—an image that has particular resonance for men, who are still encouraged to stand up and fight for their rights. That means most people are wrong. Very few divorces ever go to trial, and almost all divorces are resolved with a negotiated settlement. But the manner in which settlement is pursued shapes the rest of your life. When you give in to the impulse to fight, you end up with a great deal of collateral damage. So if ever there was a time to choose self-control and peaceful negotiation, this is the time.

For fathers who have been married more than a few years, the divorce experience may be very different from that of their wives. The first significant difference—and one that may come as a surprise—is that only one-fourth to one-third of divorces are initiated by men. We will explore the reasons for this in subsequent chapters. Second, even though more men get custody of their children than did so 20 years ago, only about 10 percent of men are the primary residential parent, even today. The mother retains not only custody but also, at least for a time, the marital home. It is usually the man who is expected to move out and establish a new household and pay child support and alimony in amounts that can reach one-half his earnings.

Divorce is ultimately about change—in parenting patterns, in residences, and in economic and emotional security. And it is more often the man upon whom most of the change, particularly in the early stages of the divorce, devolves. When all this change is combined with a deep sense of rejection, the total experience can be quite traumatic. It is the mission of this book to give men a guide for negotiating these transitions successfully.

My goal is to help men make wise choices early in the divorce so that the reorganization of their families is done well and with a minimum of angry struggle. Is it better to fight a divorce battle or to seek a constructive and gentle transition for all members of the family? To fully understand that choice and the currents that tend to push men toward destructive fighting, we must look at some of the social trends that are redefining what it is to be a man and what is expected from husbands and fathers.

Traditional expectations of men are clearly under assault, and what used to be accepted as reasonable male behavior is now in question both at home and in the workplace. But that does not mean that there is any clarity. To the contrary, men are expected to be aggressive yet gentle, to be good providers but also be nurturing at home, and to be manly but temper it with visible displays of emotional sensitivity. For many men it can seem more than confusing.

In large measure, the place where new expectations are felt most acutely is in marriage. The holy grail of marriage, at least for women, has become intimacy, in which husband and wife share feelings, become vulnerable, and obtain access to each others' thoughts, all as part of a pursuit of more emotional closeness. The presumed outcome of all this is continual passion, emotional equality, and hitherto unprecedented connectedness. For someone who was raised on John Wayne movies, the transformation to the new sensitive male has been a bemusing experience. I recall watching my daughter reject several suitors whom I thought were perfectly acceptable candidates because she felt that they were just too traditional in their views of women. Just when I was about to ask if her expectations weren't a bit much, she found the man who met these expectations and married a gentle, sensitive, and quite remarkable man. So clearly the "new man" exists, but I suspect he is in the minority, while most of us have dinosaurian echoes of the "old" man. After mediating thousands of divorces, I have an understanding of the conflicting demands being made on contemporary men.

Where changing expectations of men have played out most dramatically is in divorce. Changing tides in divorce are nothing more than an almost-perfect reflection of changing tides in marriage. And it should come as no surprise that women now initiate the majority of divorces. In fact, I suspect that most of the increase in the divorce rate over the past 50 years reflects the dramatic increase in the number of women leaving their husbands because they are dissatisfied with their marriages. A few continue to leave husbands for traditional reasons of adultery, cruelty, failure to provide, and substance abuse. But most leave their husbands for the simple reason that they are unhappy, and the unhappiness arises because they do not feel fulfilled emotionally. And so men who have done all the things that they thought they were supposed to do to live up to their part of the bargain are getting dumped in record numbers. And just as men have difficulty figuring out how to behave in the new marriage, so do they also have trouble figuring out how to behave in the new divorce.

A useful metaphor for divorce is a difficult passage in a river. There is a beginning, often characterized by lots of rough water. But there is also an end to this section of the river. Navigate well, and almost all divorcing families can come through in pretty good shape. On the other hand, this part of the river is tricky; it has rapids, sudden turns, dangerous rocks, shoals, and treacherous whirlpools. Foolishness, belligerence, and ignorance in running the river can sink your boat or put it on the rocks. In this book, I am the riverboat pilot who is intimately familiar with this stretch of the river. I have been down this stretch with thousands of people, and I know where the hazards are located. I will show you how to steer and how to stay in the channel. If you do it with grace, a little class, and a lot of common sense, you will come through the journey unharmed—and so will your children.

A

MAN'S GUIDE

TO A

CIVILIZED

DIVORCE

"Your father loves me very much, in his own way, and I love your father very much, in my own way, and that's why we're getting a divorce."

One

THE DECISION TO DIVORCE

THE DECISION TO DIVORCE is one of the most difficult determinations a person makes in life. People often spend years mulling over the decision and make that move only after long and agonizing reflection. Besides being an ending, the decision to divorce is also the beginning of two streams of events. First, filing for divorce triggers legal, emotional, and financial processes in which couples must decide, or have decided for them, how they will convert one household into two. It requires decisions about how children will be parented, how each person in the family will be supported, and how marital property will be divided between the spouses.

The second stream of events is the building of new lives. New households must be established. New routines and protocols must be negotiated and developed. New relationships and new social lives must be built and nourished. After all, the purpose of getting divorced is to build a new life and have another chance with someone new. People divorce because they are unhappy and wish to be happy. And for about 80 percent of the divorcing population, that means eventual remarriage.

The success people have in rebuilding their lives is closely related to how they go about getting divorced. Those who have bitter divorces have a much harder time rebuilding their lives than those who have peaceful divorces. I am convinced that the anger generated by the divorce process itself is often more intense and lasts longer than the anger that arises from the failure of the marriage. I also am convinced that people can choose how they will get divorced. You can choose to have a good divorce, but you can only do this if you understand what a "good divorce" is and what emotional and behavioral dilemmas must be confronted along the way to this goal. If you understand, then the decision to divorce is only the first of many decisions you will need to make carefully and consciously rather than by reflex and impulse.

This book, then, is built on several premises: (1) a good divorce is possible and highly desirable; (2) for a good divorce to happen, the parties must engage in emotional, legal, and practical behaviors that are difficult, even counterintuitive at times, but that will yield the long-term results they seek; and (3) these behaviors can be learned and acquired through understanding of the psychological and legal dynamics of divorce.

What Is a Good Divorce?

The idea of good divorce may strike some as oxymoronic. After all, do not all divorces involve pain and dislocation? Aren't all the changes and disruptions of divorce bad things for everyone? Don't all divorcing couples hate each other and seek to do each other harm? How can the notion of good divorce make any sense?

I contend that there is such a thing as a good divorce and that it is an attainable goal for almost all divorcing couples. In my experience of mediating more than 3,000 divorces, I have found that at the beginning of a divorce there is a surprising amount of residual goodwill between couples. This can either be supported or eroded by the divorce process. Maintaining and utilizing goodwill will allow you to end up with a good divorce.

What is a good divorce and what is a bad divorce? A good or bad divorce is characterized by what kind of relationship exists after the divorce is final. Good divorces are easily distinguished from bad ones in six basic areas.

1. An emotional divorce occurs. The spouses are no longer tied to one another by intense emotions of either love or hatred. They can rebuild their lives unencumbered by emotional baggage from the divorce.

2. Both rebuild their lives. The spouses have succeeded in creating new lives for themselves. This does not necessarily mean a new marriage, although often that is the case. It means that each person has established new routines, a satisfying social circle, and activities that are not distorted by emotions left over from the divorce.

3. Both think the agreement is fair. In many divorce settlements, each spouse walks away bitter and angry and feeling exploited. Such abiding feelings usually preclude subsequent cooperation. In a good divorce, both people feel that they have been treated fairly and need not devote further energy to seeking vindication.

4. The former spouses are able to cooperate as parents. The couple has established a functional parenting style that includes a satisfactory residential structure and schedule, a workable agreement regarding finances that bear upon the children, and a civil mode of communicating with one another about the children. While no longer married, they still function as parenting partners.

5. Children are comfortable in each household. After a divorce, each parent will establish a household, social circle, and, for most, a new relationship with a significant other. A hallmark of a good divorce is the children's degree of comfort in each household 5 years after the divorce. This means that each parent is supportive of the other parent's new life and that each parent gives the child permission to be comfortable in the other parent's household.

6. The former spouses can resolve disputes themselves or through mediation. The lives of couples do not remain static after a divorce. Changes in employment or finances, new relationships, and other factors create new circumstances not fully anticipated in the divorce settlement. As children grow, their needs change as well. New circumstances often demand changes, usually in the areas of parenting and money. In a good divorce, the couple has built the skills to work through these changes without animosity and with cooperation. If they cannot agree on their own, they go to a mediator they trust to help them. They do not resort to the legal system.

If a good divorce sounds like a contradiction in terms, the way to achieve a good divorce sounds even more paradoxical. It involves overriding reflexes and behaving in a counterintuitive fashion. These reflexes are natural during times of turmoil and hurt—rage, humiliation, sorrow, and the desire to lash out. Men in particular are culturally inclined to fight when their feelings have been hurt. Threats, sarcasm, and belligerence that may seem an appropriate response to hurt will only prove destructive in divorce.

This chapter will introduce you to some of the dynamics of the divorce process—a unique intersection of legal, emotional, and practical issues. You will also understand that the decision to divorce does not arise in a historical or psychological vacuum, and what implications that has for your own divorce.

Why Is This Happening?

To some people, it feels as if everyone is getting divorced. They wonder what is happening in the world to cause this apparent breakdown in the institution of marriage. They also look at their own crumbling marriage and wonder what happened. Typically, people ask "What did I do wrong?" or "How did our marriage fail?" I have found that these questions are best addressed with a little historical perspective.

To begin with, it is not accurate to say that the institution of marriage is breaking down or going out of style. On the contrary, most people, even those who have been divorced, want to be married. Within 2 years of divorce, 80 percent of men have remarried; within 5 years, 75 percent of women have remarried. Although more people are living together and more people are marrying later than they used to, we still have about 2 million new marriages every year in the United States.

But marriage as an institution has changed considerably in the past century. The expectations of husbands and wives have evolved with the times, and the definition of a "happy marriage" has expanded from the strictly pragmatic to include the emotional. Two sets of events were most influential in bringing about this change.

The first set of events includes World War I and World War II. These two wars required the complete industrial mobilization of the economy and brought millions of women off the farms and out of the homes and into the factories. As women became used to being the breadwinners and managing households without the husbands who were off in the military, they became ever more independent and assured that they could make it on their own. Even though domestic roles for women were once again glorified during the Eisenhower era with popular cultural images like Ozzie and Harriet, it was too late to put the genie back in the bottle.

The second impetus to the increasing liberation of women was the advent of reliable birth control. This made sex outside of marriage safe enough to permit both single and married women to engage in their own sexual adventures. The economic independence of women coupled with a newfound sexual freedom has given women the same freedom long held by men: the ability to escape from an unhappy marriage. For centuries men could escape simply by deserting or, if that was inconvenient, they could carry on with a mistress. Because men don't get pregnant, the greatest risk to the man is an unwanted out-of-marriage offspring.

But whereas men could escape, women could not. Women who engaged in extramarital sex could be cut off without support, and the courts generally had no power to order a man to share his property with his wife. Now this has changed as women's roles have changed and evolved in the wake of the feminist movement.

In addition to these sets of events, the final impetus to divorce has been the elaboration of the concept of romantic love in the late twentieth century. As disseminated broadly by movies, television, and popular culture generally, an image—perhaps a fantasy—has grown that it is possible to have a marriage of perpetual passion and mutual happiness. This newer expectation of long-term marital happiness has essentially displaced older, more practical images of marriage that stressed the raising of children and economic constancy as the key objectives. In brief, it is quite new to think that you should leave a marriage just because you are unhappy.

The law of divorce had to change to keep pace with the culture. Most states had divorce laws that were quasi-criminal. Only the victim of very bad behavior could obtain a divorce. If your spouse engaged in infidelity, beat you, deserted you, was incarcerated, or was committed to a mental institution, you could sue for divorce on one of these "fault grounds." The theme was a request to the court to dissolve the marriage because your spouse had so violated the marital covenant that it was unreasonable to expect you to continue to live with such a person. In other words, divorce was based almost exclusively on marital misconduct. Divorce was accompanied by social stigma and rejection and was generally regarded as embarrassing, if not humiliating.

But by the 1970s it was apparent that fault-based divorce no longer matched the realities of people's expectations of marriage. People were leaving marriages not because their spouses were terrible but because they were unhappy. And where divorce statutes did not allow such divorces, people simply lied and perjured themselves to get the divorce. As divorce law grew ever more sleazy, states began to pass no-fault divorce statutes that permitted people to divorce without a finding of marital wrongdoing. And by the 1980s, virtually every state had adopted some form of no-fault divorce statute that permitted a divorce if the couple had lived apart for some defined period of time or if they pleaded that they were simply incompatible and could not live together.

The universal adoption of no-fault divorce did not *cause* people to get divorced. It simply made it easier to do once a married person decided to divorce. It also meant that one spouse could not hold the other in an unhappy marriage by refusing to cooperate. If one partner wants to leave the marriage, there is nothing the other can do to prevent the divorce.

Although some people have willfully screwed up their marriages, the more common case is two people who simply couldn't adapt to the practical demands and strenuous tasks of everyday family life, combined with expectations of deep emotional intimacy. I think that there is little benefit to be had by lengthy deliberations of whether or not you have failed.

Why the Majority of Divorces Are Initiated by Women

I just took a count of the last 50 divorces I have seen recently in my office. Of the 50 divorces, 38 were initiated by the wives, 3 were decided mutually, and 8 were initiated by husbands. Although this is not a scientific random sample, it is consistent with what I have witnessed for years and consistent with what I hear from colleagues. Women initiate the majority of divorces. I strongly suspect that if we were able to analyze the data, we would find that it is women who account for more of the recent increase in the divorce rate than men. Every week I see couples in which the wife says some variation of the following:

"My husband here is a good man and a good father. He has been an upstanding member of the community and a good provider. He has not deserted me, has not abused me, has not been unfaithful, and has been a good friend. But I want a divorce. I have simply fallen out of love and I am not happy in the marriage. My husband just can't communicate with me the way I need. He doesn't understand my need for intimacy and just can't communicate his feelings or respond deeply to mine. Before I'm too old I want another chance to find someone with whom I can connect, someone who can be my soul mate and can understand me the way I need to be understood. I just can't imagine living this way for another 20 years. That's why I want a divorce."

Although it's not just women who have this expectation, it is mostly women. In private conversations, women frequently complain that they just can't get their husbands to spend enough time listening and connecting emotionally. It's an understandable desire and certainly has become a common expectation in contemporary Western society. But whether most men can meet the expectation is not at all certain. It's unimportant here whether men are essentially different in emotional style than women as a matter of culture, genetics, or both. But I know few men who have the same need for intimate and self-revealing conversation as most of the women that I know. For men whose wives are leaving them, this presents many conundrums. "Am I supposed to be different than I am? Is the next woman going to do the same thing to me? I've done all the things I was supposed to do. How is it fair that she is leaving me just because she can't figure out how to be happy?"

Where the Emotional and Legal Processes Collide

One of the things that makes divorce such a unique and often-troubled experience is that it involves a complex interaction between two very different
processes. First, divorce is a difficult emotional process. It causes intense
feelings of sadness, humiliation, abandonment, disappointment, rejection,
and rage. Most of all, divorce engenders fear, particularly fear of loss.
People fear loss of identity as spouses and parents, loss of economic security, loss of control over their lives, and loss of dignity. So the emotional
process of divorce is one in which people have to manage all these feelings
at the same time that they have to reorganize their lives. As with any other
transition, there are stages through which most people pass, beginning with
initial turmoil, followed by struggles with change, and eventually with
adaptation and adjustment.

Interacting with the emotional process of divorce is the legal process of
divorce. Marriage is a legal status created by the state. When we marry, we
make the state of California or New York or whatever the third party to our
relationship. So when we want to end the relationship, we must get the permission of the state. The state, through its court system, must decide that
we have acceptable reasons to divorce—it must find grounds for divorce—
and it must then dissolve the marriage. As a condition of its consent, the
state demands certain reassurances. It wants to know that our children are
supervised and provided for. It wants to know how each spouse will be supported so that neither becomes a ward of the state. And it wants to know
how marital property has been divided so that there are not perpetual
clouds on the title to property. Each state has its own statutes and common
law to govern how these things are decided.

So, if you want to divorce, you must submit to the legal process. At its
simplest, it requires some formal documents to have the court obtain jurisdiction and then some kind of hearing to satisfy the court that you have
complied with the state's requirements and addressed its concerns. At its
most complex, it can require numerous court hearings, discovery procedures, and trials in which judges decide issues of children, money, and
property.

Whether the legal divorce process is simple or complex has a great impact on the emotional process of divorce. Particularly when there are chil-

dren, the manner in which the legal divorce is managed sets the emotional tone for the entire family. Generally, the more contact the couple has with the legal system, the more bitter the divorce. When the divorce is over and the lawyers disappear, the couple is left perpetually furious with each other and unable to agree on issues related to the children. Conversely, the more issues the couple is able to resolve for themselves, and the more that each feels a sense of ownership of the agreement, the easier it is to move on and to cooperate for the benefit of the kids.

In this interaction, cause and effect move in both directions. Decisions made about legal strategy and tactics affect the emotional process of divorce. But the way the partners act on their feelings influences the way the legal process operates. For example, if a husband is angry that his wife has rejected him and he acts out his rage by cutting off her access to money, he leaves her little choice but to seek rescue from the legal system. Because he has now demonstrated that he is not to be trusted, she hires a lawyer who obtains a court order for support, thus taking away the husband's ability to act capriciously—or to become more cooperative voluntarily. Now that the wife has seen that she is better off relying on her lawyer than on her husband's goodwill, she is likely to conduct the entire divorce in a legalistic manner. Had the husband, instead of trying to instill fear, tried to make her feel safe and secure, she probably would have been more inclined to work cooperatively with him to resolve the issues of the divorce.

People bumble their way into bitterly litigated divorces because they fail to understand the consequences of their behavior. When we are frightened, deeply humiliated, or enraged, it is easy to strike out and attempt to inflict pain on the other party. But in the matter of divorce, acting out on one's feelings is what sends lawyers' kids to college.

The critical decision is whether you will act on your immediate feelings or whether you will act in your long-term best interests. To do the latter, you must not become so overwhelmed with emotion that you are unaware that you have a choice, and you must understand your long-term interests. If you can control your emotions and reactions, you may be able to both control the tone of the divorce and to minimize your contact with the legal system.

Themes of This Book

There are four major themes to this book: (1) A good divorce is possible, (2) negotiating a mutually beneficial settlement agreement is the central task of the divorce, (3) there are three phases of divorce, and (4) obtaining a good divorce requires you to act like a grown-up.

A Good Divorce Is Possible

The first theme of this book is that a good divorce is possible when you manage both the way you express your feelings and the way in which you interact with the legal system. (The legal system is a bad fit with the needs of divorcing families, and I will explore this at length in chapters 4 and 5.) It is only by managing your own behavior that you minimize your contact with the legal system and thus maximize your chance of a good divorce.

Managing your behavior requires that you manage your feelings. Despite popular notions that women are emotional and men are not, I believe that men and women both have all the same emotions. Both experience pain, humiliation, anger, and loss. You may be very angry that your wife has given up on the marriage and on you. You may be feeling guilty if you are the one who is leaving her. You may feel betrayed if you think she is with another man. You may fear for your future and the future of your children, and you may be indignant if you think you are being treated unfairly. All of these feelings are normal and not gender-specific. But there do seem to be differences in the way men and women act on their feelings.

In general, women talk about feelings and talk about them and then talk about them some more. Women usually talk to other women about how they feel. Women expect each other to "share" their feelings and intimate thoughts. Indeed, one of the abiding disappointments women have about their husbands is that the men did not turn out to be like girlfriends. Their husbands do not like to talk about their feelings and are less than enthusiastic about listening to their wives express how they are feeling.

For the most part, men talk about their troubles to the extent that talking helps to solve a problem. If I am troubled by something and I cannot solve it right now, not only do I not want to talk about it, but also I find that talking about it just makes me feel worse. Just because I feel something doesn't mean I want to talk about it. I also find that men are better able than women to suppress difficult feelings or to at least compartmentalize them. When I have to get something done, I cannot afford to be distracted by whatever difficult feelings I am wrestling with at the time, so I put the feelings in storage while I get on with the task at hand. There is clearly a lot of cultural influence here. In Western culture, men more than women are expected to manage their feelings without making a lot of noise. Complaining about hurt feelings or about being afraid is, for many, unmanly.

The principal exception to this is the management of anger. Western culture permits men to act out on their anger. The Western hero is slow to anger, but when he finally gets angry in the face of injustice, challenges to his integrity, or humiliation, he also gets ready to fight. To accept public humiliation or disrespect without a fight makes you a wienie. And here is the challenge that divorce poses for the way many men manage their feelings.

The adversarial system is a highly choreographed system of fighting with clear winners and losers. The myths that surround the soap opera of the courtroom portray lawyers as killers, attack wolves, hired guns, and gladiators, all images that conjure up aggression and fighting. Here fighting is acceptable because it leads to "justice" and the vindication of truth. These images are tailor-made for the proclivity of men to manage their anger by fighting. But if you fight in divorce, you end up with a mess. So divorce may require you to manage your feelings in a counterintuitive manner. This is where you do not want to fight. It is a time to meet aggression with gentleness, to duck rather than counterattack, and to talk more than you are inclined. Classic "manly" behavior will have to be modified if you are to get through this without a mess.

A Mutually Beneficial Settlement Is Critical

The second theme of this book is that the negotiation of the settlement agreement is the central task of the divorce. As we shall explore further, a negotiated settlement is the outcome in 99 percent of all divorces. The constructive and peaceful negotiation of the divorce settlement can serve as a blueprint for the rest of your life. Paradoxically, the negotiation of a good settlement agreement between you and your wife is a collaborative process that, like all such processes, requires a measure of trust, civility, and mutual respect. Even though you regard your relationship as irretrievable, you will have to pay attention to relationship issues to negotiate well with her. Chapters 7 and 8 will help you approach negotiation and use a mediator to facilitate the negotiation of your agreement. First you must understand how to manage your feelings through these processes.

The Three Phases of Divorce

The third theme of this book is that there are three phases of a divorce: beginning, middle, and end. The beginning is when you decide to divorce, come to grips with the initial crisis caused by the decision, and then begin to settle down and deal with the implications. The middle of the divorce involves the decision making about how the family will become two households, who will care for and provide housing for the children, and how to manage the economic issues. Finally, there is the end of the divorce. This includes the signing of a separation agreement, obtaining a formal dissolution of the marriage, and beginning new lives. Clearly, how you manage the beginning shapes how you will experience the middle and the end. How you behave during the beginning and middle shapes how well you will be able to build a new life. I will remind you throughout the book that you can consciously choose how this will be done—and you can choose well or poorly.

Divorce for Grown-Ups

The fourth theme is that to have a good divorce will require you to act like a grown-up. I earn a good part of my living mediating divorces. I have observed that the essential distinction between the behavior necessary to succeed at mediation and the behavior that typifies conventional adversarial divorce is precisely the self-discipline that distinguishes between childish and adult conduct.

To have a successful divorce requires you to exercise control over your emotions. It requires that you behave reasonably even when you don't feel reasonable. It requires that you act on your long-term interests rather than your immediate feelings and that you devote sufficient time to determine what your long-term interests are. It also requires that you understand not only your needs but also the needs of each member of your family, and then seek a distribution of resources that is fair to everyone. If you have children, you will, of necessity, have to deal with your soon-to-be ex-wife for many years, and you need to avoid poisoning the relationship between you even if you believe that she is being provocative and unreasonable.

In short, you have to be a grown-up or, if you think that is impossible, fake it convincingly.

AN AMICABLE DIVORCE

Two

GOOD DIVORCE, BAD DIVORCE

IN CHAPTER 1, WE INTRODUCED THE PREMISE that there is such a thing as a good divorce, that it is viable, and what it consists of. This chapter will bring this seemingly alien concept to life by presenting you with two contrasting case histories. By following the stories of Jack and Laura and of Bill and Jane, you will get a clearer picture of the contrast between a bad divorce and a good divorce, with particular focus on the choices each couple made to take them in one direction or the other.

CASE STUDY: Jack and Laura

Jack and Laura have been married for 17 years and have two children, 14-year-old son Ari and 11-year-old daughter Julie. When they married, Laura was a struggling commercial artist and Jack was beginning a career as a banker. Five years ago, Jack was promoted and is now earning $130,000 a year, with an annual bonus that can reach $30,000 in a good year. Laura had taken 10 years off to devote to child rearing. A few years ago, she resumed her career and is now working part-time for an advertising agency that specializes in nonprofit organizations. She earns $15,000 a year. They save very little. Four years ago, they bought a new house; it was a financial stretch, but they both liked the house and they thought it was a good decision.

Although the marriage started out well, affections began to cool between the partners about 2 years after Julie was born. Jack was devoting long hours to his job and Laura was engrossed in the details of suburban motherhood. The frequency of lovemaking declined, and contact between Jack and Laura increasingly focused on mundane details of schedule and housekeeping. Jack was often irritable, and when Laura tried to confront him about his temper, he simply stonewalled her. She became increasingly detached.

Laura was disturbed to discover that she was attracted to a man at work. Afraid that she might end up having an affair, she asked Jack to go into marriage counseling with her. At first he was reluctant, saying that nothing was wrong with the marriage, but she insisted, so he complied. After 6 months, Jack decided that he wasn't getting much from the therapy and quit going. Laura continued in individual psychotherapy.

The marriage continued to limp along until finally, after 2½ years of therapy, Laura decided that the marriage would never heal and told Jack that she wanted a divorce. Jack was incredulous. He acknowledged that the marriage wasn't the best but stated that they had an obligation to work it out for the benefit of the children. Laura insisted that she had had enough of Jack's emotional coldness and distance and was too lonely to continue. She also said that she didn't feel that it was good for the children to see their parents in a loveless marriage and that she was determined to have another chance before she was too old. Jack told her she was acting like a spoiled brat with soap opera expectations of life. They didn't speak for days and the atmosphere in the house went from detached to hostile.

At this point, the evolution of Jack and Laura's divorce is completely typical and unremarkable. This is the way most divorces develop, with one partner becoming disillusioned over time and finally deciding that the continuation of the marriage is impossible. It is also typical that relations in the home become strained and even hostile once the decision to divorce is in the open. Whether the divorce is resolved well or whether it becomes mean and bitter will depend on many decisions the partners make from this point forward.

*As weeks passed in hostile silence, each partner started to realize that
the marriage was truly over and that they would have to start dealing with
the reality of the divorce. Each was upset and fearful about the future, and
each sought solace from friends and relatives. Laura was determined to stay
in the house with the kids and consulted with several friends who had been
divorced. One friend, who had had been through a particularly rough divorce, encouraged Laura to find a tough lawyer to protect herself. The friend
emphasized Jack's superior knowledge of the family finances and warned
Laura that she was in danger of Jack hiding money to deprive her of her fair
share. She said that her husband had tried to do that to her and that only
the fighting attitude of her lawyer had saved the day. She also told Laura
not to cave in to Jack's unreasonable demands that she get a job because a
return to employment now would hurt her chances of alimony in court. She
gave Laura her attorney's phone number and encouraged her to make an
appointment.*

*Laura received similar advice from others she consulted. Her mother told
her she was worried, that she had always thought Jack was not very nice,
and that Laura needed to be careful or she would find herself on the street.*

*At the same time, Jack was getting similar advice from his buddies. "Di-
vorce is war," they told him, and he'd better get ready to "fight" so that
Laura didn't "screw" him out of his kids and the money. He, too, received
several names of lawyers reputed to be ferocious. His friends also warned
him to raid the bank accounts before Laura did and to make sure that Laura
didn't run up outrageous bills on her credit cards. Jack's friend Will told him
a horror story about a friend of his whose wife went on a spending spree
and ran up $30,000 in credit card debt before her husband cancelled the
cards. This really upset Jack, because he and Laura had had disagreements
from time to time about credit card spending.*

*That night when Jack went home, Laura asked to speak with him. She
told him that things were so unpleasant in the house that she thought he
should move out so they all could get some peace. Jack was taken by surprise and offended that Laura just assumed that he would have to leave.
"Why should I have to move? You're the one who wants the divorce—you
move if you don't like it here with me. Besides, money is tight and I don't*

think I'm getting a bonus this year. I don't see how we can afford to keep this house and a second house too. I'll move when we sell the house."

Now Laura became upset. "What makes you think I'm going to sell the house? I have no intention of moving. It's too much disruption for the kids. All the psychologists' books that I have read say you're supposed to maintain continuity for the sake of the children."

"Well," answered Jack, "If you want a separate house, you go get a full-time job so we can afford it." "I'm not going to do that," answered Laura, "This is the time when the kids need the most attention. Maybe I'll get a job when they are a lot older, but certainly not now when they need me." "I'm not leaving!" said Jack, and he stormed off in disgust, leaving Laura steaming.

The next morning Jack commiserated with his friend Will, who suggested that Laura was acting just as he had thought she would. Will encouraged Jack to get tough. Jack called Myron Gold, one of the lawyers to whom his friends had referred him, and made an appointment. He cancelled Laura's credit cards. Then he went to the bank and withdrew most of the money in the joint account and deposited it in an account in his own name. Finally, he sent Laura an e-mail telling her that she was no longer to use the credit cards and that he would pay all necessary bills and give her $400 a week for routine expenses. When Laura read the e-mail, she became enraged. She thought that Jack was trying to intimidate her and decided to show him she wasn't going to be bullied into submission. She made an appointment with attorney Marilynn Edens for that afternoon.

The couple is now in trouble and well on the road to a bad divorce. They have both sought and received advice from well-meaning but woefully ignorant friends. Jack has acted precipitously and foolishly by his unilateral demonstration of financial control. All he has demonstrated to Laura is that she can't trust him to be fair with her and that she needs to be rescued by a "tough" lawyer. And each party has chosen a lawyer because of an aggressive reputation. Neither has asked friends for the name of a fair and reasonable lawyer. Remember the river metaphor at the end of the introduction. Here, the couple has failed to realize that on this journey they are in the same boat. What happens next will be a result of the lawyers' personalities and styles. That adversarial attitude will color the rest of the decisions the couple will continue to make.

Laura thought her interview with Marilynn Edens went well. Edens listened to her story and assured Laura that Jack couldn't get away with his antics. Edens said that Laura would probably get permanent alimony and that she would not have to move from the house. She also advised Laura that she didn't have to get a full-time job and that it was unlikely a court would require her to do so. The attorney said that in her experience, the best way to deal with a bully was to haul him into court and get a judge to order him to pay reasonable support and not to make any unilateral changes in the family finances. Finally, Edens said she would need a retainer of $7,500 to begin representing Laura. She suggested that Laura borrow the money from a family member until Edens could get a court order requiring Jack to pay Laura's legal fees. They made an appointment for the next day when Laura would sign a retainer agreement prepared by the lawyer and would pay the retainer.

The next day, Laura signed the agreement and paid the retainer with money borrowed from her father. Edens said she would start working on an order to show cause to present to the court the next week and would also start drafting a complaint for divorce alleging extreme cruelty on Jack's part. She took a long statement from Laura detailing all the mean things Jack had done. She also said that for what it was worth, she would send Jack a letter demanding that he restore the money to the joint account, reactivate the credit cards, and have his lawyer call her so they could explore possibilities for a settlement.

When Jack showed the letter to his lawyer, Gold frowned and said, "I'm afraid that your wife has chosen a very difficult lawyer." In his experience, Edens was a real "ballbuster" and never settled a case until she first dragged it out. He didn't like Edens and was not bashful about saying so. He advised Jack to prepare for a war of attrition and told him that with someone like Edens, only tough lawyering would work.

Gold told Jack not to put the money back or restore the credit cards unless a judge ordered it. Gold stated that it was best early on with Edens to establish that they were not afraid to go to court. Gold told Jack to stay in the house because leaving Laura in possession of the house would provide no motivation to get the case resolved. Gold did say there was a good chance that the judge would let Laura stay in the house at least until the children graduated from college, but that there were some judges who might order the house sold. Gold said that it was better to see which judge was assigned to the case before they decided how to play that issue.

Jack paid a retainer of $10,000 and signed a retainer agreement. Gold also sent Edens a letter telling her he was representing Jack and that they would not put the money back in the joint account nor reactivate the credit cards. He suggested that Edens send him a proposed budget and that they would be willing to negotiate temporary support.

The next day when Jack was in his office, the sheriff came by and served Jack with the complaint for divorce filed by Laura's lawyer. Jack was embarrassed to have the sheriff show up at his workplace because it set the office's gossip mill into motion. But Jack was even more upset when he read the things that Laura had said about him in the complaint. The complaint was a public document that described Jack as an emotional brute and cruel person. Jack was now determined to stop at nothing to get back at his wife for humiliating him.

Judge Wilkins heard Laura's motion for support and request to freeze all marital assets. After considering the affidavits submitted by each side and hearing the lawyers' arguments, the judge ordered Jack to continue paying the household bills and to pay Laura $500 per week. He also ordered Jack to restore one credit card for Laura's use but limited Laura's ability to use it to $300 per month. The judge ordered the lawyers to complete discovery within 6 months and set a provisional trial date for 9 months away. Both lawyers advised their clients that it would be unlikely to get a trial date for at least 18 months. Because the judge would not order Jack to move out and would not order Laura to get a full-time job, the couple was left with the status quo for at least another year.

Now both partners settled down to a period of limbo, and things in the house grew genuinely poisonous. Family dinners were no longer possible. Jack adopted the attitude that he didn't have to tell Laura when he was coming or going and was totally uncooperative about scheduling time when he would be in charge of the kids so she could go out. If she wanted to go *out, she could hire a babysitter at her own expense, he reasoned. Laura stopped doing Jack's laundry or running errands on his behalf. Neither spoke to the other unless absolutely necessary and then only in a curt tone. If a problem arose with the children, they would discuss it, but Jack would often dismiss Laura's opinion. After 3 months of this, both children started to have problems. Julie became sad and withdrawn. Ari's report card for the first time ever had three Ds.*

Laura took both kids to her therapist, who recommended therapy for both kids. He said that it was not unusual to see depression in children who were living through a tough divorce. Laura decided to put both children in therapy, but when she told Jack, he said that it was out of the question, he didn't believe in therapy, and she was being overprotective. Laura said she was taking them anyway, and Jack said he wouldn't pay for it. So Laura went to see her lawyer, who filed a motion with the court to compel Jack to pay for therapy for the kids. The judge ordered the children evaluated by a court-appointed psychiatrist. The psychiatrist interviewed the children and concluded that both were depressed and needed psychotherapy; she also said that Julie probably needed antidepressant medication. Upon receipt of the evaluation, the judge ordered Jack to pay for the therapy. The fees for the lawyers and the psychiatrist were $4,200 for this round in court.

The couple is now settling into the posture of litigants. They can cooperate about nothing, and conflicts must be resolved by the court. They are acquiring an essentially uncooperative parenting style that will last well after the divorce is over. Their children are depressed and struggling.

By refusing to work together, they have lost the ability to navigate. They cannot avoid the rapids and rocks along the way, and they have made the journey more difficult than it has to be. Worse still, the children are along for the ride.

Jack and Laura continue their tug-of-war. Jack starts dating, but Laura can't because she never knows whether Jack will be in or out. Jack meets a few women, but most are not receptive to a man who is still living with his wife. Both are lonely. The friends they made over the years as a couple now pull away. The couple no longer goes to church together, and neither feels comfortable in the church because everyone knows the couple is going through an unpleasant divorce. Jack would like to move out and Laura is desperate for him to move, but his lawyer continues to counsel against it. Laura is offered a great full-time job and is tempted to take it, but her lawyer tells her she will be forfeiting part of her alimony claim.

After about 9 months of this, a trial date is scheduled and the lawyers and parties hold a meeting to explore settlement. The meeting goes poorly. The two lawyers don't like each other, and their animosity is evident. Edens takes a tough line, insisting that her client get half of Jack's salary as alimony. Gold rejects this as ludicrous and says that no judge would ever give her anything even close to that. Edens demands that her client stay in the house until the youngest child graduates from college. Again Gold tells her that is ridiculous and that he won't have his client living in a two-bit apartment just because Laura refuses to have any change. Laura insists that the kids can't handle more change. Jack tells her she is being selfish. The meeting breaks up without agreement, and the couple goes home still in limbo. By now, Laura has joined the kids in taking antidepressant medication.

Four months later they had another trial date scheduled, but this time the judge said he wanted to have a conference to see what was holding up a settlement. Again the couple went to court with their lawyers, but this time Jack and Laura sat in a waiting room while the lawyers went in to talk with the judge. After about 40 minutes, both lawyers came out to speak privately with their clients. Edens told Laura that the judge was inclined to let her stay in the house with the kids, but only until the younger child graduated from high school. She also said that the judge would grant her only $30,000 alimony a year for 8 years. Laura was bitterly disappointed by that because it meant she would have to work full-time or give up the house. But Edens told her that it really wasn't worth going to trial because they already knew what the judge would order.

Gold had a similar talk with Jack. He explained that the inclination of the judge was clear. The judge would let Laura stay in the house until Julie graduated from high school. This meant that Jack would be unable to get access to his equity in the house for 10 years. Jack would have to move out, and the judge suggested that Jack move within 60 days. Gold also told Jack that the judge was going to award $30,000 in alimony to Laura for 8 years

*and would not order her to get a full-time job. The judge would also order
child support in addition to the alimony. Jack felt that this was calamitous
and asked Gold why they had gone through all this trial preparation if the
case was simply to be resolved in a closed-door conference with the judge.
Gold assured Jack that he was willing to go to trial if Jack wanted. On the
other hand, Gold said that it was his experience with this judge that once
the judge indicated his viewpoint, he was very unlikely to change it in a trial.
It would just cost Jack a lot of legal fees for no gain. Gold urged Jack to accept the terms he had just described because he was unlikely to get a
better result at trial.*

*Both Jack and Laura reluctantly agreed to the proposed settlement, but
neither felt that justice had been done, and each thought that the process
had unfairly favored the other. They went home bitter and furious at each
other.*

The couple has paid lawyers to engage in extensive preparation for a
trial that never takes place. Instead, the lawyers reach a settlement that
neither Jack nor Laura feels is fair. Jack and Laura are resentful and both
feel betrayed, not only by each other but also by their lawyers and by the
legal system as a whole.

E P I L O G U E : 3 years later

*Although Jack has been out of the house for almost 3 years now, relations
between the former spouses have not improved. He and Laura have been
back to court twice in the past 2 years. The first time the couple returned to
court, Jack took Laura to court because he believed she was interfering with
his visitation rights with the children. Both kids, who were supposed to
spend every other weekend with Jack, seldom came. They both complained
that Jack's apartment was too cramped. According to Laura, the children
complained that Jack was grumpy all the time and that they particularly
disliked his new girlfriend who always seemed to be hanging around. The
judge ordered that the children go to Jack's as scheduled, whether they
liked it or not. So now when the children visit Jack they are sullen and uncooperative.*

The second time the couple returned to court, Laura took Jack to court because she said he was often late on his support payments. The judge ordered that Jack's support payments be deposited to Laura's account directly by Jack's employer, much to Jack's embarrassment. Jack is bitter about the divorce and thinks he got the bad end of a bad deal. Laura tried for a long time to get by on the alimony ordered by the judge and what she could earn working part time. But Laura got so far behind on her credit cards that, in desperation, she took a full-time job. Now she has a full-time job as well as almost all the responsibility for the children. She is angry that she gets so little time off from the kids. Recently she asked Jack to switch weekends so she could go on a trip with a friend, and he angrily refused. Neither Jack nor Laura is happy, and both kids are having troubles.

Jack and Laura have had a typical conventional divorce. They both followed the advice of their attorneys, but neither feels that they have much to show for it. There was no trial, and the case was settled after a very unsatisfying day in court. Unfortunately, Jack and Laura never acquired a new way to deal with each other around issues of the children, so they are now unable to cooperate. The resulting problems of the children are not surprising. Laura and Jack never had the opportunity to work out any cooperative financial arrangements, so both feel mistreated and neither feels content. Neither has any investment in the success of the other, and if Jack does marry the new girlfriend, she is almost assured of a tough ride as a stepmother.

Although the divorce is over, Jack and Laura have never crossed the river and are still not on solid ground. The saddest part of this scenario is that it was largely unnecessary. It is also repeated thousands of times a year by divorcing couples.

What Constitutes a Good Divorce

The measure of a divorce is twofold. First, we want to know how it turned out. Is the family adapting well to the divorce? Do both partners feel that the settlement is fair, considering the circumstances? Are both parties rebuilding socially? Do they wish each other well? Are they able to cooperate on matters affecting the children? Do the children have rich and robust relationships with both parents? Are the children continuing to develop normally and reaching appropriate developmental milestones? Are the children comfortable in both homes? Do the children believe that they have the permission of each parent to like the new mate of the other parent? These are the questions we ask when we want to know whether the divorce was successful. Often it will take 5 years to tell because not everyone adapts at the same pace. But ultimately, people get divorced because they want another chance. If they succeed at that, the divorce was successful. If they stay attached by acrimony and bitterness, it was not.

So this raises the second question—how was the divorce conducted? There is a powerful correlation between how the divorce was conducted and how it turns out. The behavior of the spouses during the divorce sets the tone for after the divorce. If the spouses regard each other as having conducted a war or each thinks the other has been unfair, the aftermath of the divorce will likely be bitter. Moreover, each one will hold the other personally responsible for everything said and done by the other's lawyer. Whatever the lawyer did as a legal maneuver or whatever negotiating position the lawyer took during settlement discussions will be interpreted not as a logistical strategy but as an emotional proposition. Thus, when Jack's lawyer argues that Jack should not have to pay for therapy for the kids, Laura understands that to be Jack's proposition that the children do not matter. Even though Gold knew that the judge would probably order Jack to pay for therapy, his use of the argument as a stratagem proves again to Laura that Jack is vicious and insensitive. This, in turn, justifies to her whatever unreasonable claims she might make, as both parties now regard the other as uninterested in fairness.

Contrast Jack and Laura's story to Bill and Jane's.

C A S E S T U D Y : Bill and Jane

Bill and Jane have been married for 20 years. Bill is 47 and Jane is 45. They have three children: Bobby, 17; Maury, 15; and Nancy, 14. Bill is a systems analyst for a defense contractor and earns $110,000 a year. Jane is a teacher by training but stopped teaching when Nancy was born because the needs of three children were too great for her to manage both job and parenting responsibilities. They have gotten by on Bill's salary, but they have not managed to save much.

For the past few years, Jane has felt restless and uneasy in the marriage. It is clear to her that the marriage was subordinated early on to the needs of the children and although she and Bill don't fight much, they don't seem to have much in common anymore, either. Lovemaking has diminished over the years and sex, when it occurs at all, is perfunctory and unsatisfying. As the children became more independent, Jane started thinking of doing something to reestablish her career. She signed up for some courses at a local college. She had long fantasized about becoming a lawyer and took some courses in law and government to see if she liked it. Not only did Jane like the courses, but she also liked the company of other students and looked forward to going out for coffee after class with her classmates.

During her second semester, Jane met a man in her constitutional law class and started to look forward to having coffee with him after class. Craig was a social worker who also was considering a career change to law. He was divorced, but he had no children. Jane found him interesting, funny, and a good listener. By the end of the semester, they were fast friends and had begun to confide the intimate details of their lives. Jane felt a little guilty about her friendship with Craig and never mentioned it to Bill.

Jane began to feel increasingly dissatisfied with her marriage and found herself being short and impatient with Bill. Bill was on the passive side and tolerated Jane's behavior because he thought it was some "woman's" thing that would pass in time. But as Jane became ever more distant, Bill finally confronted her; he was stunned to learn that Jane was so unhappy with him. Although wary of counseling, Bill suggested that the two of them find a marriage counselor and try to fix what was wrong. Jane reluctantly agreed.

They went to therapy for a few weeks. Each repeated what he or she wanted from the other. Jane said that she wanted more attention and romance and wanted Bill to court her more. She wanted Bill to be more expressive and to share more of his feelings with her so that she felt that she had an intimate partner, not just a roommate. Bill just said that he wanted *peace. He wanted Jane to settle down and stop complaining. He said he would try to be more "emotional" but wasn't sure that he could give Jane what she wanted. Not much happened in the counseling because neither really thought that the other had much commitment to the process.*

Finally the counselor began to ask some difficult questions. Did they really want to be married, and were they willing to do the hard work necessary to make a success of the counseling? Jane blurted out that she really wanted a divorce. She did not think she could be happy with Bill and wanted to be free to pursue a new life. She had had many discussions with Craig about this, and he had encouraged her to make the break. Although they had not slept together, Jane knew there was a definite "buzz" between them and thought that they would end up lovers if she were free.

Bill was surprised by Jane's revelation and, after a little thought, started to feel ambushed. He believed that Jane had never intended to work on the marriage, but that she was just using the therapy to find a safe place to break the news that she wanted a divorce. He was very angry with Jane and refused to talk to her for days. After a week of this, however, Bill told Jane that he would not try to hold her in a marriage that she did not want. He told her that he could manage the children and that because she wanted the divorce, she should move out and get a job. Jane was furious. She had devoted her entire adult life to their kids and home, and she sure wasn't going to just move out and leave it all behind.

At this point, Bill and Jane are experiencing very similar emotions to those of Jack and Laura. Bill feels betrayed by Jane and does not understand what he has done wrong. He regards her as someone fickle and untrustworthy because she is prepared to violate her marriage vows because of some nebulous idea of happiness. Jane feels that Bill is emotionally stunted in his inability to express affection and that he will never change. She regards his anger as an ominous sign of how he might become nasty. They are both angry and distrustful of one another.

Both Bill and Jane then sought solace and support from friends. Each received the typical advice given by friends. "Don't make any concessions." "Be prepared to fight." "Get the toughest lawyer you can find." Jane went to see a lawyer suggested by a friend. The lawyer advised her that she would get permanent alimony and custody of the kids if she waited long enough. Jane also was told that she would be able to stay in the house until the youngest graduated from high school. But the lawyer advised her that there was no way to force her husband out of the house until the judge gave her exclusive possession when they went to trial in about a year. Jane was upset because she couldn't imagine the family living so long in the tense environment that was developing.

The kids suspected something was going on and had begun to ask questions. Jane told them that Bill was sleeping in the guest room because his snoring had been keeping her awake. But the steely silence that existed between the parents was enough to convince the children that their parents' marriage was in trouble.

Bill also sought legal advice. The lawyer told him not to move out and that it was reasonable to expect Jane to resume teaching in order to help support herself and the kids. When Bill told the lawyer that news had reached him that Jane was seeing some guy at the college, the lawyer suggested hiring a private detective to follow Jane and gather proof of her infidelity, something that would give them some leverage in settlement discussions. The lawyer said that under the circumstances, and considering the ages of the kids, Bill had a better-than-even chance of winning a custody fight and getting both the kids and the house.

But Bill was troubled by his lawyer's attitude. He could see how following the lawyer's advice might get him some advantage, but at what price? Sure he was mad and would have liked some sense of vindication, but what was it going to do to the kids to have to live through such a battle? And where was the money going to come from to pay these legal fees? They didn't have much savings, and the only way to come up with the $20,000 that the lawyer estimated it would cost to go to trial was either to liquidate part of his retirement fund or to take out some of the equity from the house. And Bill knew that Jane faced the same financial dilemma. Could they really waste this much money and still be able to help the kids with college?

Unlike Jack and Laura, both Bill and Jane are having misgivings about the scenario that their respective lawyers are presenting, and each is uneasy about the enormous financial commitment that is being asked of them. By not signing the retainers and thinking it over first, Bill and Jane are still in control of the divorce.

Bill felt at a loss. All his family and friends had goaded him on in his efforts to find an aggressive lawyer to look after his interests. Suddenly Bill remembered that the marriage counselor they had seen seemed like an experienced and reasonable person. Although it seemed strange to ask a marriage counselor for advice about getting divorced, Bill really needed an objective perspective, so he called the marriage counselor to seek his advice. Was there any way for him to avoid the expenses of a legal battle?

The counselor suggested that Bill consider divorce mediation. He told Bill that in mediation, Bill and Jane would be in charge of negotiating a settlement with the assistance of an experienced mediator. And although Bill and Jane would use lawyers as advisers, the role of the lawyers would be limited to advice and the couple could avoid losing control of the process. The counselor suggested two mediators he had used in the past. Bill researched both mediators and suggested to Jane that they consider mediation.

Jane was skeptical. Wouldn't Bill overpower her in the negotiation? Who would represent her interests there? How did she know if the mediator would be fair? Bill pleaded with Jane to at least discuss the matter with the counselor. She called the counselor, who encouraged her to at least have one meeting with the mediator and then decide if she wanted to continue. The counselor explained that mediation was completely voluntary and Jane had nothing to lose but an hour of her time. Under those conditions, Jane agreed to one meeting with the mediator to explore whether mediation was a realistic thing for her to do.

Both Bill and Jane are skeptical. Each is afraid that they will be taken advantage of, and neither has heard of mediation before. Both must override their preconceptions of how divorces are transacted and ignore the advice of their family and friends, who think that they are "nuts" to try to work things out on their own.

The couple went to see Mary Miles, an experienced mediator. Mary had been a divorce lawyer, but she became disillusioned with conventional law practice. She found it difficult to participate in a process that caused so much harm and became involved with divorce mediation; finally, she limited her practice to only mediation.

Mary Miles listened to the couple for a while and then suggested that they should be able to resolve the issues in about 8 or 10 sessions. Jane liked Mary's calm manner, her knowledge of the law, and her ability to handle people. Jane felt reassured that Bill wouldn't be able to bully her and that Mary would ensure a fair process. Mary asked each of them how they saw the major issues. Jane said that she wanted to go to law school and wanted Bill to support her until she was able to establish a career, some-thing that would probably take 5 or 6 years. Jane wanted Bill to move out so that she could continue to live in the house with the children. She wanted the children to see their father and to maintain a good relationship with him but felt that she should be the primary parent because she had always been.

Bill told Mary that he felt strongly about staying with the kids. He didn't see why he should have to move out. All their savings were in the house, and if he moved out he wouldn't be able to buy another house for 5 years. Owning his own house was very important to Bill because he spent his spare time in his garden and his workshop and would be unable to have those things if he moved. Bill disagreed that Jane had to be the primary parent. He did lots of things with the kids, had coached their teams, and helped them with their homework. He was as good as Jane at cooking and taking care of the house and did not accept the assumption that Jane had to stay with the kids. He also felt strongly that Jane should get a teaching job to help out. Two households were more expensive than one, and they were already using up his entire salary. How could they make it if Jane didn't go to work? Bill said that it was not his problem that Jane wanted to go to law school, and if she wanted to do that, she could go part time and take out student loans. But she needed to get a job.

This made Jane angry, and she said it just showed that Bill was not inter-ested in helping her. The mediator calmed them down and requested indi-vidual meetings with each in the following week. All subsequent meetings would be joint meetings, but the mediator explained that she wanted an op-portunity to get to know each of them a little better.

In mediation, the couple's issues and opposing viewpoints were aired. Both Jane and Bill felt that the mediator had listened carefully and that each had been given the chance to speak. While neither was completely convinced that the issues could be resolved in mediation, both were willing to give it another try.

The following week, Jane and Bill had their individual meetings with Mary Miles. For the first part of the meeting, Mary just listened and occasionally probed. She encouraged both clients to tell her everything on their minds about the divorce. Then she began to probe for options. Why could the house not be sold so each could afford a less expensive house? How much equity was in the house and what were townhouses and smaller houses selling for in the area? When Jane worried that a move would be too disruptive for the children, Miles pointed out that a move within the same town that did not involve a change in schools or friends was not really very disruptive and that the kids could manage it if their parents were cooperative.

Mary asked Jane if she thought the case could be amicably resolved if it meant that Bill would have to live in an apartment. Jane acknowledged that it was unlikely and that some solution had to be found to keep Bill in a house. The mediator also asked Jane why she assumed that it was her job to take care of the children. After all, Jane had assumed that responsibility for 17 years. Now that the kids were more independent and she wanted to pursue a new career, wouldn't it be fair to her to have Bill do more of the work so she could do well in law school? Jane had never thought of the issue in those terms. She knew that mothers who "gave up" custody of their kids were regarded as bad mothers. If she let Bill assume the primary role, wouldn't that mean that she was a bad mother? "Only if you insist on framing it that way," the mediator said. "I'm sure you and Bill could work out a shared parenting agreement that shifted more of the burden to him but kept you in an important close role with the children." Jane said she would think about it.

When Mary met with Bill, he told her his two concerns were not having to live in an apartment and not having to pay long-term alimony. That's why he was so insistent about Jane getting a job immediately. Mary asked Bill to analyze how much money Jane would earn as a teacher over the next 10 years and then compare that to what Jane would earn if she went to law school for the next 3 years and then worked as a lawyer in a firm for the *subsequent 7 years. Bill did some calculations and discovered that Jane's total income would actually be higher if she went to law school. He realized that then Jane would be better able to help with the cost of college that would become almost crushing with all three children in college at the same time. Bill agreed to look at the subject anew.*

Mary Miles has given the couple a private and safe forum in which each was able to articulate concerns and objectives. She was then able to lay out the various options under consideration and explore how to best meet those objectives. Bill and Jane felt validated and understood, so they were able to examine their respective positions and to realize that compromise might be possible. The goal of their divorce became a mutual one.

Over the next few meetings, Bill and Jane worked out their settlement agreement. They refinanced the house to get enough equity out for a down payment on a townhouse for Jane. They decided that in 2 years the present house would be sold and the equity divided so Bill could buy a smaller house. Bill agreed to pay alimony to Jane until she finished law school and for 1 year after that if she needed it. The joint custody agreement allowed the children to spend most of their time in the house with Bill, but they would spend weekends and any other time they desired with Jane. Bill and Jane knew finances would be a little tight, but with Jane taking out student loans, they believed they could make it.

Both Bill and Jane had to alter their original scenarios of what their divorce would be like. But each felt they had reached a viable and reasonable solution.

E P I L O G U E : 5 years later

Five years later the family is doing well. The oldest child is graduating from college this year, and both younger children are doing well in their colleges. All three went to state colleges and universities, and the family was able to manage the financial strain. Jane graduated from law school this year and is starting as an associate in a major law firm. Her first year's salary is twice what she would have been earning as a teacher. She is happy in her new career.

Nothing came of Jane's relationship with Craig, but she did meet a man her last year of law school, and they are well on their way to a long-term relationship. Bill remarried 2 years ago and is quite happy in his new life. Bill and Jane are not friends, but neither are they hostile. They have been cooperative regarding their children and both view the children's successes with pride.

The children all like Bill's new wife and the man Jane is dating. For this couple, the divorce was a success.

Comparing the Outcomes

Both of these stories are based on real couples, and although many details are omitted for purposes of brevity and protection of the parties' privacy, each serves as a good example of its type.

In chapter 1, we outlined the six features of a good divorce. Let us look at our two couples in light of those components.

Emotional Divorce

People divorce in order to begin new lives and hope that their new lives will involve new mates. One cannot begin anew without truly ending the prior relationship. Many couples on the cusp of divorce recite a wish to come out of the divorce as friends. That is not likely. It is extremely difficult to go from an intimate relationship to a platonic friendship, and it is unlikely that a friendship can survive all the hurts necessarily attendant on a divorce. A warm cooperative relationship is probably the best that can be hoped for. It is possible, however, to come out of the divorce with an active enemy. A spouse who emerges from the divorce feeling humiliated and poorly treated may never be able to let go of powerful feelings of anger and betrayal. There is a big difference between remembering that you had feelings of intense anger, and actually regurgitating and re-experiencing those feelings. People who have had decent divorces are able to get on with their lives so that the feelings toward their ex-spouses, both positive and negative, become progressively weaker and in time play no part in their new lives.

The opposite of love is not hate. The opposite of love is indifference. When we let go of a former love or spouse, in time we hope that we are simply indifferent. There may be some fond memories and there may be troubled memories. But what is important is that our feelings for the person are no longer powerful and are no longer able to mobilize our emotions.

Bad divorce is characterized by just the opposite. After a bad divorce, one or both spouses cannot let go and must stay connected with the other. The most efficient way to do that is to stay engaged in continuous conflict during which the divorce is never final. The more extreme couples in bad divorces become chronic litigants, ever dragging each other back to court trying to win in the latest squabble. Because they are never able to fully disengage, they are never able to acquire the necessary distance and indifference that are prerequisite to really starting over. The ongoing conflict affects all aspects of the divorced family's life. Visitation with children is forever in a tangle. Fathers show up late or cancel visits at the last minute. Mothers interfere with and sabotage the father's time with the children. Chronic litigants often infect each other's new marriages, and new spouses give up because life is a perpetual battle with the former spouse. The endless cycle of provocation and litigation poisons the parents' ability to cooperate for the benefit of the children, and the children often develop depression as a result. And if you damage your children, they in turn ruin your life.

In our two case studies, Jack and Laura, the first couple, are on their way to chronic conflict. Because each feels cheated and humiliated by the other, they are having a hard time putting the divorce—and the harsh emotions that go along with it—behind them. Each has trouble letting the other live in peace, and as a consequence neither is thriving. Our second couple, Bill and Jane, managed to get through their divorce with their civility and sense of self-respect intact. They are doing well and are clearly separated from each other. They have a good divorce.

Rebuilding Lives

A key indicator for how good or bad a divorce was is whether or not people have rebuilt their social lives by 5 years after the divorce. Even in what we call a good divorce, there usually are many social losses associated with the change. Many couples that were friends of the divorced couple drop one or both of the partners, while a few manage to maintain friendships with both divorced partners. Newly single people often report surprise that long-term friends seem to avoid or forget about them. The family of each divorced partner generally pulls away from the former in-laws even though some try to maintain a cordial relationship for the benefit of the children. So for many divorced people, particularly men, loneliness is a common result of divorce. Women tend to have more close women friends with whom they exchange intimacies. Men are less likely to have intimate male friends; golf buddies are not the same as intimate friends with whom one can be open and vulnerable.

Even church membership is not much of a resource for divorcing people. Few churches have developed ministries for their divorced couples. Because there are few formal or ritualistic events for reintegrating the divorced couple as single members of the congregation, one or both spouses end up leaving the church and either joining another church or doing without church membership.

Most newly divorced people need to consciously rebuild their social lives. People who are divorced eventually reach a point where they are ready to look around to see if there is another potential mate out there. The initiator of the divorce typically does this first and may have begun to clandestinely date others even before the divorce was announced. The noninitiator may need more time before beginning to date. For most people, dating is not a great pleasure and is fraught with insecurity and awkwardness. An entire singles and dating industry has grown up to serve this population.

Most people succeed in rebuilding their social lives within 5 years following their divorces. About 80 percent of men are remarried within 2 years of divorce, and about 75 percent of women remarry within 5 years. The sad irony is that about 55 to 60 percent of those remarriages will end in divorce. There are some people who never regain a social footing; usually these are the people who had the worst divorces. Some are so bitter that they are unable to trust anyone enough to build a successful new relationship. Others have created so much economic disarray that they just can't get themselves reorganized; they end up financially struggling and bitter.

Still others have so messed up their children that they are unable to find a potential mate willing to live in the chaos generated by the would-be stepchildren.

In many ways, the ones who had the easiest divorces adjust better and rebuild with greater success. It is easier to create second families when the children of the first marriage are not a source of perpetual disruption. It is easier to court and be courted when you have adequate amounts of time away from your children. (When you are dating and courting, your children are a liability rather than an asset.) Finally, it is far easier to build a new relationship when you are no longer riveted to the first. Prolonged litigation and conflict lasting after the divorce is over distracts you from building a new relationship and may leave you without the emotional energy to have a successful connection to anyone new.

Jack and Laura illustrate what happens when the divorce is not resolved well. They are unable to free themselves from the anger and results of their divorce. The maladaptation of their children prevents Laura from finding someone new and causes difficulties with Jack's new girlfriend. It is not uncommon that the foundation of the second divorce is laid brick by brick during the first. Jack and Laura are going to have to get finished with each other before they will be able to build successful new lives.

Bill and Jane, on the other hand, have emotional and practical closure regarding their relationship and divorce and are able to move on unimpeded.

Both Thinking the Agreement Is Fair

Jack and Laura came away from court with a settlement agreement, a fact that would suggest that both agreed to the terms. About 99 percent of all divorces are eventually resolved by a negotiated settlement. But in about half of those cases, the couple is back in court within 2 years, continuing the fight over the children and support. With a 50 percent failure rate, there must be something essentially defective in those settlement agreements and the process that produces them. Recall how Jack and Laura got their settlement. They sat passively in the courtroom hallway while their lawyers met with the judge behind closed doors and "worked it out." Neither party participated in creating the agreement, and both felt that it was imposed on them. Neither of them had any commitment to living according to the agreement. Neither came away with any sense of ownership, and neither was inclined to honor even the letter—much less the spirit—of the settlement. As a result, Jack and Laura are locked in continuing conflict and cannot finish with the divorce or each other.

In contrast, Bill and Jane negotiated directly, without the intervention of a coercive court system. They had all the time they needed to negotiate, explore options, and be creative about using their resources to attend to the needs of the entire family. They did it almost by themselves, they own it, and they are prepared to live by it. Because each thinks it is fair, Bill and Jane are able to move on and successfully disconnect from each other.

Ability to Cooperate as Parents

One of the most important indicators of a good divorce is the emergence of a working partnership as parents. Children need both parents, and they need both parents to have functioning homes in which they feel physically and emotionally comfortable. Children also need their parents to cooperate with each other so the children are not presented with quarreling parents unable to provide nurturing, guidance, and discipline. Many divorcing parents have to acquire a new model for communication because their old patterns, whether based on friendship and mutual affection or on bitterness and acrimony, are no longer applicable.

I suggest to clients that they address each other as they would a colleague or customer. Such communication is characterized by respect and cordiality—even warmth. What it does not include is intimacy. There is a job to be done and another human you have to work with. Intimate observations or angry responses that would be inappropriate in business are also inappropriate between divorced parents. You have no emotional claim on each other, so communication reflecting such a claim is out. Your only goal is to make your settlement work. A civil working partnership is difficult to achieve when you are still seething at each other or when the children have been inappropriately recruited as allies of one parent against the other. All that emotional stuff that flows from a bad divorce makes it unlikely that people can achieve the cooperation a parental partnership requires. Jack and Laura don't have it; Bill and Jane do. It has a great deal to do with how each pair divorced.

Children That Are Comfortable in Each Household

The adjustment to divorce is a long-term undertaking, and I use 5 years as the benchmark period. If, 5 years after the divorce, both former spouses are reestablished socially and the children are at ease with the new lives of each parent, we have strong indications of a successful divorce. But for that to occur, several things must have occurred early in the divorce. First, neither parent will have recruited the children as allies against the other. Rather, each parent would have been clear with the children that they have no role in the disputes between the parents and will have encouraged the children to like and respect the other parent. Second, each parent will have promoted the other parent as loving and competent, and neither parent will have used the children to sabotage the other parent. Finally, each parent will have encouraged the children to like and respect the new spouse or significant other of the other parent. Each child will feel that she has each parent's consent to be comfortable in the other parent's household.

By this standard, Jack and Laura have failed, while Bill and Jane have succeeded. Because Jack and Laura were unable to finish their divorce with a mutual sense of justice, neither can support the other as a parent. Their continual return to court to fight over kids and money inevitably leads to the involvement and alienation of the children. In contrast, Bill and Jane are able to cooperate as parents. They are able to move on to new lives and integrate the children into those lives without continuing hostility and bitterness.

The Former Spouses' Ability to Resolve Disputes Themselves or through Mediation

Divorce is about change. If things go well for each of the former spouses, their lives will evolve as they build new relationships and adapt to living in separate households. New jobs and new mates may require relocation. Lay-offs and promotions will change economic circumstances. Children change as they get older. They grow more mature, start dating, and start driving your car. So if you are divorced with children, the support and parenting arrangements may have to be modified from time to time. The important question is whether the parties are able to resolve issues of change as they arise and how they will manage when they don't agree about what to do.

I regard the ability to resolve differences amicably and constructively as the ultimate indicator of a good divorce. In our two case studies, we see Jack and Laura unable to let go of their conflict and so unable to resolve any disputes without going to court. They will be "married" to each other through conflict as long as they have dependent children, and that conflict will continue to contaminate their lives. Bill and Jane, on the other hand, are able to resolve differences and disputes, dispose of them quickly, and move on.

I always encourage couples whose divorces I mediate to incorporate mediation clauses into their separation agreements. The clause creates an obligation to return to mediation whenever an issue arises that the couple cannot resolve by themselves. In most cases, this keeps the couple out of court and allows them to find solutions to their problem, often in a single hour-long session.

In this chapter we have laid out the makings of a good and a bad divorce. It will be important to keep these paradigms in mind as you begin the process of divorce. They will help you focus on the ultimate objective and avoid the petty skirmishes that send you off course and make any victory a Pyrrhic one.

In the next chapter, I will explain how to manage the beginning of divorce.

"*Dear, I'd like to roll our marriage over
into an amicable divorce.*"

Three

MANAGING THE BEGINNING OF THE DIVORCE

AS YOU BEGIN THE ARDUOUS JOURNEY of your divorce, it is important to understand the emotional process. You need to learn more about not only your own emotions, but also those of your wife. The first important problem to understand is the issue of mutuality in the decision to divorce.

Very few divorces begin when two married people wake up one morning, look at each other, and simultaneously announce that it is time to end the marriage. Usually one of the partners reaches the decision first. That person, the initiator, has typically spent anywhere from 1 year to 5 years thinking about a divorce and making emotional adjustments. The initiator has learned to cope with the disappointment of realizing that the marriage cannot work and may even have gone through a period of mourning, unbeknownst to the spouse. The initiator has the advantage of having had time to prepare for the divorce.

For example, she may have already begun to build a new life by making new friends separate from her spouse, or by returning to school to acquire a new degree or credential that will augment a job search. He may have lost 20 pounds, taken up exercise, acquired new hobbies, and otherwise begun a new and separate life. By the time the spouse is informed of the desire to divorce, the initiator is usually well along in or has completed the process of detachment and adjustment. By the time the initiator breaks the news, the marriage is dead. He or she has already resolved to move on.

The critical question for the divorce is this: Where is the other spouse in this process? The other spouse may be anywhere on a continuum from totally thunderstruck to resigned acceptance. "I don't understand. I thought we had a great marriage. We never even had a fight." Or, "Well, I guess you're probably right. I thought it might be worth another crack at counseling, but this has gone on so long it's time to get it over with." The reactions of most noninitiators fall somewhere in between.

After many years in the practice of mediation, I believe that how the difference in psychological state between the initiator and noninitiator is managed is the most important factor in shaping the divorce.

CASE STUDY: Dave and Wendy

Last week Dave told Wendy that he wanted a divorce, and the couple is in turmoil. Married 18 years and with two children, Dave and Wendy have been struggling for 10 years. At first, the struggles involved money. The couple was never able to arrive at a workable protocol for managing the family finances. Dave was the more conservative about money. He believed it was irresponsible to spend money that they didn't have and objected to using credit cards when they were short of money. He believed that you lived within your means and saved part of your pay every month, no matter what.

Wendy was the spender. She was slow to balance her checkbook and resistant to disciplined budgeting. A free spirit, Wendy had no problem with buying things on credit. As a result of their conflicting money styles, paying the bills became an opportunity for angry words and mutual frustrations. Their conflicts gradually escalated to attacks on each other's character and personality.

Dave called Wendy immature and irresponsible. Sometimes when she argued in favor of some expenditure he thought unnecessary, he would call her shallow; once he told her she was just plain stupid. Wendy was so hurt by this that she wouldn't speak to him for days. When she did speak to him, she retaliated at the first opportunity. Wendy told Dave he was dull, emo-

tionally withholding, and stodgy. She called him selfish and controlling. Over time, each became a virtuoso at insulting the other, and their mutual anger grew.

As their mutual disapproval grew, they each withdrew affection. Sex was an early casualty, and civility became increasingly problematic. They tried marriage counseling, but neither felt it was useful. Wendy decided to get a part-time job so she would have her own money. But on the first of the month when bills had to be paid and Dave demanded that they pool their money, she balked. "I got a job so I could have some money that you didn't control, and now you want to tell me how to spend it. I am not giving you all the control!"

A deadlock evolved and hardened over the years, and each partner's view of the other also hardened. Dave came to regard Wendy as selfish and narcissistic. He asked himself how he could have married her, how he could have so messed up his life. He brooded because the marriage was such a disappointment. He blamed Wendy because they were in debt. He blamed her for being sexually withdrawn. He felt they would be fine if only she hadn't turned out to be so self-centered.

After years of growing estrangement, Dave finally came to believe that the marriage was a failure. What was wrong could not be fixed. At 45 years of age, he was approaching the point where he did not have unlimited time at his disposal. If he was being forced to start over, he had better get going.

Divorce is about change. It requires at least one, and often both, of the partners and their children to move to new homes, adjust to new economic circumstances, build new social lives, and learn new routines for managing households. Change is difficult, and none of us like it very much—particularly when we regard the change as making our lives more difficult or less comfortable. But in order for a family to adapt well to divorce, it is necessary that everyone accept a fair measure of change. The question is whether both divorcing partners are willing to do so. It is at this point where the difference between initiator and noninitiator becomes so important.

In the case study above, Dave is the initiator. When he tells Wendy, she is likely to be caught by surprise. The initiator has had the necessary time to think through the divorce. The initiator comprehends that there are painful changes and dislocations but sees the gains as outweighing the losses. For the noninitiator, who has not yet come to terms with the end of the marriage, the divorce and all its ramifications are only about loss.

In time, most noninitiators come to terms with the divorce and become ready to accept the necessary changes. But the operative word is *time*. Pushed too fast, these partners will dig in their heels and refuse to budge. "You want this divorce and I don't. So *you* figure out how to solve all the problems. You move out and leave the kids with me, and you figure out where the money will come from to pay for all this." Hearing this, the initiator believes that the other spouse is not going to be reasonable and concludes that the only thing to do is to hire a lawyer and begin the fight. So the initiator's sense of timing, coupled with an understanding of what the spouse is experiencing, is very important.

If You Are the Initiator

Dave has been thinking how to tell Wendy that he is ready to end the marriage. His first impulse is to tell her that he is fed up and can't take it any more, that the sooner he gets away from her, the sooner he will be happy. Luckily, Dave has a counselor who helps him shape a different message.

Telling Your Wife

You need to tell your wife with all the gentleness you would use if you were telling someone that a loved one had died. Choose a time when the two of you are alone and unlikely to be interrupted. You are about to break some bad news that will, in all probability, evoke strong emotions. Determine in advance that you will not use strong language or an angry tone, regardless of her reaction.

Dave said, *"Wendy, I have some difficult news to share with you. I have reached the conclusion that you and I need to divorce. We have both tried, but it is not working between us and I do not believe that it will work. I think the marriage is over and that we have to separate."*

Note the neutral language. Note that you are making "I" statements. You are reporting the state of your own feelings and are not characterizing hers. Now be prepared for a response and listen when she talks to you. Her response may be anything from agreement to urgent denial.

"How can you even think such a thing? There's nothing wrong that some

hard work can't fix. We have children to think of; how could you even con-
sider doing this to them?"

Be prepared for an angry assault.

"This is just another example of you trying to run away from responsi-
bility. You are selfish and only thinking about yourself. I have given you
everything I could. I've poured myself into making this family and this home.
I don't deserve this and the kids don't deserve this. Grow up and stop acting
like an adolescent!"

Do not retaliate. This is not the time to defend yourself or to justify your
decision. The following, though understandable, is self-destructive:

"Don't lecture me about growing up. I'm leaving because I'm sick and
tired of your childishness. I'm sick of living in this messy house. I'm sick of
living without sex or affection, and I'm sick of you never doing your share.
Whatever I've tried to make the marriage work, you undermined. You
messed up our attempts at counseling and stonewalled me whenever I
asked you to change. This is more your fault than mine, so you grow up!"

The above may feel good for about 3 minutes, but it will produce
nothing but a bitter fight. You have sought to justify yourself by attacking
her and have guaranteed a contentious and angry fight at the beginning of
the divorce. Consider the alternative:

"I know this is very painful and I am very sorry to do this, but I am at my
wits' end and just can't see an alternative. I don't have the feelings that we
would need to make our marriage work. There is too much distance be-
tween us to overcome. The marriage is over. I am worried about the chil-
dren and I am concerned for you. The marriage has to end, but I will do
everything I can to do it decently and fairly."

Notice that there is no defense here; only the reiteration that you regard
the marriage as over and you will do your best to manage the divorce fairly.
You will need to do two things in order to pull this off. First, you must feel
the sense of correctness of your decision. If you feel conviction in your decision to divorce, it will be easier for you to hold your ground and not engage in self-defense. Second, you must be aware that anger, recrimination,
and defensiveness will spawn further anger on her part and will work
against your desire for a reasonable and amicable process.

If you are operating from a stance of emotional conviction and if you have overcome your anger and your desire to return her comments with counterattacks, you will be able to maintain your calm and your kindness. You may have to repeat your determination to end the marriage several times in the face of intense emotional attack by her. If you get angry and engage in a struggle, you forfeit the opportunity to model the behavior you want her to imitate. Now is the time to demonstrate your commitment to a peaceful transition. Her attacks on you will abate if you hold firm and don't retaliate. It takes two to fight. Your refusal to engage will reap large dividends later.

Give Her Time

After you tell your wife that you want a divorce, you need to give her the time to assimilate the information. Although both of you are anxious about the future, this is not the time to engage in discussion about the details of the divorce such as whether to sell the house or whether she needs to get a job. Acknowledge that divorce will require some important changes, but reiterate that you will work with her to achieve a fair and workable arrangement. Tell her that there is no rush to decide these things and assure her that you will be available to talk more when both of you are ready. Avoid the following bad example.

> *"Don't think that you can have it all your way. You better get used to the fact that we are going to have to sell this house. And unless you want to starve, you'd better get out there and find a job like I've been asking you to do for years."*

I have seen too many people begin divorces this way, and all it does is scare the wives into running to a lawyer for protection because the husbands have just demonstrated their indifference to their wives' welfare.

Here's a summary of the rules for telling your wife that you want a divorce.

▶ Use "I" statements.

▶ Use neutral language.

▶ Do not blame her for your decision. Model peaceful behavior.

▶ Be clear that it is over.

▶ Do not discuss proposals about the details of the divorce.

▶ Do not retaliate if she attacks or criticizes you.

▶ Reassure her that you want to work with her to achieve fairness
and the best arrangement for all of you.

▶ Tell her there is no hurry to resolve everything and that you will
wait until she is ready.

▶ Suggest or agree to divorce counseling.

Just as the noninitiator must learn to recognize and control strong emotions, the initiator must rise to the same challenge. It might help to realize that both of you ultimately want the same thing—a peaceful, fulfilled life for yourself and your children

If You Are the Noninitiator

If you are not the one initiating the divorce, you will have to cope with the feelings of rejection and indignation that arise when your wife tells you that she wants a divorce. Unless you haven't been paying attention, you have to know that the marriage has been failing. You haven't had sex in a long time. Your wife has been going her own way and probably leading an almost separate life. You have been in counseling one time or more and the counseling has not been successful. In all probability, you have been aware of your wife's discontent and you have been unhappy with things yourself. The difference is probably one of pain threshold. You have been willing to press on—perhaps for the benefit of the kids, perhaps because the idea of all the change involved has simply been too frightening. But at some level you are not totally surprised.

This does not mean, however, that you are ready for divorce. Though disillusioned with the marriage, you have not developed your own scenario for the future. So what do you do now? The thought of trying to finance two households on a budget that has been supporting only one is very scary. You ask yourself, "How will I afford it? Does she expect me to move out and just leave her with everything? Why is she doing this now? Is she having an affair? What about the kids?" The litany of questions can leave you lost and irate.

What should you do at this point? For starters, you should defer the adoption of any firm positions until you can gain a reasonable perspective on the divorce. It is reasonable to ask your wife to give you some time—a few months—to get a grip on your emotions. Psychotherapy is useful now because you need someone to help you organize your thoughts and feelings. Close friends may be helpful if you have some who will listen without judging or offering advice on how to manage the divorce.

Paradoxically, you may have the impulse to turn to your wife to help you because for so many years she is the one you have consulted when you were troubled. It may be painful to realize that you can't turn to her for solace and even worse that she is the author of all this pain. Just because you have strong emotions now doesn't mean that you have to tell her everything that you feel. It's okay to tell her that you feel hurt, scared, lonely, and rejected. But it is not okay to begin to characterize her as a terrible person or to begin attacking her.

What You Need as the Noninitiator

Here is what to ask of your wife.

▶ Reasonable time to absorb the news and the implications of the divorce before you have to act

▶ That she not press you to negotiate or make important decisions about the divorce until you have had time to think about it

▶ Reasonable time before she tells other people, with the exception of the few confidants that she has probably confided in anyhow—you do not need other people asking about the divorce until you are ready to talk about it

▶ That she not discuss the divorce with the children until the two of you can do it together and at the proper time

▶ That she maintain an atmosphere of cordiality and respect in the house until such time as the two of you separate

▶ That she go with you for several sessions with a divorce
counselor to manage the feelings that you both are experiencing

▶ That when you are ready, the two of you will seek a good
mediator to help you negotiate the divorce settlement so
that you don't get lost in litigation

Here is what you should *not* do.

▶ Try to talk her out of it—it won't work

▶ Threaten legal action or threaten to injure,
humiliate, or punish her in any way

▶ Threaten to "take the kids away from her"

▶ Threaten economic retaliation

▶ Engage in a debate about who is at fault or who should have
behaved differently in the past; it does not matter any more

Common Problems Encountered Early in Divorces

Many of the challenges couples face early in a divorce stem from the fact
that they have little or no prior experience and no way of identifying
common pitfalls. Here are some common problems.

The Greek Chorus Phenomenon

*In the first weeks after Dave tells Wendy, both of them talk about the deci-
sion with their close friends. Wendy talks to Susan, whose sister is presently
going through a rough divorce. Susan urges Wendy to be very careful that
Dave doesn't do something sneaky like her brother-in-law tried to do to her
sister. She tells Wendy many horror stories about men taking advantage of
their wives and to find a good lawyer to protect her rights. She offers the
name of her sister's lawyer.*

*Dave has a similar discussion with his fishing buddy, Hal. Hal went
through a divorce 10 years ago and is eager to help Dave avoid the mistakes
he made. "Be careful that she doesn't get to the bank accounts before you*

do. My ex-wife had some shark lawyer who convinced her to raid all the ac-
counts and transfer the money into accounts in her name only. By the time I
figured it out she was in control. It's better for you to get there first."

One of the perverse things that appears to characterize most divorces is
what I have come to call the Greek Chorus Phenomenon. The Greek chorus
is an ancient dramatic device in which a group forewarns a character in the
play about impending events. In divorce, both partners inevitably attract a
group of well-meaning but woefully ignorant people who offer advice
about how they should manage their divorce. Such notable experts as your
drinking buddy, coworker, brother, and other assorted friends and relatives
may believe that they know enough to give advice. However, their expertise
is drawn from TV programs, bad movies, worse books, magazine articles,
and perhaps their own divorces or those of their friends and family. The
problem is that very few of your advisers know anything about the real
world of divorce. They all tend to assume that divorce has to be an ugly war
of attrition in which you should be prepared to fight. They also assume that
your spouse is out to cheat you and do you out of what is rightfully yours.
The most common advice the Greek chorus gives is to fight, to assume the
worst, and to get to the bank before your wife empties the account.

I almost never hear about friends who counsel you that divorce can be
managed with decency and civility, that you should act gently and gener-
ously, and that you should demonstrate peaceful intentions rather than hostile
behavior. Whatever the reason, amateur advisers seem to get some strange
pleasure from getting you agitated and warlike. That is most destructive.

Do not discuss your divorce with anyone but professionals. Discuss it
with your counselor, mediator, lawyer, financial planner, or accountant. But
don't discuss it with relatives, friends, or coworkers. If one of them brings
it up, thank them for their interest and support, assure them that you are
getting all the advice you need, and politely decline the offer of free consultation. This particularly applies to your parents, whose protective instincts
may motivate them to join a battle that may not yet exist. If you have children, you should tell your parents that this is a time when their grandchildren could use some extra attention and encourage them to maintain a
warm relationship with your wife. It is sad when we see grandparents

squander the goodwill of a former daughter-in-law or son-in-law because they have become embroiled in a battle in which they do not belong.

The Impulse to Reconcile

It's been 2 weeks and Wendy and Dave are living together in strained silence. One night Wendy comes to Dave in tears and says, "I just can't accept that after so many years we're just going to throw everything away. I can't get it out of my mind how much this is going to hurt the kids. And I can't get it out of my mind that you and I are not going to be together anymore. I know we have had a bad time for a while, but I think we could fix it if you were willing to try. I am willing to do anything we have to do. What do we have to lose? Please, please let's try again." Seeing Wendy in tears has always weakened Dave's resolve, and he wraps his arms around her to comfort her. It makes him feel guilty that she is so sad. "Why not try again?" he thinks to himself. "Okay," he says after a minute's reflection, "I'm willing to try if you agree to go into counseling and really work on the marriage." That night they sleep together for the first time in many months.

They find a marriage counselor and see her once a week. But within a month, Dave is feeling that he has made a terrible mistake. In counseling Wendy is taking all the stubborn positions that have always driven him nuts. They are not making any progress. A month later, in the middle of a contentious session, he calls a halt. "I can't do this again. I can't take any more. I'm really done this time. I want a divorce."

In many, if not most, divorces, there is at least one effort to reconcile. The typical scenario involves the plea of the noninitiator to "try again." The initiator, out of guilt or fear of appearing hard-hearted, reluctantly agrees. In most cases the couple agrees to try counseling one more time. The problem with such attempts is that they are usually too late. By the time the initiator has announced an intention to divorce, the marriage is dead; there is nothing for the counselor to work with. Under the best circumstances, the counselor will help the couple realize this quickly and then engage in divorce counseling to help them part with mutual understanding and civility. But more often than not, the attempt at reconciliation leaves the partners angrier and increases the ill will.

Does this mean that you should not give in to your partner's pleas for reconciliation? Unless you are genuinely ambivalent about the divorce and still believe that the marriage can be turned around, I think you should refuse. To agree to a reconciliation attempt that you know in your heart can't work is cruel and prolongs the inevitable. It is better to be gentle but clear that the marriage is over and let your wife know that you will do whatever you can to help her through the process.

The Death Spiral

Another common problem I see early in divorces is a situation I call "The Death Spiral." Once the decision to divorce has been made and communicated, couples enter into a very difficult period in which it is easy to bumble into a bad divorce. Although many people assume that divorce must always be bitter, my experience suggests otherwise. Even though there is acute emotional pain early on, most couples retain a surprising degree of affection and goodwill. If that is not squandered in the early months, it can provide the basis for a decent divorce. The challenge is how to manage all the tumultuous emotions swirling through the house. Although some couples separate as soon as the divorce is announced, most couples will continue to live in the same house while they decide how to manage the separation. For some couples it's a matter of finances. Others stay together because they can't agree on who will leave or whether they will sell the house. Many men remain on bad advice from their lawyers, who tell them not to leave the house until the divorce has been resolved.

Living in the same house after the decision to divorce is very difficult for several reasons. The first is the couple's role confusion. They are used to turning to each other for advice and solace. In some cases they may have been estranged for so long that this doesn't apply. But with most couples, at least one of them, particularly the noninitiator, is inclined to seek help from the other. But when the other is the source of the pain, it doesn't help to seek relief from the spouse. People who are divorcing but living in the same house don't know how to act with each other. Should they sit down to dinner as a family as they did for many years? Should they try to have conversations with each other or should they not? Should they live in separate bedrooms and, if so, who moves out of the master bedroom?

What about friends? Do they continue to socialize with other couples—with the process uncomfortable for all—or do they just live separate social lives? And what about dating? Living in the same house, each is acutely aware of when the other comes and goes, and jealousy is fed by vivid imaginations.

For people trying to live in the same house after deciding to divorce, growing hostility is almost inevitable. Without established protocols and with communication difficult, there are many opportunities to accidentally step on each other's toes. Unrealized expectations, insensitive remarks, mistakes about who was supposed to pick up the children when, and many other missteps and misunderstandings are inevitable. But here is the problem: When my friend steps on my toe, I automatically assume that it was accidental and unintentional. I say, "Ow!," he apologizes, and it is forgotten. But if the person who steps on my toe is my adversary, I'm not so sure it was accidental. Maybe he was being malicious and trying to inflict pain. The event is the same, but the intention imputed might differ. If I conclude that he was trying to hurt me, I become angry. Not only will I be wary of him in the future and make sure he can't get within reach of my toes, but I may retaliate to show him that I'm no wimp and that I can push back. Now suppose that it really was an accident, but I decide it was intentional. My retaliation strikes him as a hostile act, and he reacts with distrust and further retaliation. Within a short time, we are at war.

This is the death spiral of relationships that can easily occur early in the divorce. It is inevitable that each partner step on the toes of the other, at least figuratively. As each begins to infer hostile intent, the other begins to retaliate, and the atmosphere rapidly becomes poisonous. Psychologists call such reactions "negative attribution." Each one simply starts to assume the worst about the intentions of the other. For children, such a household becomes a living hell. In fact, this scenario is a leading cause of depression in children.

I do not suggest that this "death spiral" occurs only when people occupy the same house, but living in the same house during the divorce increases the likelihood. It is vital to be careful about how you communicate with your wife. It is understandable that you are both touchy and reactive. You must make a concerted effort to steer away from confrontations, maintain a civil and respectful tone, and exercise the consideration you would expect of any adult roommate. You also need to duck when she is provocative to you. You are not a trout that has to rise to every fly on the surface.

If you are the initiator and she does not want the divorce, she may continually try to engage you. And if the only way she can do this is with provocation and conflict, be prepared for her to push your buttons. Your response must be calm, polite, and nonretaliatory, even if you bite your tongue until it bleeds.

If you are the noninitiator and are angry about the divorce, you may be tempted to punish your wife for the pain she is inflicting upon you. In either scenario, you can avoid the death spiral if you are capable of the requisite restraint. This may be a particular challenge to those who follow some "macho" creed of never backing down from a fight. If this is you, you may want to reflect on the difference between acting manly and acting stupid.

The Temptation of Temporary Separation

Yet another challenge many couples face in the beginnings of their divorces is the temptation to try a temporary separation. On hundreds of occasions I have had couples come to my office and tell me that they were not there for a divorce but just wanted a "temporary separation" to see if they would miss each other and should get back together. In a few cases both are sincere. The initiator is ambivalent and the noninitiator wants a reconciliation. And in a few cases, they separate, continue to work on the marriage, and eventually get back together. But that happens in very few cases. More typically, the idea of separation is a smokescreen to allow them to separate without having to use the word "divorce."

There are some people who seem to believe that it is kinder to amputate an arm an inch at a time. So the initiator tells a little lie to the other spouse. "I just need a little space and a little solitude to think things through and get my head straight. After a while I believe this confusion will lift and I will be better able to decide if I think the marriage will work." The noninitiator eats it up because it holds out hope and puts off the need to cope with the sad feelings of the divorce. So the initiator moves out and uses the illusion of temporary separation to grease the exit ramp. Sometime thereafter, the other spouse ends up bitterly disillusioned when she finds out that it was a ruse and that there was never an intention of moving back in.

When couples tell me they want to have a temporary separation, I have a simple acid test. "Tell me," I ask, "during this temporary separation is it your intention to date other people, and if you do, is there an agreement to remain celibate, other than having sex with each other?" If the initiator answers that he will indeed date during this period and that monogamy is not an acceptable rule, the other spouse will usually figure out the real agenda and declare that the marriage is over and that divorce, not separation, is the objective.

I have seldom seen a marriage improved by a temporary separation. In fact, the separation itself tends to further damage an already damaged relationship. Most therapists I know agree that if you want to work on a marriage, you stay together and work on it. Most of the time when someone is talking "temporary separation," that person is really talking divorce but is trying, for one reason or another, to cushion the blow. I think it is a bad idea because it invariably gets the divorce off to a bad start with the noninitiator coming up feeling doubly betrayed. If you really are talking temporary separation, I would expect to see the following:

▶ No dating of others during the separation

▶ A fixed time limit for the separation, after which you
either get back together or decide to divorce

▶ A continuation of couples counseling

▶ No alteration of the financial status quo
or permanent division of assets

▶ A temporary plan for the management of income and spending

If you want something significantly different from what I have described, you really want a divorce but do not have the courage to say it. I strongly urge you not to use this ploy.

Roleplaying: Villains and Victims
Another challenge many people face in the early stages of divorce is falling into predictable roles. These overly simplistic identities of the initiator as

the villain and the noninitiator as the victim often lead to the cliché bad divorce. Managing your anger when you are rejected is a difficult but crucial task at the outset of your divorce. Anger can be a way to shirk responsibility for your own feelings. When you get angry at someone, you are able to focus all your hurt feelings on the behavior of that person. If it's her fault, it's easy to believe it isn't your fault. The more intense and elaborate your own anger, the less you have to feel difficult feelings about your own actions. By blaming others, we avoid blaming ourselves. We construct ever more elaborate explanations for our predicament, all starring the person we are blaming.

The Victim's Song of Woe

As the noninitiator processes intense feelings of anger and blame, it's easy to slide into the role of victim. "I didn't do anything wrong. I am completely innocent and am therefore being victimized by the bad behavior of my wife. She is being selfish (childish, irresponsible, mean, etc.). She has abandoned me (and the kids); she is having an affair and is betraying me; she has led me on all these years and never really loved me; she has used me all this time and now that she doesn't need me, is dumping me. She should be punished."

As the victim recounts and lists all the terrible things his wife has done and all the character deficits she has, his story gets ever more elaborate. Because all the wrong rests with her, because you are innocent and she is guilty, because you are the victim, she must be the villain. Victims need villains and villains should be punished. In the context of divorce, villains should be punished by having to accept responsibility for all the nasty consequences of divorce. That is, all those unpleasant changes that divorce requires should be heaped on her. Why should you suffer? Why should the kids suffer? She has brought this about, so let her pay. Let her move out and leave you and the kids in the house. Let her get a job and support herself and maybe even pay child support. You have struggled and worked all these years to save some money and build a pension account. Let her go build her own and leave yours alone. She ought to get nothing because she deserves nothing.

There are two problems with a victim's posture. First, it helps to reinforce the illusion that some day you will be vindicated and she will be punished. But the judicial system doesn't do this very well, as we have seen. And then there is the second problem. If you want to punish her for her wrongdoing, the only available forum is the courts, and that means a long process of litigation with all the emotional and financial exhaustion it produces. The only punishment you will inflict is that the two of you will have an awful divorce and that she will suffer as much as you will. You can leave her broke, but you will be broke also. You can disrupt her relationship with the kids, but yours will also get disrupted. The solace won by a victim's role will be very temporary.

To make matters even worse, when one parent assumes a victim's role, the impact on the children can be devastating. The victim parent behaves so pathetically that the children feel that they have to rescue that parent. They take it upon themselves to comfort and reassure him. And as the victimized parent confides in the child and seeks comfort, he recruits the child to share his anger at the mother who is initiating the divorce. "Mommy is breaking up the family. She wants to leave you and me." Assuming that this ploy is successful—and it frequently is—the child comes to the rescue and becomes angry with the other parent. Because the child is now taking care of the victimized parent and is alienated from the other parent, that child has effectively just lost both parents.

During the onset of divorce, children are understandably needy and require extra attention and nurturing by both parents. In this scenario the children find themselves being caregivers instead of being cared for by their parents; they end up becoming emotional orphans.

A second version of a "victim mentality" scenario takes place when the noninitiator extends the "poor me" attitude to a "poor children" attitude and uses this line of reasoning to launch a custody battle, ostensibly in the best interests of the children. I am convinced that the majority of custody fights involve men whose wives have initiated the divorce and who are holding onto the kids in the hope of also holding onto the house and the familiar structure of their lives. "You want this divorce, so why don't you move out and leave me and the kids here? Why should all our lives be disrupted just because you decide to break your vows and have a second adolescence?"

This sentiment often then leads to an attempt to portray the wife as a poor mother and to convince everyone that the children would be better off in the care of their father. This portrait of the mother often gets painted when she is leaving the marriage for another man, and it is tempting to argue that her immoral behavior proves that she is unfit to be the primary parent.

When you are feeling rejected, when your ego is in tatters and your sense of identity as father and husband is suddenly shattered, it is easy to fall into self-deluding beliefs as a way to seek solace for the pain. It is also easy to assume a pose as protector of the children, when what you are really doing is trying to minimize the dislocation the divorce will bring to your life. If you believe that your wife should move out of the house, it also means you will not have to move. If you believe that the children should stay with you, it means you will not have to cope with the painful feelings that living apart from them will bring. The more of your old life you can preserve, the more you can shift the dislocation of divorce to your wife, the less you have to change. And when you slide into this thought pattern, you are in trouble because you are probably ensuring a hotly litigated divorce.

If you can honestly acknowledge your feelings, you will see that you probably are not looking at the best interests of the children, but at your own fears and emotional needs. Assuming the posture of a victim is about the worst thing you can do. You need to avoid this at all cost lest your divorce become a total mess.

The Challenge of an Affair

This particular challenge, when one spouse has an affair, is so important and complex that it warrants its own section. Affairs are one of the most difficult issues of divorce. When one spouse learns that the other has been involved with someone else, the intense feelings of betrayal and humiliation can destroy the ability to trust, and a good divorce becomes unlikely. "If I couldn't trust you with other women, how can I trust anything you say about money?" The feelings are complicated by the fact that the affair may turn out to be of long standing. If it is you who have had the affair, your wife wonders whether you have been lying not only about the affair but about everything else as well.

I recall a divorce in which the wife had caught the husband in an affair 8 years before the divorce and had confronted him. The husband had been contrite and had promised never to see the other woman again. The couple had gone to marriage counseling to work on their relationship and had, seemingly, transcended the affair and continued the marriage.

Eight years later, the wife discovered that the husband lied and had continued his relationship with the other woman. Not only had he continued to maintain the other relationship, but it turned out that he had been paying her rent, bought her a convertible the same year he explained to his wife that they could not afford a new car for her, and, worst of all, paid for a breast enlargement operation for the girlfriend. Although this guy sets a record, in my experience, the acute rage and pain caused by his behavior are common in divorce.

Most affairs are not as flagrant as this example. Often a spouse is lonely because his marriage has grown stale or sour. He is tempted by opportunity, and he enters a relationship with someone new. Frequently it is a coworker he has known for some time and who has lent a sympathetic ear and slowly become a comforting companion. She understands the work that he does, is economically independent, and is a friend. The relationship blossoms from a friendship to something more, almost on its own steam, so that before they know it they are in bed together. Faced with the stress of a declining marriage, the affair feels very good. There are very few marriages, even good ones, that can stand up to an affair. It's like comparing yesterday's black coffee to today's frothy cappuccino: One just can't be compared to the other.

Do affairs destroy good marriages? Or are they only a reflection of marriages already gone bad? I have certainly seen otherwise viable marriages, ones that could have continued at least for a while, ended by affairs. I have also been aware of an increasing number of marriages in which affairs have been revealed and the marriage continued after some intense counseling. The majority of affairs develop after the marriage has deteriorated significantly. I have seen few cases in which otherwise happily married and emotionally satisfied people get involved in affairs. In most affairs, the affair is a symptom of something already seriously wrong with the marriage.

It is not unusual for people to have affairs as marriages unravel, and it is not surprising that the initiator of the divorce has begun to connect to other people as she accepts that her marriage is over. Having an affair is a way of reassuring yourself that you are still attractive and that you will be able to rebuild a social and emotional life after the marriage. So that which would have been unthinkable during the marriage becomes more acceptable as you depart. But it is not acceptable to your partner. Now to the strong emotions that accompany any breakup is added the indignation and rage of feeling betrayed. For a man to be publicly cuckolded is a source of deep humiliation. For a woman to be betrayed by a wandering and lecherous husband makes her an object of sympathy and him an object of scorn. So there is no understating the emotional impact of an affair revealed.

The Impact of an Affair on the Divorce

The greatest danger about the revelation of affairs is that it makes it so much easier for the aggrieved spouse to make the affair the central explanation of the divorce. Consider the story of Jim and Casey.

Jim and Casey had been struggling with their marriage for years. They fought over money, about disciplining the kids, because Jim did not feel that Casey was an adequate housekeeper, and because Jim felt that Casey talked to him in a disrespectful way. Yet no matter how often Jim pleaded with Casey to change, she angrily rejected his requests. Over a period of 5 years, they each engaged in mutual stonewalling and each grew more distant from the other. Sex diminished and then stopped altogether. Casey gained 30 pounds and Jim did not find her sexually exciting. When he told her that her weight was a problem for him, she was hurt and angry but did nothing to solve the problem. As the two withdrew from each other, each spent more time in pursuits that didn't involve the other. At times, each wondered if divorce was desirable, but they did nothing to move in that direction because it was too scary.

Then Jim took a new position working as an account manager for a bank. Jim's new employer used a team approach and Jim was teamed with Sally, an attractive single woman with whom he quickly established a good rapport. Jim and Sally were a successful team from the beginning and soon were winning praise for their recruitment of new business. Working with Sally was fun for Jim, and he enjoyed going to work in the morning because he looked forward to spending the day with her. Their skills were complementary, and Sally was generous with her praise of her colleague. They were frequently together having lunch with clients and often found them-

selves together in the evening when both stayed late to work on a new account.

Jim and Sally started to become emotionally close and began to share the details of their lives. Jim told Sally about his frustrations at home, and Sally told Jim the details of her divorce a year before. A friendship slowly developed over 6 months. Gradually, Jim found himself fantasizing about sex with Sally and felt that she was interested in him, too. One night, after winning a big account, they went out for dinner to celebrate. As the evening drew to a close, Jim kissed Sally for the first time and found her warm and responsive. Within a few weeks, they had slept together and the affair was on.

Two weeks later, Casey heard a rumor through a friend that there was something going on between Jim and a woman at his office. Alarmed, Casey called a lawyer she knew to get the name of a private detective, whom she hired to follow Jim. Within a week the detective provided Casey with all the evidence she needed, and she confronted Jim that very night. Surprised and feeling ambushed, Jim acknowledged that he had met someone with whom he enjoyed spending time. Casey was furious and told Jim she wanted him out. He moved out 2 days later, and Casey immediately filed for divorce on grounds of adultery. Casey told her friends that Jim had left her for another woman, and that was the story she told throughout the divorce.

It is rare that a perfectly good marriage succumbs to an affair. The story of Jim and Casey is the typical case. When a marriage goes sour, it is usually a joint effort. Upon a little investigation, we usually find that each partner contributed to the demise of the marriage. Marital fault is usually not one-sided, but there are many people who resist taking responsibility for the divorce. It is easier and more comforting to be able to play the victim.

But this psychologically comforting posture has an unfortunate consequence when it comes time to craft a settlement that distributes the dislocation fairly among the family. If the noninitiator is able to take refuge in a dramatic story that puts all the blame on the other, then he or she is also able to justify in her mind that it is the guilty party who should absorb a disproportionate share of the adverse consequences of the divorce. "You were bad, you suffer" is the posture taken. The difficulty with the affair is that it becomes the story that liberates the "victim" from any responsibility and thus makes it much more difficult to negotiate a reasonable settlement.

It compounds the already existing dynamic of anger and victimization experienced by the noninitiator of the divorce.

In the divorce that followed, Casey never deviated from her position as the aggrieved victim of Jim's infidelity. Her position throughout the divorce was, "You did this to us, so don't expect me to make this easy on you." She punished Jim as much as she could by telling the children that the divorce was caused by Jim's affair, and before long their teenage daughter refused to see Jim. Casey refused to do any of the things she could have done to ease the transition for the family. She refused to consider getting a job and refused to consider selling the house that they couldn't afford.

Although the case was settled the day before the trial was scheduled, the outcome was bitter. It was years before Jim was able to have a relationship with his daughter. When Jim eventually married Sally, the daughter refused to attend the wedding and exhibited nothing but hostility toward Sally. Casey finally got a job but had lost 3 more years of a career. And Casey and Jim never were able to have a cooperative relationship involving the children.

Casey was able to use the affair to avoid responsibility for her role in the failure of the marriage. That was ultimately to her detriment, and it guaranteed the family a bad divorce.

If You're the One Having an Affair

Having said all this, the question remains: How should you manage the issue if you have been having an affair? What do you do? Do you tell or conceal? If your wife finds out, how do you manage it so that it doesn't produce an ugly divorce?

I submit that it is not necessary for you to reveal to your wife that you are having an affair. It's kind of late in the game to obsess about honesty and integrity. If you have been discreet, your affair is not public knowledge, and your wife is unaware of it, you accomplish nothing by telling your wife now. It will probably focus her exclusively on the affair, justify her assuming a victim's posture, and generally poison the divorce process. Further, if you hope to marry your girlfriend someday, identifying her now as a "homewrecker" assures that your children will be programmed to resent her.

If your wife already knows, it is another matter. Now your attention must be on damage control, lest the affair become the central legend of the divorce. Your wife will be angry and extremely upset. She will feel hurt, rejected, frightened, humiliated, and betrayed. You need to spend a lot of time listening without trying to defend yourself. Defending yourself is the last thing you should do. Apologies and expressions of contrition help. It is only after your wife has had an opportunity to tell you how she feels that she will be ready for any discussion that acknowledges that the marriage was dying before the affair. If you are lucky and if you listen long enough, she may be ready to hear the message and to join you in seeking a constructive divorce.

There is no point in your assuming a belligerent posture. Nothing could be dumber than to tell your wife that her own behavior is what caused you to have an affair. Although you will tell her that you believe the divorce would have happened anyhow, your posture of contrition is necessary if she is ever to cooperate with you. At some level of consciousness, she knows that she contributed to the divorce, but that will never emerge for her if you get into a cycle of attack, defense, and counterattack.

If Your Wife Is Having an Affair

When it comes to extramarital sex by women, we have always had a double standard, and it is only recently, and only in modern countries, that we have come to relax that perspective. There is a culturally shaped predisposition for men to react to the affairs of their wives with particularly intense rage. This can have just as distorting a consequence for you as if the situation were reversed. Consider the story of Max and Sue.

Max and Sue had been married 15 years when Sue told Max that she wanted a divorce. Max was stunned. Although they had had some problems over the years and had only had sex twice in the last 6 months, Max had always believed that he and Sue would work it out. They had two children, ages 6 and 8, and they did many things together as a family. Max was surprised and blindsided by Sue's announcement. Through several long evenings Max tried everything he could to talk Sue out of divorce. He pleaded for the benefit of the children. He pleaded that all they needed was some more time to weather this crisis. He urged Sue to return to counseling with him.

Sue, however, was resolute. She told Max that she simply didn't love him anymore and felt the life had drained from their relationship years ago. She said that she had agonized about this for years and had struggled unsuccessfully with her growing sense of isolation and loneliness. For years, she had pleaded with Max to talk to her, to share his feelings with her, and not to exclude her from what was happening inside him. But she regarded Max as closed off and guarded. She needed intimacy and a close connection and had come to believe that she would never get it from Max. Approaching 40, Sue was determined to have one more chance of closeness with someone before she was too old. Although she didn't believe it would do any good, she agreed to a short round of counseling with Max in the hope that he would better understand her decision.

So they went to counseling every week for a month. Here Max argued for a continuation of the marriage, but Sue held her position and insisted that the marriage was over. As Max became more frustrated, he also became angry. He started to realize that Sue was proposing to dismantle the life he had struggled to build. In passing comments, she had tried to assure him that she wanted him to see the kids as much as he wanted to. And as she spoke, it dawned on him that she expected him to move out and leave her and the kids in the house. Now he really became angry.

Then Sue dropped a bomb. During the last session, when Max was again pleading for another chance, Sue told him that she had started to develop a relationship with a man she met at work and that she really wanted to be able to pursue that relationship because she had gone so long without warm companionship. Max was beside himself with anger and betrayal. He felt that Sue had tricked him into counseling knowing that he was hoping to fix the marriage, even though she had already decided on divorce. In Max's mind the divorce had nothing to do with their relationship. Sue was just using their marital difficulties as a pretext to leave the marriage for another man.

Max felt that he hadn't done anything wrong in the marriage, but that Sue had betrayed her marital vows and had engaged in adultery. He was the wronged party, and he vowed that Sue would pay for her behavior. Max asked around at work for the name of the most aggressive lawyer he could find. The next week he filed for divorce, seeking custody of the children and seeking to deny Sue any alimony or marital property. The divorce was a

3-year-long mess with legal fees well into six figures. Max didn't get custody. Because the relationship had become so poisonous, visitation with the kids was difficult and awkward. The judge awarded Sue alimony and awarded her half the marital property. Max is now bitter and disillusioned. He vows never to marry again.

The advice for you here is consistent with our discussion about affairs. If you find out that your wife has been having an affair, you have the right to grieve and to feel angry. But the same principles apply to you about choosing between acting out your feelings and acting on your long-term interests. If you have children, you owe them the most peaceful divorce you can manage. And in most states, your fantasy of punishing your wife for her infidelity will run aground eventually because few judges are willing and few states permit marital fault to be expressed in the economic resolution of the divorce. There are a few states in which adultery by a wife is a complete bar to alimony and in which you can even sue her paramour for alienation of affection. But usually it's not going to matter in the long run, and your angry litigation will only leave you both poisoned by the years of struggle.

It is not likely that your great marriage was destroyed by your wife's affair with another man. If you truly believe that, you are confused. I suspect that your marriage was in trouble long before she met the other man and that you had ample warning that something was wrong between you. If you don't acknowledge to yourself that you played an important role in the decline of your relationship, not only will it affect the way you act now, but it will also prevent you from learning from the experience. It is undoubtedly a blow to your ego to find out that she now prefers another man and it is a blow to your pride to think of her in bed with another man. But you do not have to act out like a character in a bad novel. You need self-restraint, and your children need you to exercise self-restraint. Look ahead 5 or 10 years before you decide what to do. In divorce, everything you do by instinct is wrong.

Now that we've talked through the early stages of a divorce and outlined its monumental challenges, it is time to move on to proposing the collaboration. Here is where you will work out the details of your divorce and shape your new relationship for your new lives.

"The New Year is approaching, Miriam—traditionally a time of new beginnings. I suggest we use the occasion to dedicate ourselves to restoring that atmosphere of trust and mutual respect which characterized the early years of our marriage, and that in that spirit we continue to work together toward what I sincerely hope will be an amicable divorce."

Four

PROPOSING THE COLLABORATION

AFTER YOU AND YOUR WIFE have worked through the initial
emotions of your divorce and made it through some early pitfalls, reality
has set in; it's time to get to work. At this point in your divorce, you'll need
to propose collaboration to your wife and recruit her for the process. In this
chapter, we'll talk about that process and then go over some important
guidelines for relating to your wife during the early stages of the divorce.
Then, I'll review some of the emotional tasks you need to complete as you
get underway.

Proposing the Collaboration

It is ironic, but in order to have a successful separation and a good divorce,
you and your wife must work together, perhaps like you never have before.
Separating well is a complicated task that can be accomplished only with
collaboration.

Even if you choose to do it through lawyers and lawyers fighting, in
the end the two of you will still have to reach agreement about how to
manage the children and the income and how to divide your property. The
only question is whether you will choose an efficient way or an ineffi-
cient way.

Negotiation does not mean that you will each act as if you have only joint goals. But it does mean that you will recognize that you have many goals in common and that the ability of each of you to thrive will be largely determined by how well the other thrives. So you have some hard work to do and many difficult choices to make. The last thing you need is to place a lot of drag on the system by engaging in a mutually self-defeating struggle.

It may seem surprising, but whether you are the initiator or the noninitiator, you can propose the collaboration. Try to set aside your emotions now and take the lead in proposing that the two of you collaborate to achieve a decent divorce.

When I say you're "proposing" this to your wife, I mean that in quite a literal sense. I'm actually going to recommend that you sit down with her and offer her a formal proposal on how you'd like to move forward in your divorce. Because mutual trust may be low, you will need to be patient when you propose this to your wife. Try to choose a neutral time and place, where you'll both be as comfortable as possible.

Here are five key talking points when making the proposal.

1. WE BOTH SEEK A DECENT DIVORCE.

"I have been thinking about the divorce and how we should go about it. I think it is important that we both do it decently, and I hope that you think the same way. I am aware how easily some couples get into litigation and spend years torturing each other before a settlement is worked out. I think it would be a shame if that happened to us."

This is the basic proposition. It casts the divorce as something that requires both of you to act on in concert.

2. WE BOTH WANT FAIR RESULTS.

"The divorce will be a difficult transition for us and for the children. We need an agreement that allows the children to retain solid relationships with each of us. We need to divide our resources so two households can thrive. I want you to know that I am committed to working with you to accomplish a fair and equitable division of income and property. I also am committed to doing it in a way that allows both of us all the time we need to figure this out."

The reference to fairness is important, but note that you do not propose specific settlement terms at this time.

3. WE SHOULD USE MEDIATION.

"I have been doing some reading and believe that we should use a mediator to help us negotiate our agreement. A good mediator can help us identify options that we might not think of and can help us keep talking when we get stuck. I hope you will join me in finding the right mediator for us."

Introducing mediation is important. If you have done your homework, you will have books, articles, and Web sites that you can provide to your wife so she can do her own research.

4. WE SHOULD USE LAWYERS CAREFULLY.

"I am not asking you to do this without the help of a lawyer. I am asking that each of us use a lawyer to advise us when we need advice, but that we not ask them to take over and speak for us. We each should be free to obtain all the advice we need to do this well, whether that advice comes from lawyers, accountants, or psychologists."

A common error is to insist that neither of you consult lawyers out of fear that the lawyers will make a mess. But if your wife is frightened or regards you as having a negotiation advantage, your insistence on her not having a lawyer will be enough to frighten her away from mediation. There is every reason to consult with lawyers, but to choose lawyers who will support you in mediation rather than taking control of the negotiation.

5. WE BOTH NEED TO COMMIT TO NOT WALKING OUT.

"I am proposing that we make a mutual commitment to keep talking until we resolve all issues and that neither of us use the threat to quit when we are frustrated. I promise to stay with it until both of us are satisfied that the agreement works."

A commitment to staying in negotiation even when you have serious disagreements is important for getting you past the rough spots.

From a woman's perspective, your commitment to not cutting off communication is very important to reassuring her that she is safe.

You'll notice that the proposal is cast very positively, in terms of agreement. At this time, notice that you're not talking about any specifics. For example, it would not be good to propose that she agree in advance to some particular custody arrangement as the price of your cooperation. Right now, you're just agreeing to cooperate! By demanding concessions and agreement at this time, you would create fear in your wife that you have many nonnegotiable positions and that negotiation with you will be fruitless.

It's natural that you'll have concerns about how your wife will respond to your proposal. How she responds to your proposal may depend on many things, but particularly on how you have behaved to this point. If you have avoided angry outbursts and a lot of blame and guilt-inducing statements, and if you have not made threats about cutting off money, there is a good chance she will accept your proposal.

In my experience, initiators are more likely to be open to mediation than noninitiators. So if your wife is the initiator, she is very likely to welcome your proposal. She wants closure and clarity as soon as she can get it because she is emotionally ready to move on.

If you are the initiator, you may meet some initial resistance. The more patient you can be and the less insistent on a quick response, the greater the chance that your wife will, in time, agree. Remember that her own Greek chorus is encouraging her to fight just as yours is doing. If she is frightened and if she is being told by friends and acquaintances that she had better protect herself, the slightest threatening behavior from you will confirm her fears and send her running to a lawyer for rescue. So go easy and go slow.

Guidelines for Relating to Your Wife

Between the decision to divorce and the physical separation, you and your wife are stranded between two worlds: your past life together and your future lives apart. It is only natural during this period of limbo that emotions run high. Even the slightest miscue can lead to an explosion that could irrevocably damage your chances at a good divorce. The problem is that, because the relationship has changed, it is hard to know how to act.

Managing Day-to-Day Interactions

So how do you relate to each other? Even though you and your wife are divorcing, you are still together and still have many of the expectations of a married couple. She may still be your primary confidant, so you may be inclined to turn to her when something is troubling you. However, she is also the person you are divorcing and the feelings of rejection are still palpable. She is both friend and stranger at the same time, as are you to her.

While you are in this stage, it's likely that you and your wife may get into discussions that begin as pleasant recollections from the past, only to see them deteriorate into two conflicting versions of history. You may each ruminate about the future, only to find yourselves in a fight over how much support she seeks or whether she will agree to sell the house. Your situation is volatile, and what begins as a simple discussion soon becomes a battle with hurt feelings.

This is all part of the process of parting, and the sooner you acquire new expectations of each other, the better off you will be. Many couples come to me for mediation and express hope that they can come out of the divorce still being friends. It is very difficult to ratchet a relationship down from an intimate one to a friendship. Friends expect to be able to turn to each other for emotional sustenance, encouragement, and ap-proval. Calling on each other for help or emotional reinforcement is tricky because intimate conversation between you triggers so many old and unresolved issues. You are the source of so much pain to each other that the pain is simply inconsistent with a friendship. So talk of friend-ship, more often than not, can just lead to further disillusionment with each other.

So, instead of aiming for friendship, the model that I return to repeatedly in this book is the appropriate dialogue with a business colleague. We expect business colleagues to be friendly rather than to be friends. When you talk to a colleague, you are careful to maintain a cordial and respectful tone. You do not engage in bursts of anger and you do not attack each other's character. You can agree to disagree, and you can negotiate amicable resolutions.

Because your relationship with a business colleague is limited to your common purpose, your communication is also limited. This helps ensure the relationship is long term; you do not stress it by demanding interaction outside of what is necessary to achieve a common goal.

This is especially important if you have children, as you and your wife will have to cooperate around child-related issues for a long time. You will have to be able to share relevant information, cooperate with each other to achieve common but limited goals, and resolve conflicts related to those goals on the occasions when such conflicts arise.

Although it is quite difficult to shift gears suddenly and move from an intimate relationship with complex expectations to that of business colleagues, you need to begin consciously moving toward the transition. As mentioned before, during the very difficult period after you have decided to divorce but before you have separated, it is easy to do great damage. Each of you may still be testing old agendas with each other. Each may look for approval and then feel angry when it is not forthcoming.

That's why now is the time to learn how to steer clear of trouble. You must be polite and cordial. Let your wife know when you are coming and going. Do your share of work in the house and have no expectations of personal service from her. Do your own laundry and shopping. Think of yourself as housemates, not spouses; you need to exercise the independence of a housemate. Do not burden your wife with your fears and do not expect to have intimate discussions. That is what you have friends for. That is what you use a therapist for. The sooner you and your wife achieve a respectful and cordial distance, the better off you both will be.

I also urge that you suggest divorce counseling for the two of you. Divorce counseling is not marital therapy and is not intended to achieve reconciliation. Divorce counseling uses a skilled therapist to help the two of you have any unfinished discussions about emotional issues that will help you both accept that the marriage is over. Ideally, divorce counseling provides a safe place where each of you can say things that you feel the need to say and ask questions that are still unanswered. Frequently in such counseling, the noninitiator of the divorce seeks answers about why you want a divorce and sometimes tries one last time to get you to agree to try again. It is a useful forum, because the therapist can interrupt to ensure that each of you are heard, can intervene to help you frame statements to minimize injury, and can provide the opinion of an independent third party that the marriage indeed seems to be over. It is also a safe place to try and obtain your wife's agreement to join you in managing a decent and gentle divorce. It gives you an opportunity to assure her that your intentions are to be fair and gentle and to meet your responsibilities to her and the children. A competent counselor should be able to help you do this in a few sessions. As in the choice of any professional, check out the counselor's credentials and experience carefully because an incompetent counselor can do more harm than good.

Managing Your Finances

Needless battles over money derail more divorces in the early stages than any other issue. Money is a source of power, so to be without money makes us feel powerless. At this point in your divorce, you want to avoid any behavior that will frighten your wife about money. Here are some simple rules.

1. Make no unilateral change in any bank or securities account. Well-meaning but ignorant advisers and some overzealous lawyers may counsel you to raid the accounts and move the money to new accounts in your name only. The usual rationale is that if you don't strike first, your wife will, and then she will have a huge advantage. And it is true that were she to sequester the money she would enjoy a slight bargaining advantage in the war that would follow. But it would also not be difficult to obtain a court order freezing the money so that neither of

you could get at it without the consent of the other. But that is irrelevant because your objective here is trust, and trust cannot be achieved without some vulnerability and risk.

2. If there is some compelling reason that you have to make a withdrawal, such as payment of taxes, tell your wife first and secure her consent. Do not assume that she trusts you, and control your indignation if she asks for safeguards that she had not sought in the past.

3. Do not cancel your wife's credit cards or in any way take unilateral measures to control her spending. If you think that her spending is a problem, take the question up with your counselor or mediator. It is often necessary to negotiate temporary support or money management arrangements. By insisting on a bilateral agreement, you establish the premise that you and your wife can work out the details in negotiation and that power struggles through lawyers are unnecessary.

Managing Parenting Issues

At this stage of your divorce, it's critical to maintain the parenting status quo. If your wife has been the parent in charge of the children, now is not the time to assert your equality as a parent. Your relative parenting roles will be negotiated soon, and in your anxiety to maintain your role as father, do not precipitate threatening struggles over the children.

One of the most painful aspects of divorce is informing the children. I have seen many couples mess up this sensitive task by handling it unilaterally or precipitously. So develop a plan with your wife for you to together tell the children about the divorce. This is absolutely a joint task, and you may want some joint counseling about how and what to tell them.

Managing the News of Your Breakup

This is the time to develop a plan with your wife to break the news to relatives and friends. You can assume that she has discussed this already with intimate confidants, so don't be surprised to discover that some people already know. Nevertheless, offering to consult with your wife on the timing of the public dissemination of the news is an essential courtesy to extend.

Managing Your New Social Lives

Be very discreet in dating at this time. Even when your wife is the initiator, she will not be ready to receive information that she has been replaced without your even breaking stride. Do not assume that because she is leaving you she is done with you emotionally. She may even continue to harbor strong feelings toward you and may fantasize that you will make some dramatic gesture to win her back. If your wife gets a report that you were at the movies with some other woman just 2 weeks after she told you that she wanted a divorce, her resentment may sizzle even though you think she has no right to such feelings.

Ideally, dating should wait until you are living separately, and even then there is no reason to put new relationships in your wife's face. You have nothing to prove to her, and there is no issue here of who is right or wrong. It is only an issue of maintaining civility and moving the relationship along to a businesslike collaboration. But if you are dating while you are still living in the family home, it is worth taking pains to keep that activity thoroughly segregated from your continuing life at home.

Some Emotional Tasks to Complete

As you begin to collaborate with your wife on your divorce, there are several emotional tasks that you need to complete. These tasks may take some time, but they are better to complete sooner rather than later.

Coming to Terms with the Past

Coming to terms with the past history of the marriage can take years. There is often a sense of wonder that we could have been so wrong in our initial decision to marry. How could I have made such a mistake? And if I could have made that mistake, does it mean that I can make another mistake with the next woman? In time, if you are lucky and sufficiently honest with yourself, you may figure out what went wrong so that your next relationship is more successful. Understanding what went wrong, what your contribution was, and whether there are proclivities of yours which you need to recognize are all part of the long task to be completed.

You also must let go of issues of blame and recrimination that will get in the way of the collaboration you have proposed. You can do one of three things, depending on how you are emotionally constructed. One possibility is that you explain the circumstances of the divorce to yourself in terms of everything being your wife's fault, but keep it to yourself. Again, here is the distinction between feelings and behavior. You feel one way, but act another. You do not tell her that you think she was largely at fault for the marital failure. You do not communicate that because she was at fault she should absorb the dislocation of the divorce and leave you untouched. In other words, you act as if you are partly responsible for the divorce and avoid saying things that require her to become defensive. Regardless of your feelings, you must behave in a manner consistent with the collaboration you have proposed.

A second option—which is preferable by far—is for you to actually believe that the divorce and the marital problems that caused it were a joint venture, so that your behavior can be congruent with your feelings. That may take more soul searching and more therapy than you are ready to accept.

The third choice, one that will prove deadly, is anything that has the premise "Because you were wrong (duplicitous, lazy, untruthful, self-indulgent, treacherous, etc.) in the past, it is only right and just that you should compensate me in the future." That line of reasoning expressed in discussions with your wife gets you nothing but resistance and the squandering of an opportunity to stay in control of the process. Once you raise the past, you lock yourselves into a fruitless search for a reconciliation of your two radically different versions of history. You will not ever agree and your divorce process will be a pointless attempt to vindicate the past at the expense of a constructive future.

Developing a Vision of the Future

When I teach divorce mediation skills, one of the key strategic elements I emphasize is that the mediator must help the client shift his focus from past to future. In the future there is no blame. In the future you are mostly free of the consequences of this unsuccessful marriage. And whereas you can do nothing to reshape the past—other than nurse your illusions—you can take control and shape your future. The faster you can begin to envision what your future life will look like, the sooner you can get on with the task of designing it. Where will you live? How do you want to relate to your children? How do you want to reshape your social life? Do you see yourself building a new relationship possibly leading to remarriage?

In the very beginning, when you are still reeling from the news that your marriage has ended, you will not be ready to construct a vision of a new relationship. But in fact, 80 percent of men are remarried within 2 years of the divorce. There is a high probability that you, too, will meet someone new and end up remarried or living with a woman within a few years. Try to imagine yourself in a new relationship that is satisfying and not fraught with irreconcilable disputes, one in which your own emotional needs are met and one that is full of joy. You have probably been missing those things for a long time, and it helps if you can begin to imagine yourself in such a reconstructed life. The reason it is useful to do this is that it helps you to focus on what is really important and on avoiding the behaviors that could turn this divorce bitter and interfere with your ability to achieve your future goals.

Choosing Your Objectives

As you begin to construct your vision of the future, you will need to specify your objectives in the divorce with respect to the three principal issue areas: children, money, and property. The hope here is that if you begin with a realistic objective, you should be able to come close in the negotiation with your wife. If you don't know what you want, you have little hope of getting it. Keep in mind, though, realistic objectives take into account the reasonable objectives of the other person. In other words, your wife will have her own objectives. Don't set your hopes too high—you're not likely to receive sole custody, all of the money, and all of the property in your divorce settlement.

Objectives for Your Children

First, consider the objectives that you have as a father. What parenting pattern will make you feel fulfilled as a parent and meet the needs of your children? If you set as your goal that the children should spend all their time with you, it guarantees a fight because it leaves no reasonable place for your wife in the lives of her children. So objectives are not the same as wishes or ideals or desires. Objectives are a reasonable reconciliation of your, your wife's, and your children's needs. It is a given that the children will spend time with each of you, so the only issues to be decided are the distribution of that time. Perhaps a reasonable objective is for your children to live with your wife but visit your new home every other weekend.

Objectives for Your Finances

The same balancing will be necessary when dealing with financial issues. Again, what are your reasonable objectives? Here, "reasonable" involves two issues. First, what are the settlement norms where you live? You both will be influenced by what you come to believe are the norms for distributing income and property. So if the norm is for an equal division of property acquired during the marriage, your objective to obtain all or most of the property is inherently unreasonable because it does not leave your wife with any reasonable place to go. Similarly, if your income is much greater than hers, alimony will probably be an issue. If you have been married for 20 years, alimony will likely be for a substantial term of years or even be permanent. If, under those circumstances, you decide that your objective is to pay alimony for 1 year, you are choosing an inherently unreasonable objective.

But "reasonable" is not defined only by the local norms. There is no precise calibration of such norms, and lawyers will differ significantly in their views of what those norms are. And as I say elsewhere in the book, it is commonplace to have two lawyers on opposite sides of the case argue, with absolute certainty, totally opposite positions with respect to those norms.

The second piece of the discussion has to focus on what works for you and for your wife. Obviously, it is easy to slide into a zero-sum game in which you regard everything that she gets as something that you lose. But all that happens when you do is that she mirrors you and adopts the same position. So the conceptual key to negotiating a good divorce is a set of objectives that is related to everyone's reasonable objectives. We will talk about this more in chapter 8 as we discuss how to negotiate.

"I now declare you divorced, reversing my decision of three years ago pronouncing you man and wife."

Five

AN OVERVIEW OF DIVORCE LAW

IT IS 9 A.M. IN THE UNION COUNTY COURTHOUSE. *Margie and Don Franklin wait nervously in the hall outside of Judge Green's court-room. They are waiting for their lawyers to arrive because they are getting divorced this morning. Margie's lawyer, Marshal Gold, and Don's lawyer, Ann Gardner, arrive. The judge is ready, so Margie and Don follow their lawyers into the courtroom.*

Although both spouses feel nervous, they know that there will be no surprises today. The four of them met last week to work out the final de-tails of the settlement, which was signed 3 days ago. The settlement de-tailed all the necessary agreements they negotiated about how they would manage their child, how much child support and alimony Don would pay to Margie, and how they would divide the marital property. There was nothing left to fight about. The divorce was filed 8 months ago and was based on the fact that they had been separated for a year. Margie's lawyer filed the complaint, so Margie was the plaintiff and was called to the witness stand first.

After the bailiff swore her in, her lawyer asked her a series of questions they had rehearsed the day before.

Q: *Where did you live?*
A: *24 Hillside Avenue, Union, New Jersey.*

Q: *Did you marry Don Franklin on February 4, 1988?*
A: *Yes.*

Q: *Is this a copy of your marriage certificate?*
A: *Yes.*

Q: *Are you and your husband living together?*
A: *No.*

Q: *When did you separate?*
A: *In January, about a year and a half ago.*

Q: *Is there any reasonable prospect of reconciliation between you?*
A: *No.*

Q: *I show you a document titled* Separation Agreement between Don Franklin and Marjorie Franklin, *dated June 4, 2003, and ask you if you recognize your signature on page 17.*
A: *Yes, that is my signature.*

Q: *When you signed it, did you understand it?*
A: *Yes.*

Q: *When you signed it, did you do so voluntarily and free of any duress?*
A: *Yes.*

Q: *When you signed it, did you believe that it was fair?*
A: *Yes.*

Q: *Do you still regard it as fair, and are you requesting the court to incorporate this agreement into the judgment of divorce?*
A: *Yes.*

Following this cryptic exchange, Marjorie's lawyer told the judge that he had no further questions. The judge asked Don's lawyer if she had any questions and she said no. The judge then told Margie she could step down and ordered that Don be sworn to testify.

Don took the stand and was asked a series of questions by his lawyer almost identical to those that had been asked of Margie. He answered the same as she and was then excused by the judge. When the parties and their lawyers were seated again, the judge spoke.

"I find that the parties were lawfully married in New Jersey on February 4, 1988, that they separated during January 2002, and have lived apart ever since. They have established that this court has jurisdiction over the marriage and that they have satisfied the requirements of the law for a divorce by living separately and apart for longer than 18 months.

"The parties have submitted a separation agreement, and both have testified that they signed it knowingly and voluntarily, and that both regard it as fair. This court makes no independent finding with respect to the merits of that agreement and orders that it be incorporated into the judgment of divorce. Counsel will submit the appropriate judgment to me for my signature. Have a good day."

The judge signed the judgment of divorce and the divorce was over. The proceedings lasted all of 10 minutes.

Scenes similar to this occur every business day in every county of every state in the country. People are often surprised by the anticlimactic and perfunctory way that it ends—with no drama, and lasting only a few minutes. This is the way most divorces end. How they got there and how they came to be resolved is the subject of this chapter.

What Is a Divorce?

The answer to this question starts with another question: "What is a marriage?" A marriage is a public ceremony sanctioned by the state that creates a new legal status for the two people getting married. Marriage gives a man and a woman certain rights and obligations with respect to each other. Each acquires the right to inherit part of the other's estate. Each acquires certain economic responsibilities for each other. Each can demand that the other maintain a monogamous relationship. All of these are inherent in the legal status created when they make the state a third party to the relationship.

Marriage is intended to be permanent. If you want to end the marriage, you must get the permission of the state. To do this, you must offer compelling reasons to the state why the marriage should end. Only the state can dissolve the marriage bonds because only the state can create the bond of marriage. Divorce is simply the reversal of the stated edict that you are married.

Because it is the state that declares you married and only the state can declare you divorced, it is the state that establishes the rules that apply to the dissolution of your marriage. The court of each state is the institution that carries out the law of the state. That is why you have to go to court to get divorced.

There are three sets of legal requirements that have to be satisfied before the court will grant you a divorce. First, you must establish that the court has jurisdiction over the marriage. Jurisdiction is based on residency, so you must establish that you have been residing in the state long enough to qualify as a legal resident. Once the jurisdiction of the court is established, you must establish that you have grounds for divorce. Grounds are the reason you offer to the state why it should dissolve your marriage. Each state legislature has passed laws concerning the reasons that that state will accept as a basis for divorce.

Having established grounds and jurisdiction, you must then satisfy the court that you have resolved the issues of divorce: custody of the children, support of the children, support for each spouse, and division of the marital property. If you have agreed on all these things, the state will grant your divorce. If you have not agreed, the court will conduct a trial, after which the judge will decide all of these issues and then dissolve the marriage. So divorce is about how we establish jurisdiction, grounds, and the resolution of the issues of divorce.

More on Jurisdiction

You get divorced in the state where you reside, whether or not it is the state where you got married. In this country, certain powers belong to the federal government and other powers are reserved for the states. The regulation of marriage is a power of the states, and therefore each state establishes its own laws on divorce. Each state decides for itself how long you have to reside before you qualify as a resident. Many years ago, when divorce was hard to obtain, certain states such as Nevada made it easy to establish residency and easy to get divorced. Because you could establish residence in a few weeks, many people seeking a "quickie" divorce would fly to Reno for a month and come back divorced. A problem arises because a state cannot easily exercise jurisdiction over property in another state, so the quickie divorce dissolved the marriage but often left other issues unresolved.

Jurisdiction is generally not a problem in divorce; you get divorced in the state where you have been living together. On occasion, it is a problem when one spouse has moved to another state, established residency, and wants to obtain the divorce in that state, believing that state's laws will be more favorable to the filing spouse.

Grounds

The young couple sat in my office looking solemn. They were a Chinese couple, both in the computer programming business, who had immigrated to this country 5 years before. When I asked how I could help them, the wife replied that she wanted a divorce from her husband. But the husband quickly stated that he did not want a divorce. He said that no one in either of their families had ever divorced and that to him, divorce was unthinkable. Looking at her, he asked "What have I done wrong?" "You have not done anything wrong," she said," I am just unhappy being married to you, and I want a divorce." "Happy?" he asked incredulously, "What does happy have to do with anything? We are married. We have children. What does happy have to do with it?"

Although laypersons think that grounds for divorce are important, grounds are, in fact, among the least important aspects of a divorce, and almost no divorces ever go to trial today on questions of grounds for divorce. Before the advent of no-fault divorce, only the spouse who had been victimized by the illicit conduct of the other spouse could sue for divorce. All divorce grounds were what are today called "fault grounds." The premise of your complaint for divorce was that your spouse had engaged in behavior that violated the covenants of marriage so egregiously that it would be unreasonable for you to be required to continue the marriage to that person. The most common offense that could serve as grounds was infidelity. Universally, adultery was grounds for divorce. Another common ground was desertion. If your spouse left you and refused to return for a period of time defined by statute, this was considered grounds for seeking a divorce.

Depending on the state, there are other grounds as well. Extreme cruelty, addiction and alcoholism, incarceration in a prison or a mental institution, or sexual deviance are all recognized as grounds for divorce.

Note that none of the above include simple human unhappiness as grounds for divorce. Before the current era, divorce was a punitive quasi-criminal proposition. But this definition of divorce started to change after World War II. The modern definition of romantic love began to displace more traditional notions of marriage and many people, particularly women, began to expect and demand more emotional satisfaction from their marriages. It was no longer acceptable for the spouse just to be a good provider, be monogamous, stay sober, and not beat you. People expected to be happy together, and endurance was no longer the antidote for marital unhappiness. People who were unhappy in their marriages wanted to be able to divorce without the consent of their spouses or the interference of the state. They wanted to be able to escape and remarry and were increasingly unwilling to be held in the marriage against their will. State legislatures began to respond by adding new grounds to their divorce statutes, and by the 1980s, virtually every state had adopted some variation of a "no-fault" ground for divorce.

No-fault grounds usually fall into one of two categories. The majority of states provide that if you can prove that you and your wife were incompatible or have differences that can not be resolved—irreconcilable differences—you can obtain a divorce. The second category is some defined period of separation. If the two of you have lived in separate homes for a period of 6 or 12 or 18 or 24 months—depending on the state—the court will take that fact as proof that your marriage is dead and dissolve the marriage. No-fault grounds do not require the consent of the other spouse; one person can no longer hold the other in an unhappy marriage.

Does It Matter if the Divorce Is No-Fault or Fault Based?

Most states, but not all, take little note of allegations of marital fault. Even though statutes may permit the court to take such behaviors into account, few judges are willing to do so. The modern view of divorce tends toward the position that both spouses have contributed to the demise of the marriage, even in cases where one of the spouses has had an affair. I recently saw a couple in which the wife was ending the marriage after having had an affair. Two years earlier, on the day the wife was having a double mastectomy, the husband had not been there because he was trying out for a TV game show. Given his remarkable insensitivity, how many people would really condemn this woman for seeking emotional comfort from another man?

As a practical matter, in most states it does not matter whether you proceed on fault grounds or no-fault grounds. But this fact has not yet fully entered the public consciousness. Too many people labor under the misapprehension that they can go to court and punish their errant spouse. Most end up disillusioned when, after spending 2 years and five figures on legal fees, they get to court and the judge is not interested in the issue of misconduct. Many people want to punish the divorcing spouse but in the end have to settle without such vindication. So here is the point. Grounds don't really matter. Almost no one goes to trial on issues of grounds for divorce. Anyone who wants a divorce can get one and can be neither stopped nor punished. In the end, there is no comfort for anyone but the lawyers in court struggles over grounds for divorce.

The Issues of Divorce

The issues of parenting, child support, alimony, and division of marital property must be resolved in order for you and your wife to obtain an uncontested divorce. These are also the issues that the two of you must resolve in order to lead a successful life.

Why the Court Wants These Issues Resolved

When a marriage ends, the state wants to know how the children will be cared for and supervised. Who will support the children? Who will supervise them and keep them out of trouble? Who will be in charge of ensuring that they grow up as lawful, productive members of society? The state fulfils the role of *parens patrie*, the parent of last resort. If you abandon your children, it is the state that must care for them, a task it assumes with great hesitation. Thus the state, through its courts, wants to know who will be in charge of the children and how the divorced parents will manage the rights and duties of parental responsibility. This concern is expressed in the issues of custody, visitation, and child support.

The state has a similar concern with respect to the maintenance of the spouses. Alimony is a legal requirement that the court can impose on either spouse to prevent the other spouse from becoming a ward of the state.

The third concern of the state is related to clear ownership of property. Because the family is an economic as well as a social unit, the dissolution of the family can leave questions behind about who owns what. Commerce and social order require that title to property be clear and unambiguous. You cannot buy land, businesses, or even cars if you cannot prove that the seller is the undisputed owner. So the division of marital property is important to the state as a matter of both social order and social justice. Married people have certain rights to each other's property. When one spouse dies, for example, the other has a right to inherit at least part of the estate. If you and your wife own a house with a right of survivorship and one of you dies, the other automatically receives full ownership of the house. If these rights were not terminated upon divorce, it would produce confusion whenever a third party attempted to purchase the property. So the state requires that property be divided into two bundles—his and hers—upon divorce.

The concerns of the state about children, spouses, and property have evolved over the years into what is now modern divorce law. Custody, visitation, child support, and division of marital assets are the issues of divorce that must be resolved to satisfy the state. Although we will delve more deeply into each of these later in the book, it will help if you have an overview of the issues now.

Custody

Over time, custody has become a poisoned concept that has come to mean a win/lose struggle in which one parent "loses" the kids while the other parent "wins" the children. Some states have recognized this and reworded their statutes to substitute "parenting" for "custody." There are three questions to answer with respect to parenting (or custody, whichever term you choose).

The first question is one of residence: With whom will the child live?

Will the child live exclusively with one parent and not with the other? Will the child live with both parents? And if the child lives with both parents, what will be the residential pattern? How many days and nights with the mother? How many days and nights with the father?

The second question is one of nurturance. Who will take care of the child on which days? Who will see that the child is fed, clean, entertained, educated, and clothed? Who will tuck him in at night, read a bedtime story, take her camping, and teach her stuff? How are these tasks, responsibilities, and pleasures to be divided between the parents once they are living in different households?

The third question is one of guardianship or decision making for the child. How and by whom are important decisions to be made concerning the child's health or education? If the child needs medical treatment, who chooses the doctor, or who decides whether she has an operation or takes a drug? Will the parents consult, or will one parent have the unilateral right to make such decisions without regard to the wishes of the other?

Today, courts have become psychologically oriented and recognize that children need both parents, even if one of the parents has more responsibility than the other. So the issue of custody has become the issues of custody and visitation. One parent is awarded custody, but to ensure that the other parent maintains contact with the child, the noncustodial parent is awarded rights of visitation with the child. Moreover, custody is no longer a vehicle of punishment, but is to be awarded by the court to the parent that the court finds to be better able to raise the child. (Throughout most of the twentieth century, that parent was the mother, with the father awarded visitation rights.)

Today, because most cases are settled by negotiation, the parents can choose any arrangement that works for them, and many have gone beyond the traditional custody/visitation model to some form of shared parenting. The important fact to you is that you and your wife can now shape any parenting arrangement that you wish and the court will not usually second-guess you. So let's review the concepts used to discuss this issue.

SOLE CUSTODY: Sole custody is an arrangement in which one parent is designated as the sole custodial parent and is put in charge of the child. The sole custodial parent has exclusive responsibility for the child, has exclusive decision-making authority over the child, and has exclusive residence where the child lives. The other parent, typically the father, has specified times when he can visit the child but has no authority with respect to the child.

JOINT CUSTODY: Joint custody became popular in the 1970s and is today recognized by most states. Joint custody means that both parents hold the residential, nurturing, and decision-making roles jointly, and more or less equally. Typically, there is a residential schedule in which the children spend approximately half of their time with each parent, and the parents have equal authority to make decisions for the children.

JOINT LEGAL CUSTODY: This term evolved in the last 20 years as the bloom came off the rose of joint custody. Many people found that equal sharing of the responsibilities of parenting did not work for them. These couples found that a more traditional pattern in which the children live principally with one parent and spend alternate weekends and some other times with the other parent actually worked better for that family. But although the second parent, again usually the father, would not have an equal role in caring for the child, he was unwilling to suffer the ignominy of the designations "noncustodial" and "visiting parent." In order to avoid the symbolic disenfranchisement of that parent, he was granted joint legal custody, entitling him to be consulted on major decisions affecting the child. Instead of being called the custodial parent, the parent with whom the child lives most of the time is designated the parent of primary residence or the primary residential parent. This designation has probably become the most common one used.

SHARED PARENTAL RESPONSIBILITY: This term has been adopted by some states to replace the concept of custody. It generally assumes that both parents will be involved in decision making for the child and that the residential arrangement can be anything from one of the parents being the primary residential parent to the parents each having equal time with the children.

The Role of the Children

Many people on the cusp of divorce ask if the children can decide with whom they will live. Generally, children, particularly young children, do not play a role in the decision. In most states, the preferences of the children are accorded more weight as they get older, and a child of 15 or 16 will have great influence if the parents cannot agree. From a psychological perspective, asking children to choose between parents is quite destructive because it gives children a kind of power that frightens them—no matter how they choose, they worry about betraying one parent. When you and your wife start to make the decisions about parenting, you will already know the preferences of your children, and there is little to be gained by asking them. You do your children a great favor by *not* asking them and by acting like parents by making the important decisions yourselves.

Can Parenting Arrangements Be Changed Later?

Until a child reaches the age of emancipation, the court retains ultimate jurisdiction over the child. This means that you can always go back to court to seek a change in the parenting arrangement. You and your ex-wife can make any changes at any time if you are both in agreement, but unilateral change against the will of the other parent can be made only with the permission of the court.

Child Support: Who Pays?

Supporting the child financially is the responsibility of both parents. Child support refers to the arrangement that has been worked out to share the expenses of the child. In the typical scenario, where the child lives primarily with one parent, that parent administers the financial needs of the child. She buys clothing; pays the medical bills; and pays for lessons, gifts, activities, school supplies, and the myriad other expenses that children require. Generally the pattern of spending after divorce simply reflects that which existed before the divorce. Because the primary residential parent spends most of the money budgeted for the child's needs, the other parent makes child support payments to defray the costs of raising the child.

Although monthly child support payments are typical, some parents do it differently. When the incomes of the parents are more or less equal, and when they have a full shared parental pattern in which each parent has the children half the time, each parent will simply pay the room and board expenses of the children when they are with that parent. Then they will keep track of expenditures for clothing, lessons, and other expenses of the child and share them equally. Cost sharing in this manner may be more satisfying for some parents even as it requires somewhat more complicated administration.

The Amount of Child Support

How much children cost depends on many things, including the family's income, where the family lives, and choices made by the parents. If you decide you want your children to attend a private school, you will spend up to $30,000 a year for this choice. If you believe that your children have to be dressed to the height of fashion, you will spend more than if you are less enthused about dressing in the latest styles. Because these choices can vary so widely, deciding on how much to spend on the children—and therefore how much child support should be paid—can become a subject of hot dispute. About 15 years ago, the federal government imposed on all states the requirement that each state establish minimum child support guidelines for divorce. The purpose of the guidelines was to establish a floor under child support amounts so that a judge could not order clearly inadequate support or no support at all. We have seen several generations of guidelines as states have attempted to make them acceptable to more parents. You will need to investigate the guidelines in your state. Don't be surprised to discover that they are too low to reflect the pattern of spending you have chosen in the past for your children.

Changing Child Support over Time

Child support is subject to change as the needs of the child and the financial capacity of the parents change. Children are entitled to share in the good fortune of their parents, so if you are paying child support and you sustain a dramatic increase in income, you can expect that you will be asked to pay more child support. Child support ends when a child is emancipated, generally when a child reaches age 18 or upon graduation from high school, whichever occurs first. A number of states, particularly the more urbanized states, will delay emancipation until the child graduates college. If you live in such a state, you will be expected to contribute to the cost of putting the child through college. No state that I am aware of has extended the requirement of child support past undergraduate education.

Many separation agreements provide for periodic review of the subject of child support. Ideally, you and your wife will work out a relationship in which over time the two of you will negotiate changes as appropriate. On the other hand, if change is needed and you are unable to resolve the issue between yourselves, you can always resort to the court for adjudication. I encourage all my clients to include mediation clauses in their settlement agreements so that if a dispute of this kind arises, they return to mediation to resolve it.

Alimony

Alimony is the toughest issue in divorce. It is also the subject of least consensus among lawyers and judges. Alimony, also called spousal maintenance or maintenance support, is paid to a former spouse. The statutes that deal with alimony are gender neutral—either spouse can be required to pay alimony to the other. With the rising incomes of women, it is no longer unusual to see cases in which women pay alimony to their husbands. But alimony is most frequently paid by men to women. Most divorces do not involve alimony payments. We have terribly inadequate data on divorce, so there are no precise statistics available. A study that was popular in the late 1970s claimed that fewer than 14 percent of women received alimony. I can't vouch for that statistic, but I suspect that not more than one-third of divorces involve alimony.

Some women earn salaries comparable to their husbands' and do not need alimony. So the cases in which alimony is an issue involve couples in which there is a significant disparity of income between the parties, a fairly long duration of marriage, and a demonstrated need of the wife for alimony.

The way in which these standards are applied is influenced by cultural factors such as attitudes toward sexual equality. Paradoxically, as the women's movement gathered momentum in the 1970s, there was a backlash against alimony. "If they want to be independent, let them be independent" was the attitude of a male-dominated judiciary and legal profession. But as time went on, the pendulum shifted back toward more alimony cases as it became increasingly evident that it was necessary to assist women who had been economically disadvantaged by their marriages. There is reason to believe that on average, a woman loses 3 percent of her career salary ceiling for each year out of her career. So a woman in her forties who stayed home for 12 years to raise children is at a severe disadvantage when reentering the work force. Alimony as a hot issue also reflects the very struggles that often contributed to the marital breakup. Power struggles over spending, demands by husbands that women return to work to supplement family income, and economic pressure caused by too much spending are all emotional issues that may contribute to the tensions that destroy a marriage. So, when a woman seeks alimony, many men experience the demand as a reprise of the very behaviors that they think caused the divorce.

Types of Alimony

There are three types of alimony, generally defined by their duration and the condition that causes alimony payments to end.

PERMANENT ALIMONY: Permanent alimony, sometimes called lifetime alimony, is paid until the recipient spouse remarries or until one of the parties dies. In large measure, alimony is neither permanent nor for a lifetime because very few women will remain unmarried and receive alimony until they die. Further, most husbands die before their ex-wives. And most state courts have some law in place that recognizes that a man paying alimony has a right to retire eventually, and that when he retires he cannot continue to pay the same alimony he paid before he retired. So it is a misconception to think that alimony gets paid forever.

REHABILITATIVE ALIMONY: Rehabilitative alimony is a modern concept that recognizes that while the wife should eventually be self-supporting, she needs time to retrain or recredential to a point where she can earn enough to support herself. Rehabilitative alimony is usually linked both to a number of years or to a "rehabilitative" event such as the wife getting her MBA or other credential. In most cases, rehabilitative alimony will be paid for a specified number of years, during which it is assumed that the wife will be rehabilitated. In some states the court will extend the alimony if for some unanticipated reason the wife is unable to achieve independence in the prescribed amount of time. Illness, economic events, or other unforeseen circumstances may arise that require a year or two more. But rehabilitative alimony is not for a long period of time and rarely exceeds 4 or 5 years. Its premise is clearly that the wife should become economically self-sufficient within the predictable future.

ALIMONY FOR A TERM OF YEARS: This is a hybrid between permanent alimony and rehabilitative alimony. It simply means that alimony will terminate in the specified term. If the term is 10 years, alimony will cease at that point, even if the wife is not self-supporting. The assumption is made that she had the opportunity to achieve self-sufficiency and that she should not remain dependent any longer. Alimony for a term of years may be appropriate when the wife is not sure what she wants to do as a career and doesn't want to be tied to the achievement of a credential such as a 4-year college degree.

REDISTRIBUTIVE ALIMONY: Redistributive alimony is the final, and seldom used, type of alimony. Suppose a wife supported her husband through medical school and sacrificed for years so that he could establish a lucrative career. Just as he begins his career, he falls in love with another woman and leaves his wife. There is little marital property to divide, and he is just starting to earn a good income. The wife has never given up her career and is able to support herself, so the traditional standards of alimony, if applied here, would result in her receiving nothing. Redistributive alimony evolved to award the wife some share of the husband's enhanced income which was made possible by the wife's invested time and energy.

Alimony and Taxes

Whereas child support is paid with after-tax dollars, alimony is paid with pretax dollars. Alimony is taxable income to the payee and not taxable to the payer. The payer deducts alimony paid from gross income before calculating taxable income. (To be precise, alimony is an adjustment to gross income rather than an itemized deduction.) One practical effect of this, which we will discuss in depth later, is that alimony sometimes shifts dollars from a high tax bracket to a lower tax bracket. So if a man who is in the 35 percent tax bracket pays $100 in alimony to his ex-wife, the net after-tax cost to him is $65 because he would have to pay $35 in taxes even if he did not pay alimony. If his wife is in the 15 percent bracket, her net income from the alimony is $85. Because of this tax aspect, alimony can become a useful financial planning tool in the divorce.

Division of Marital Property

For most couples, the division of marital property is a simple matter because the structure of their assets is simple. Most couples own a house; a couple of IRAs; a 401(k) plan; two cars; and a nominal collection of savings accounts, savings bonds, and a few shares of stock. Offsetting this is a car loan, some credit card debt, their mortgage, and perhaps a home equity loan. For such garden-variety divorces, the property gets divided equally, and the biggest issue is when to sell the house. But for couples who have greater complexity in their assets, the law of property division offers a complicated tapestry of statutes, case law, appraisal techniques, and tons of issues to fight about. Modern property division is a lawyer's dream because it justifies almost endless disputes over who gets what, how much it is worth, where it came from, and whether it even is marital property. So if your assets deviate at all from the simple middle-class marital estate, you will have to understand something about the modern law of equitable distribution.

Systems for Dividing Marital Property

Today, most states are "equitable distribution" states. Only nine states (Arizona, California, Idaho, Louisiana, New Mexico, Nevada, Texas, Washington, and Wisconsin) are still community property states, where property acquired during the marriage is automatically defined as joint property and is divided equally between the spouses at divorce.

Equitable distribution does not mean equal distribution. To the contrary, the law of equitable distribution formally rejects any numerical formula. Equitable distribution is defined by what it is not: It is not equal distribution, and the person whose name is on the title doesn't necessarily keep the property. The essential difference is that the judge is empowered to order the transfer of property from one spouse to another so long as the property is defined as "marital property" and is not exempt from equitable distribution. Moreover, the judge is admonished to distribute the property between husband and wife in such manner as is "equitable and just."

Since its inception, equitable distribution has evolved into a complex jumble of rules and procedures that has complicated even simple divorces. In chapter 13, I will explore at length the details of equitable distribution. For now, it is sufficient that you be aware that this is an area of divorce in which it is easy to lose control and to succumb to a lot of legal mumbo-jumbo that renders even the simple divorce unnecessarily complicated and impenetrable.

An Overview of Legal Procedure

Because divorce is, ultimately, a legal process, you need to know how a divorce gets into and moves through the court. As noted before, about 99 percent of all divorces are resolved before trial and end with the negotiation and drafting of a settlement agreement followed by the hearing described at the beginning of the chapter. There are two distinct aspects to a divorce: the negotiation of the settlement and the obtaining of the divorce through the court.

Ideally, you negotiate the settlement before there is any contact with the judicial system. Whether the settlement is the product of mediation or of negotiation between your lawyers, there should be no filing of any court documents until agreement has been reached and the settlement agreement is signed by you and your wife. The more you deviate from this and negotiate your settlement after one of you has filed for divorce, the higher the financial and emotional costs of divorce will be. Unfortunately, the most common pattern in the United States is one in which negotiation follows litigation, what some people have called "litigotiation," or what is also called the litigated settlement. Here are the steps in the formal divorce process.

The Pleadings

A divorce begins with the filing of a document called a *complaint for divorce*. The person who files is the plaintiff, and the other party is automatically the defendant. The complaint states the grounds on which the divorce is sought. For example, in New Jersey the grounds could be that the parties have lived separately for at least 18 months. The complaint also cites the fact that the parties were married, that the marriage still exists, and that the court has jurisdiction of the divorce because the plaintiff is a legal resident of the state. The complaint states whether the parties have children and whether they have acquired assets during the marriage. All of this is what goes into the body of the complaint.

The complaint ends with a *prayer for relief* in which the plaintiff tells the court what she wants the court to do. All complaints for divorce end with a request that the court dissolve the marriage. Other complaint requests depend on whether the terms of the divorce have been settled prior to the filing of the complaint. If there is a signed settlement agreement, the divorce is considered uncontested. In an uncontested divorce, the complaint states that fact and usually requests that the court incorporate the settlement agreement into the judgment of divorce so that it becomes part of the final court order. Note that the settlement agreement is enforceable as a contract from the day it is signed, whether or not the parties are actually divorced. In addition, the agreement is enforceable as a court order.

The prayer for relief in a contested divorce case is more elaborate. The plaintiff may ask the court for custody of the children, child support, and alimony. The plaintiff also asks the court to distribute the property of the marriage between the parties.

Once the complaint has been filed with the court, a copy is "served" on the other spouse. States differ in the manner of service. In some states it can be mailed. In other states it has to be served on the defendant by the sheriff. Once the defendant has been served, he or she has a fixed amount of time, typically 30 days, to answer the complaint by filing an *answer*. In the answer, also known as a responsive pleading, the defendant admits or denies the allegations of the complaint and makes his or her own prayers for relief regarding custody, support, and property distribution. If the defendant fails to file an answer within the prescribed time, the plaintiff can ask the court to enter a default judgment in which the court declares the parties divorced and grants whatever other relief the plaintiff requested. In some states, if there is a signed separation agreement, the defendant frequently defaults, as there is no adverse consequence to doing so. The terms of the agreement negotiated by the partners and the court does nothing other than dissolve the marriage.

If there is an agreement, the case goes on the court's uncontested list and the case proceeds to a final hearing. If the case is contested, it now proceeds to litigation.

Discovery

In order to either negotiate or go to trial in a divorce, spouses need to know the details of each other's finances. In the negotiation of a simple divorce, the husband and wife simply exchange copies of their account statements and provide each other with a list of other assets. Either party can question the statements and get answers to those questions. If some asset, such as the house, requires an appraisal, the partners jointly choose an appraiser. In the sense that each one is "discovering" information, this process could be called an informal discovery.

In litigation, discovery also involves finding out about each other's assets and property, but it is a more formal process run by lawyers in preparation for trial. Lawyers are often reluctant to accept the statements of the adversary at face value. These days, lawyers are also concerned about being sued for malpractice, and many insist on a full and formal discovery. Even though this discovery often turns out to be unnecessary, many lawyers argue that they cannot do their jobs responsibly without comprehensive and exhaustive investigation.

In a litigated divorce, every issue at dispute is subject to discovery. In order to prepare for trial, lawyers need to find out all possible details of the other party's case and to assemble the evidence they will introduce. Modern litigation, unlike what you may have seen on television, is not based on surprise. Each side is entitled to know all the details of the other's case. So if you are going to introduce expert testimony about any issue including custody, child support, alimony, or equitable distribution, you have to provide your wife's lawyer with a copy of your expert's report. If you are going to introduce documents into evidence, you have to provide copies as well. Discovery generally takes three forms: production of documents, interrogatories, and depositions. This process has the effect of dragging out the divorce and running up the legal fees.

PRODUCTION OF DOCUMENTS: Each side can make a demand for production of documents for any documents that can arguably be relevant to the case. So in a typical case you could be required to produce copies of:

▶ Every bank statement for every account
  you have had in the last 5 years

▶ Every check you have written and every deposit slip for 5 years

▶ Every statement for every securities transaction you have made
  in the last 5 years

▶ All tax returns for the past 5 years

▶ Every statement for any debt you have incurred in the past
  5 years (even if the debt has been paid), including copies
  of every application you completed for each of those loans

▶ All deeds you have signed or received for any real property

▶ Statements for retirement and pension accounts for 5 years

▶ Any appraisal of real property you may own

▶ A list of all assets, including household goods and jewelry,
  you may own

▶ All employment contracts, partnership contracts, or buy-sell
  agreements for any business interest that you own

▶ The written report of any expert witness
  that you intend to call at trial

▶ Any other document that might be relevant
  to any fact you intend to prove at trial

As you may gather, even a relatively simple case can generate hundreds, if not thousands, of documents.

INTERROGATORIES: The second form of discovery is written questions that you must answer in writing and swear to the accuracy of the answers. Questions can include anything that might be relevant to any aspect of the case. If adultery were at issue, for example, you would be asked questions about the person with whom you are alleged to have had an affair, including when and where you met, and what you did every time you met. If custody is an issue, you can be asked any question bearing on your role as a parent—past and present. You will be asked questions about your job, your career, your finances, and anything else that your wife's lawyer thinks is relevant. Of course your attorney will be doing the same thing to your wife.

DEPOSITIONS: After answers to interrogatories have been received and documents have been produced, the lawyers will then conduct depositions. A deposition is sworn testimony taken in the presence of a court reporter, who prepares a transcript of the proceeding. The witness is sworn in and examined under oath. Your wife's lawyer will take your deposition and your lawyer will take your wife's deposition. At deposition, the lawyer is not limited to questions that would be admissible at trial, but can ask any question the answer of which might be relevant. The deposition of a party to divorce can easily last a day or more. Each lawyer is also entitled to take the deposition of every witness that the other will call to testify at trial. And each lawyer will take the deposition of every expert that the other will call at trial. In a highly contested divorce trial, the expert witnesses called could include:

▶ Psychologists and other mental health experts testifying about the fitness of each parent

▶ Forensic accountants testifying about the value of the business and true income of a self-employed spouse

▶ Economists and employment experts testifying about the employability of your spouse (bears on alimony)

▶ Economists testifying about the lifestyle and historical living standard of your wife (bears on alimony)

▶ Appraisers testifying about the value of real estate, antiques, or anything else of value

▶ Actuaries testifying about the value of a pension

▶ Private detectives testifying about anything they were hired to investigate

Note that for each of these categories of expertise, I assume there will be more than one expert because each attorney hires a separate expert to contradict the testimony of the other's experts. A complicated case can result in 30 or 40 days of depositions at a cost of at least $5,000 a day or more. This is where the legal bill starts to fly.

All of this is in preparation for trial, but trial seldom occurs. Discovery ends up being the background for 11th-hour settlement negotiations, and rarely is extensive discovery necessary to settle the case. Although lawyers argue that they must prepare every case as if it will go to trial, much of the discovery conducted just costs a lot of money and takes a great deal of time. If you do find yourself in litigation, you will want to question your lawyer closely about this because this is where your costs skyrocket.

In mediation, we conduct only that discovery absolutely necessary to make informed decisions. Experts' reports, when necessary, are prepared by a single neutral expert so that there is only one instead of his-and-her expert reports. Generally the amount of information necessary to negotiate an agreement is a small fraction of the discovery many lawyers claim is necessary for trial.

Motion Practice

Depending on how crowded the local court calendar is, years can pass between the beginning and end of a contested divorce. During that time, many issues can arise on which the parties do not agree, and these issues have to be submitted to the court for resolution. This procedure is called a pretrial motion. Such motions can include a request that the court order temporary custody and visitation rights regarding the children; order one spouse to pay support to the other, pending trial; order assets frozen; order one spouse to pay the other's legal fees; and order discovery. The court can appoint its own experts upon motion by a party and can do anything that, in the judge's broad discretion, is necessary to further the cause of justice.

Motions begin with a written application to the court that is served on the other side. The second party has a limited time to file responsive pleadings, and the court schedules a hearing. The judge can choose to hear testimony or can decide the matter based on affidavits submitted by the parties. Motions can become like minitrials and can be very expensive for the parties. In a complicated, high-conflict case, a divorce can involve six or more pretrial motions. Motions can also be filed after the divorce is over. If one party believes that the other is not abiding by the orders of the court, that party will file a postjudgment motion to enforce the judgment of the court. High-conflict couples can file motions year after year, so that the litigation never ends. Motion practice is an indicator that the divorce has gone bad, and the more frequently you have to go to court, the more difficult your postdivorce life is likely to be.

Trial

Divorces that are litigated to the bitter end come to closure in a trial before a judge. The judge hears evidence and testimony and then rules on any aspect of the divorce on which the parties have not agreed. By the time a case gets to trial, most couples have agreed on custody issues and may even be in agreement on some economic issues. The judge will conduct pretrial conferences with the lawyers, attempting to settle the case without the necessity of trial. Even if some issues remain unresolved, the judge is usually able to settle some of them and narrow the scope of trial. At the conclusion of the trial, the judge makes her findings and orders that a judgment of divorce be prepared for her signature. The parties are now divorced.

"Just another of our many disagreements. He wants a no-fault divorce, whereas I would prefer to have the bastard crucified."

Six

HOW TO GET DIVORCED
WITHOUT A LEGAL MESS

BEFORE YOU GET INVOLVED WITH LAWYERS AND LITIGATION, you need to know something about the legal system and the way it will manage your divorce. Divorcing couples have reported that they felt as if they had lost control of their lives. In this chapter, I want to show you how and why this can happen. The adversarial system has its own way of seeing the world, its own values, and its own norms. Understanding that system may help you to retain control of your own divorce.

Understanding the Adversarial System

In western society, people have long been ambivalent about lawyers. On the one hand, lawyers are often seen as sharp, analytical thinkers. But on the other hand, lawyers are often perceived as amoral because they are willing to advocate for clients even though the client may be evil, guilty, and dishonest. To understand this ambivalence one must consider what lawyers do and how they are trained.

Lawyers are trained to be advocates. The adversarial system incorporates the assumption that when two adversaries make a rigorous presentation of the evidence that best serves their respective clients' interests, a judge or jury will be able to find the truth. Advocacy is not in itself the pursuit of truth, and therefore obtaining the truth is not the role of the advocate. Rather, that role is to persuade the fact finder to accept a particular version of the facts that serves the advocate's client. If, for example, I do my job and develop all the evidence that favors my client, and if my adversary similarly does her job and develops all the evidence that favors her client, we will both enable the judge or jury to do its job—to find the truth and do justice. My search for justice is only indirect; my participation in the process enables the system as a whole to work. This is a tricky psychological proposition and is at the heart of the public's historical distrust of lawyers. If the morality of what I do is saved only by my participation in a larger system, it requires considerable faith in the system. This is an abstract argument on which to rest one's moral position and so abstract as to evade less sophisticated laypersons.

There are several problems that spring from this system. The first, and perhaps most troubling, arises from recent changes in the process of litigation. Remember that what saves the integrity of the system is the occurrence of a trial in which the truth is found by judge or jury. What happens to the system if we do not have the trial? What happens if all we have is a negotiated settlement, in which the two adversaries, still engaged in their sincere attempt to discredit each other's evidence, are forced to negotiate a settlement of the dispute? Is justice still done? Is the truth still found? Or do we have a negotiation in which the stronger party with the most resources simply wears down the weaker party until further resistance is impractical?

These questions are by no means theoretical. In the past hundred years, the incidence of trials has decreased so much that trials are now the exception rather than the rule. About 85 to 90 percent of criminal matters are resolved by plea bargains. About 95 to 97 percent of all civil suits are resolved by negotiated settlements. And in some areas of the law, such as divorce, the negotiated settlement rate is more than 99 percent, with less than 1 percent of cases going to trial. It is conventional wisdom that it is better to negotiate a settlement than to risk the uncertainties associated with going to trial. One could even argue that, given the overwhelming norm of settlement, trials have become the pathological exception rather than the rule. In my experience, divorces do not go to trial unless at least one client or lawyer is just plain nuts.

The norm of the negotiated settlement has not penetrated legal education. What do law students study? Almost all legal education continues to be devoted to reviewing, learning, and discussing appellate cases. To get into the casebooks, a suit must first go to trial. In today's world, that limits us to less than 5 percent of the litigated universe. But then the case has to be appealed. About 10 percent of cases are appealed. This reduces our sample universe to about one half of 1 percent of the litigation universe. Actually, it is even smaller because many cases do not get published unless they are appealed to the highest court—a process that whittles the sample down even more dramatically. So the result is legal textbooks that reflect perhaps 1 case in 2,000. Add to that the fact that the published cases are representative only of the most aberrant and highly conflicted sample in the legal universe. And you can see that a very skewed, unrepresentative sample constitutes 90 percent of the modern legal education. Legal educators defend the system by saying that this is the only way to train a student to think like a lawyer. Perhaps it is, but therein may lie the problem.

A Legal Education as an Acquired Disability

The skill of thinking "like a lawyer" has two elements. The first is the sharp analytic skill and ability to focus that enables the lawyer to distinguish one situation from another and to dissect out the tiniest distinguishing characteristic of a situation to support the argument that this case is really different from another virtually identical case in which the ruling was adverse to the client represented. By learning the value of arguing each side with equal fervor, the student is gradually weaned from naive notions about truth. The truth is that the stars of law class are those students who are both meticulously prepared and verbally equipped to argue forcefully but who can turn on a dime to argue the other way when asked.

The second element of thinking like a lawyer is a commitment to persuasion that overrides one's commitment to truth. Thinking like a lawyer means defining problems as legal issues and then mustering whatever facts and legal precedents serve the position that you are engaged to advance.

But there are practically no statistical data about the outcomes of legal representation. In fact, few lawyers have ever studied statistics or acquired the insight that an understanding of sampling theory can impart for thinking about policy or strategy. Therefore, even though more than 95 percent of lawsuits are settled, there is little or no research about how settlement norms influence settlement negotiations. This means that each lawyer relies on his own experience plus whatever anecdotal information is acquired from other lawyers to decide on a strategy. A research tradition in which information is systematically gathered for dispassionate analysis simply is lacking in the legal intellectual tradition.

It is the role of the legal system to pursue justice. It is the role of the lawyer to represent her client, no matter how evil and repulsive that client may be. How does one transcend this feeling of contradiction, particularly for those who were attracted to law in the first place because it seemed the place to pursue truth and justice and to do good? We assume that if we do our job and if the system works, then justice will be done. And the way to ensure that the system works is to carefully adhere to a finely drawn system of rules and procedures that ensures fairness by denying to either side an advantage in swaying the jury or the judge.

It is this concern for procedural justice that sets the lawyer apart from the world of nonlawyers. Procedural justice is the lawyer's substitute for the more emotionally satisfying substantive justice that occupies the nonlawyer. In place of the notion that justice is about the contest for virtue, the lawyer acquires a notion that justice is about due process and an equal chance to influence the trier of fact. Lawyers become obsessed with the rules of evidence, discovery, and timing. These rules also include how people in the system are permitted to communicate with each other. For example, there is a carefully nurtured ritual that restricts ex parte communication between the judge and the attorneys and restricts communication between attorneys and the adversary client. In law, ethics involve adherence to a complex and ever-evolving set of rules, rituals, and procedures.

It is this concern for procedural justice that sets the lawyer apart from the world of non-lawyers. Laypeople cannot understand the lawyer's seeming indifference to the role of virtue. "How can you represent a guilty person?" If you do not understand and accept that the adversary system works this way and that the lawyer does good by participating within that system, there is no choice but to perceive the lawyer as amoral. It's not a big leap from amoral to immoral. In the public mind, therefore, the lawyer is inevitably tainted.

Law and Divorce

Divorce lawyers have a terrible reputation for being cynical, indifferent to suffering, and greedy for ever-larger legal fees. There are, of course, divorce lawyers who do not fit this image, but, in over 20 years in the field, I have met more people who fit the stereotype than ones who do not. It is not that divorce law attracts nasty, amoral people. In fact some of the most sensitive of students I met in law school were attracted to "family law" where they thought they could help families. How then do they make this transition from idealist to successful divorce lawyer?

Until the no-fault revolution, divorce was available only to the victim of wrongdoing, and divorce law was organized to punish the guilty spouse. In many states, divorce law had a quasi-criminal tone, and the guilty spouse could be punished with loss of the children and other, economic, penalties. As such, American divorce law still fits the adversarial system organized around the finding of wrongdoing. But the fit began to fail as expectations of marriage changed in the latter half of the 20th century and as divorce without fault—no-fault divorce—became the norm. So by 1980, virtually every state had passed some version of "no-fault" divorce that allowed people to divorce by proving that they had lived apart for some required period of time, or that they had irreconcilable differences. You no longer had to prove you were the victim of wrongdoing, but rather, you just had to show that the marriage was not working.

One would think that no-fault divorce law would make a divorce easier to obtain. But getting a divorce has become ever more difficult and complicated. It is not uncommon now for a divorce to take 3 or more years and generate legal fees well into six figures. When it gets out of hand, divorce supports legions of accountants, appraisers, actuaries, psychotherapists, and social workers of all descriptions. Divorce has become a multibillion-dollar business.

As divorce has become more complicated and inevitably resolved by negotiation, the role of divorce lawyer has become ever more intrusive. The lawyer becomes the surrogate for the client and becomes responsible for negotiating the settlement that will shape the lives of the client's entire family for years to come. Yet few lawyers know very much about family dynamics or emotional processes. Very few lawyers have any understanding about how the negotiating positions they take affect the way the clients feel about each other. So by the time the lawyers finish with their posturing and threats, there is a negotiated agreement in place, but the relationship between the spouses is so poisonous as to preempt cooperation in the future. When confronted by the emotional carnage they produce, divorce lawyers deny that their actions have anything to do with it. Rather, they insist, it is the inherent irrationality of divorcing people that accounts for all the bitterness of divorce.

CASE STUDY: Steve and Julie

After a 20-year marriage, Julie and Steve were divorcing. Things had been getting worse for years, with a gradual coldness setting in between the two. The couple's son Michael, age 15, had noticed the past year how his parents never talked at dinner, and he often found excuses to be elsewhere at suppertime. As Julie and Steve became more distant from each other, each coped in his or her own way with the growing sense of loneliness. Steve threw himself into his work. He was a manager for a software company that was launching several new products. He made his job his top priority and no longer avoided scheduling evening meetings and projects. He found companionship and purpose at work that distracted him from the distress he felt when he went home. He still hoped that Julie would come around and realize that she really had a good husband. He loved Julie but felt he could never make her happy. The last sexual encounter between the couple had taken place 9 months ago, and he missed it. Now Steve often came home after Julie had gone to bed and just went to sleep in the guestroom.

Julie was also very lonely. She was a teacher but did not find much companionship at school. Until the last few years she had devoted herself to the family, ferrying Michael around after school and maintaining a warm and inviting home. But recently Michael had morphed into a typical adolescent who wanted little contact with his parents. He spent most of his time on school, sports, and with his friends. For the first time in many years, Julie found life unsatisfying and boring. She had pretty much given up on her relationship with Steve. He had refused her many requests that they go into couples therapy, telling her that he didn't believe that some shrink could do what they could not. He told her that if she stopped moping around, regained her sense of fun, and took some interest in sex, they would be fine. She despaired that he would never understand what she needed and had no interest in finding out. Recently she had begun to flirt with a long-taboo thought that maybe the two of them needed to divorce. She was only 46 years old and while she was no "spring chicken," she still felt attractive enough to have another chance with someone new.

One week when Julie was feeling particularly down, a friend of hers suggested that the two of them go away for a weekend of square dancing, which was her friend's passion. Julie agreed and told Michael and Steve to fend for themselves for the weekend because she was going off with her friend Erica. From the time the two arrived at the resort where the meeting was being held, Julie had a great time. People were friendly and cheerful, and before long she was enjoying herself. Toward the middle of the first evening she realized that one of the men was the first boy she had ever dated many years before, named Jamie. The two of them reminisced for hours and quickly rekindled the spark they had shared 30 years earlier. Jamie was divorced and living in a city about an hour away. He was still handsome and was gentle and attentive to her. By the end of the weekend Julie was smitten, and the two exchanged phone numbers. Julie had told Jamie that she was married but feared that her marriage was not going to survive for long. The two agreed to meet at the next square dance gathering in a month.

During the month, the two e-mailed back and forth frequently. Julie was delighted to have someone who was really interested in communicating with her and who was open with his feelings. It made her feel a little guilty, though, and she didn't mention it to Steve. When she and Jamie met again a month later, the relationship bloomed quickly, and by the end of the first day the two were in bed together. Though feeling guilty, Julie was ecstatic. She decided that it wasn't fair to have missed affection and passion for so long and that it was time to get a divorce. That Sunday night when she got home, she told Steve that things had been bad for too long between them and that his refusal to go into therapy over the past year had convinced her that it was hopeless. She was unhappy, he was unhappy, and it clearly was doing no good for Michael. So she had decided that the two of them should consider divorce.

Steve was stunned. Although he acknowledged that things had been bad for a long time, he had resigned himself to the status quo and had not even considered divorce. Why not wait awhile, until at least Michael had graduated from high school? In the meantime, they would see how things went and maybe he would reconsider his objection to therapy. But Julie was no longer interested. "There's nothing to work with. I don't love you anymore, and we just don't have a marriage to work on. It has eroded and dribbled away, and I don't want to spend any more time on it. Let's do it decently, but let's do it."

Steve was so blindsided by Julie's clarity that he didn't say much. He said that he would think about it and went to watch television. The next day Steve told Julie that he thought divorce was a mistake but recognized that if she was insistent, he couldn't stop her. Steve then retreated into moody silence. He wondered if Julie was having an affair and decided to check out Julie's e-mail. Steve was a computer expert and had little trouble hacking into Julie's e-mail. And there, plain as could be, was the confirmation of his suspicion. He read all the exchanges between Julie and Jamie and concluded that was what this was all about. That evening, he confronted Julie with his evidence. Julie was incensed that he had violated her privacy and was equally angry that he was blaming other things on this. "I have lived through your withdrawal for years. I have suffered your insensitivity and your stupid refusal to do anything to help the marriage. By the time I even met Jamie our marriage was totally dead. How can you be so blind? You're just looking for excuses!"

The next day Steve made an appointment with a lawyer who had represented a friend of his. Later that week he had a consultation with the lawyer and asked the lawyer to tell him about his rights. The lawyer, Marilyn Boone, *told him that according to the law of New Jersey, a judge might consider the adultery as a factor mitigating against alimony but that it was discretionary with the judge, and some judges would not consider it as important. She also advised Steve that if the judge was not impressed by the fact of adultery that Steve would probably be ordered to pay Julie alimony for 7 to 10 years. She also advised Steve that he would win a custody fight if his son would tell the judge that he wanted to stay with his father. If that happened, she also advised Steve that he might be able to stay in the house until his son graduated from high school and that he would not have to sell the house and split the equity with Julie until that happened.*

The Components of the Lawyer's Advice and Why They Don't Work

Before you see a lawyer, you need to do some thinking about how you want to use the lawyer. Lawyers can provide a number of services, but you may only need some of those. Lawyers can give good advice as well as bad advice. The first role of the lawyer in divorce is to educate you about the law of divorce in your state and suggest how it will apply to you. For example, in the case study you have just read, Steve's lawyer advises him that in New Jersey, adultery can be a factor in—but not necessarily a bar to—a woman's right to receive alimony. The lawyer also explains to him how state law applies to other issues that will have to be resolved, like child custody, child support, and distribution of property.

Clients usually ask their lawyers to tell them about their "legal rights." And the lawyer can tell you your legal rights only to a degree. That is, a lawyer can tell you her opinion about how your legal rights might be interpreted by a judge. But because of the nature of divorce law, the lawyer usually cannot tell you with precision or certainty. With the exception of child support, which is subject to federally mandated guidelines, divorce statutes generally establish broad parameters within which judges are supposed to decide cases. For example, when parents cannot agree on custody, the judge is directed to decide in the "best interests of the child." But how a given judge will decide in a particular case is subject to considerable speculation. Your lawyer may be able to tell you if you have a strong case or a weak case, but a lawyer can seldom tell you with any certainty whether you will prevail or not.

This adds another layer to what we call legal advice because it has the lawyer speculating not about the law itself but about how the law may be applied by a particular judge. Be careful; lawyers frequently are wrong in their prognostications. Thus Steve's lawyer may be of the opinion that a judge would find Julie guilty of moral turpitude, conclude that she is morally unfit to be the primary parent of the child, and award custody of the child to Steve. And Judge Jones, who is a socially conservative judge, just might do that. But on the other hand, Judge Smith, who is not so conservative, might decide that Julie's affair, although technically adultery, really has nothing to do with her moral fitness and refuse to even consider it in making a decision. And even in the case of Judge Jones, Julie might be an attractive witness and Steve might be an unattractive witness, leading Judge Jones to overcome his social disapproval of Julie and award her custody. All of these "nonrational" factors play a role and detract from a lawyer's ability to predict with any certainty how a judge will rule.

Advice about Negotiation Strategy

In most cases, your lawyer's prediction of what a judge might do is intended as a backdrop for negotiations. Most lawyers will argue in settlement negotiations that the settlement ought to reflect what a judge would do if the case went to trial. In fact, this becomes the primary subject lawyers argue about in negotiations. So Steve's lawyer would try to convince Julie's lawyer that because Julie had engaged in adultery she should settle for little or no alimony because Judge Jones, who would probably hear the case, would rule that way. And then Julie's lawyer would argue that the marriage was already dead when Julie had her one-night affair and that she was so desperately lonely after living for 20 years with a cold fish like Steve that no judge would hold it against her. Therefore, he would argue, Julie's alimony should not be affected by her affair.

The impact of these arguments on the settlement negotiations might be affected by several other unpredictable factors. How effective is each lawyer as a negotiator? How anxious are you and your wife to settle? How willing is your lawyer to go to trial? Some lawyers are more belligerent than others. Some prefer to settle rather than go to trial, but others always practice brinkmanship and will never settle until the last minute. Finally, sad to say, some lawyers won't let a case settle until they have milked it for the maximum fee. Regrettably, there are always people who succumb to the myth that by getting the meanest, baddest lawyer in town they will acquire an advantage, when in reality it usually leads them to the predator types.

Philosophical Advice

When Steve's lawyer counsels Steve to file suit and attempt to deny alimony to Julie, he is giving both legal advice and philosophical advice. That is, he is making a judgment that the legal maneuver that deprives Julie of support is worth doing. Let's assume that the lawyer is correct in his prediction that the judge will deprive Julie of alimony. What will happen then? We can predict that Julie will be bitter. We can also predict that the couple's son will be affected by that bitterness and that the legacy of anger generated will last for a long time. When Michael graduates from high school or college and when he gets married and has children, Steve and Julie will be unable to come together with any sense of goodwill toward each other. Julie's anger at what she regards as unjust treatment by Steve will be communicated to Michael, who will feel torn between his parents. He will be confused and upset by his father's depiction of his mother as immoral and will realize that his parents can no longer have civil or cooperative communication, even when his needs are at stake. These are the completely predictable outcomes if Steve follows his lawyer's advice.

From a philosophical perspective, some lawyers are particularly handicapped by their own culture. Martin Seligman, a noted researcher on cognition and depression, reports that lawyers are the only professional group in which pessimism as a personal style is correlated with professional success. Lawyers also have the highest divorce rate, suicide rate, incidence of depression, and professional dissatisfaction rate of any profession. Moreover, the training of lawyers teaches them a notion of client representation in which the object is to shift as much of the cost and risk to the other guy's client as possible. But this philosophy disables them from assessing the needs of a family as it adjusts to the changes required by divorce. The win-at-any-cost viewpoint, though appealing from a legal perspective, can be devastating to their own clients' long-term interests.

Advice on Family Dynamics

Because the legal strategies adopted by lawyers have such an impact on the ability of the family to adapt to divorce, one would think that divorce lawyers are knowledgeable about family dynamics, child development, and the psychology of conflict. In 25 years of experience with thousands of lawyers, I have not found this to be true. The greatest obstacle to such understanding is the legal culture's discomfort with the emotional parts of life. Rational behavior refers to those of our actions driven by an understanding of our interests. Irrational behavior is that which is driven by self-destructive impulses. I think that the two of these combined account for less than 20 percent of human behavior. The rest is non-rational behavior which is behavior driven by feelings. Non-rational behavior may have either destructive or constructive consequences, but the important fact is to recognize that most behavior is driven by feelings and emotions. What this means is that the understanding of emotional life is absolutely critical to understanding complex human behavior and to intervening in an intelligent manner. And it is recognition of the emotional side of life that legal education screens out.

When it comes to giving advice on how to achieve sound family objectives, lawyers have little professional training that is helpful. Most lawyers do not give good advice about child custody issues and tend to exacerbate, rather than calm, their clients' fears. Few lawyers define their objectives in terms of what helps a family to thrive over time. Your lawyer is concerned with how to get you the most of what you think you want. She wants to help you pay the least support even if that has an adverse effect on your children and wife. She wants to get you the best deal on property distribution even if that has an adverse effect as well. Her job is to do the best for you that she can to shift the risk and cost to your wife and to shift as much of the dislocation of the divorce as possible from you to your wife. That is the advocate's job, but the job description is notoriously shortsighted and unable to anticipate the long-term effects on your emotional welfare or that of your family.

Steve was impressed with the advice given to him by his lawyer. He didn't want the divorce, but he concluded that because it was being forced on him, he ought to strike first and get the best deal he could. By showing Julie how tough he could be, he would certainly improve his bargaining position. If they couldn't reach a settlement, at least he would have an advantage in court. So he told the lawyer to go ahead and file for the divorce alleging that Julie had committed adultery and asking the court for custody of Michael and the award of child support from Julie. His lawyer asked for a $5,000 retainer and directed Steve to empty the joint bank accounts and to move the investment account into his name alone. The lawyer told him that if Steve didn't move the money first, Julie would, and then Steve would be at her mercy. So Steve followed his lawyer's advice, paid the retainer, and moved the money. The lawyer filed a complaint for divorce and directed the sheriff to serve a copy of the complaint to Julie.

Steve said nothing about the complaint being filed to Julie. He figured that the shock value would help bring Julie to her senses, and she would plea for peace. Julie was indeed shocked when the sheriff came to the school where she was teaching to serve the complaint. She was absolutely stunned by the allegations of the complaint and couldn't believe that Steve had done this to her. But the shock did not have the effect Steve had hoped for. Within a short time Julie's surprise turned to rage. She found the name of a divorce lawyer who was reputed to be one of the toughest in town. The same afternoon Julie discovered that the money had been moved and that she had no access to the family's savings. This frightened her even more.

The following morning she took the complaint she had received to lawyer Marvin Mason. Mason advised her that she would have to file an answer to Steve's complaint. He also advised her to file a counterclaim that alleged that Steve was guilty of extreme cruelty toward her, citing at length all the details of Steve's behavior. In her counterclaim, she would ask for custody of Michael, child support, alimony, and distribution of the marital assets. She would also ask the court to order Steve to put the family savings back in the joint accounts, for an order forbidding Steve from making any

*unilateral disposition of assets, and for an order of temporary support for
her and Michael. Mason asked for a $7,500 retainer and said he could not
start the case without it. But because the savings were all in Steve's control,
Julie had to borrow money from her parents. Mason filed the answer and
counterclaim and asked the court for an emergency hearing. The war had
begun, but the goal no longer was preserving good family dynamics.*

Legal Advice Revisited

We have described four components of legal advice. The formal training of
lawyers incorporates only the first, an understanding of the law. Some
lawyers acquire good negotiation skills through experience, and a few even
take courses to develop negotiation skills and techniques. But your lawyer
may or may not be a good negotiator and may or may not be a better negotiator than you are. As to philosophical expertise, a few lawyers acquire
some wisdom as they mature, but many clearly do not. The same applies to
offering psychological advice. Most lawyers are seriously handicapped by
their legal training, and few have attained anything approaching adequate
sophistication in matters of psychology.

It is important that you consult with lawyers. It is equally important that
you do not grant the lawyer greater authority than is actually warranted by
the skills and wisdom of that particular lawyer. As soon as you get beyond
advice on the law, your skepticism should grow as your lawyer proposes to
make strategic negotiations or philosophical or psychological judgments
about how you should proceed. Your lawyer's advice in these areas is
shaped more by his personality and culture than by his expertise, and you
need to stay acutely aware of that.

How to Manage Your Lawyer

Lawyers are useful tools the way my chain saw is a useful tool. Managed
safely, my chain saw cuts down a tree. Managed poorly, my chain saw cuts
off my leg. And so it is with lawyers. I want to empower you here to manage
your lawyer well. But first, I would like to address some common miscon-
ceptions that will impede your ability to manage your lawyer successfully.

Dispelling Some Myths

MYTH 1: GETTING AN AGGRESSIVE LAWYER WILL HELP YOU WIN.
There is a particularly macho myth about being tough that will get you
nothing but grief. "You have to be tough or you get rolled over." "If I start
out tough she will know that she can't take advantage of me." " She has to
know that if she messes with me she'll have nothing left when its over."
These are but a few of the postures that prompt men to go looking for the
toughest lawyer in town. All lawyers have a good dose of aggression in
their repertoires. So hire a lawyer with a swaggering aggressive manner,
and all you ensure is that you will evoke an aggressive response from your
wife's lawyer. They will have a difficult time cooperating, so you can expect a lot of pretrial motions. They will go to court over temporary support,
temporary custody, visitation, support, control over property, and arguments about discovery. Aggression begets aggression, which defeats cooperation, which is what you need if your divorce is not going to consume
you. Further, every time your lawyers fail to agree and every time they have
to go to court, it will cost each of you from $2,000 to $5,000 and further
alienation from each other. Hiring the meanest, toughest lawyer only ensures that you will have the meanest, toughest divorce.

MYTH 2: STRIKE THE FIRST BLOW. Too many people and too many
lawyers believe that by striking the first blow in court they win a strategic
advantage. So the lawyer counsels that you hire a private detective to try to
catch your wife cheating. Or that you close her credit card accounts and
drain the bank accounts before she can get to the bank to do the same to
you. Or the lawyer proposes that you file a complaint for divorce in court in
order to bring the case under the jurisdiction of the court. But the sad truth
is that there is no such strategic advantage. Whatever initial advantage may
be won will be eroded by the war of attrition that will inevitably follow.

So don't strike. Your strategy should be to reassure your wife that you
want to divorce cooperatively. Let her know that you do not intend to file
anything in court until the two of you first negotiate a cooperative agreement. Let her know that you will not cut off credit cards or move money
and that you hope she will act the same. The creation and management of a
cooperative divorce is up to you, and it is not something for which you
should count on your lawyer. By modeling for your lawyer that you will not

abuse whatever power you have, you have the greatest chance that she will not abuse whatever power she has. Trust is built over time, but it can be destroyed in a minute. Your lawyer, out of control, can quickly destroy whatever goodwill exists between you and your wife.

MYTH 3: THE COURT WILL PROTECT YOU. Many people think that judges are wise Solomon-like figures dispensing justice from the bench. In truth, the quality of judges varies widely, with the average hovering around mediocre. The judge hearing your case may or may not have much experience in family law. So, from a quality assurance perspective, it is best not to be too optimistic that you are going to get a judge with the expertise, intellectual horsepower, or wisdom necessary to do justice in your case. And even though you can take an appeal to a higher court if you do not think the judge's decision is fair, such appeals are expensive, time-consuming, and difficult to win. Even if you do prevail on appeal, most times the appellate court simply remands the case back to the same judge for rehearing.

Judges are also very busy. They do not have much time for any individual case because they are under considerable pressure to keep their calendars moving. Much of their review of documents is done by their law clerks, who are usually recent law school graduates. So the person who may be most significant in deciding your case may be a 22 year old who just graduated from law school and who has almost no experience. Because judges are so busy, they often do not take the time necessary to really understand complex legal matters. Some make decisions shooting from the hip, and when they make mistakes you have to live with them or face the expense of an appeal. So if you absolutely have no other choice, you can submit your case and your fate to this very imperfect system. But you are far better off staying as far away from the judicial system as you can and negotiating your own settlement.

MYTH 4: I AM BETTER OFF LETTING MY LAWYER TALK FOR ME. Because the legal system seems so complicated many people are afraid that if they speak for themselves, they might make some damaging admission or say something that can "be used against them" in some unknown way. So to be safe they decide that they ought to just let their lawyers do the talking for them. Unless you are particularly naive, gullible, or passive, you should speak for yourself. Divorce law is not all that complicated, and when it is, there is usually a lot of wealth involved. For most middle-class people, there is little in the way of complicated legal doctrine that will affect their divorces. Most of the problems faced by divorcing people are practical, not legal, problems. How do we stretch the income that barely supported one household so that it will support two households? How do we help the kids adapt to changed circumstances and still be okay? These are the real problems of divorce, and they are solved by reasoned, practical deliberation. The more you and your wife can do the talking, the more efficiently you will solve the problems. The more your lawyers are interjected, the more complicated, expensive, and aggressive the communication becomes. In the end, you must make the decisions that will shape your life.

Communication through lawyers is a very tricky business because the opportunity for misunderstanding is so great. Clients often end up paying many thousands of dollars in unnecessary legal fees just because the lawyers happen to dislike each other. Bad blood between lawyers makes for extra litigation because there is no trust and no goodwill, so each lawyer relies more on formal court procedures to protect him- or herself against the perceived duplicity of the other.

The serendipitous combination of lawyer personalities and styles affects emotional costs as well as legal costs. When Steve's lawyer counsels him to drain the checking and savings accounts and Steve follows that advice, the message received by Julie is that Steve cannot be trusted. When Steve's lawyer tells Julie's lawyer that he doesn't think that Steve should pay any alimony, he does so knowing that in the end Steve will have to pay alimony. But he takes this position as a bargaining ploy to keep the final alimony figure as low as possible. But what Julie hears is that Steve wants to abandon her. When Steve's lawyer also tells Julie's lawyer that child support ought to be half of what he knows it needs to be, he is engaging in another bargaining ploy. But what Julie hears is that Steve wants to abandon his children as well. She hears the lawyer's strategic ploys as if they are Steve's real intentions and holds Steve responsible for the emotional content of his lawyer's positions. Very few lawyers understand the psychological impact that these strategic maneuvers have on the other client. It is one thing to use such techniques in commercial or personal injury litigation where clients will never again have to deal with each other. But in family matters where we expect the clients to cooperate as parents for the next 15 years, the results can be very destructive. When you hand over control to your lawyer, these are the risks you assume.

Limit the Role of the Lawyer

By now you are aware that the less contact you have with the judicial system the better off you are. Similarly, the less contact you have with your lawyer, within certain parameters, the better off you are also. By all means, use your lawyer to learn as much as you need to know about the legal rules and statutes that apply to your divorce. Have your lawyer teach you, as best she can, about the law as it applies to parenting, support issues, and property issues. If there are technical issues, have your lawyer advise you about tax implications or about what valuation methods should be applied to your assets. Have the lawyer advise you, as background information only, what she thinks are the norms that would be applied if negotiation failed and the matter went to court. But use your lawyer primarily as your teacher about the law so that you can stay in charge of the negotiation with your wife. That is your chief objective.

For psychological matters, consult a good psychologist, and on philosophical matters find someone with the wisdom to advise you. Finally, count on your mediator to guide you on negotiation strategy, because it is the mediator who is best positioned to promote cooperation between you and your wife.

How to Hire a Lawyer

Hiring a lawyer to guide you requires some research and some diligence if you are going to find someone compatible. The reputations of divorce lawyers are misleading. The lawyer who is often in the news for handling controversial cases in court may be a lawyer who is too eager to litigate and totally insensitive to the delicate interaction between the needs of his client and the needs of his client's family. So the lawyer described by your friends as "the toughest lawyer in town" is probably not for you, unless you want prolonged litigation.

Here are 10 desirable things to have in your lawyer.

1. Knowledge of the law and at least 10 years of experience: To do divorce work well, a lawyer needs some seasoning. She needs not only knowledge of the law and legal procedure but also knowledge of the norms that prevail in the local legal culture. She also needs some life experience. If your lawyer has children, it is a plus when it comes time to talk about parenting issues. It's also helpful if she has had some experience coping with everyday economic issues. Don't hesitate to ask the lawyer about herself. You are going to be relying on the judgment and wisdom of this person, and you need to know something about her style, personality, and values.

2. A small law firm: Divorce is not like corporate law and does not require the complexity of a big law firm. Most divorce lawyers work in firms of 10 or fewer lawyers. Many large firms hire one or two divorce specialists to handle the divorce work generated by their corporate clients. In my experience, the fees for big-firm divorce lawyers are much larger than the fees of lawyers in small law firms. Lawyers in big firms tend to hand off as much work as they can to their associates and bill for the associates' time as well as their own. They also bill for the time of paralegals and secretaries, and every time a lawyer talks to another lawyer or a paralegal or a secretary, you get billed for both. I recently saw a case in which the husband had been represented by a sole practitioner and the wife had been represented by a partner in a major firm. Both lawyers had similar backgrounds and levels of experience. The husband's legal fee was $23,000, but the wife's legal fee was $85,000, for the same case.

3. A calm, reasoned, and pragmatic approach that assumes your case is going to settle: You do not want an excitable lawyer, and you certainly do not want a lawyer who stokes your indignation and anger. What you seek is a lawyer who calms you and counsels a pragmatic problem-solving approach to the divorce. Ask your prospective lawyer about her approach to divorce cases. Ask her how many cases she takes to trial in the course of a year. Any divorce lawyer who actually goes to trial with a case more than three or four times a year is suspect. Ask her what percentage of her cases is settled. If she settles fewer than 95 percent, she is suspect. Ask her how many of her cases settle before any court action is begun. You want a lawyer who litigates only as a last resort. Ask her about average legal fees in her practice. Ask her what kind of discovery she proposes to conduct. There are some lawyers who are so compulsive and obsessive that they won't leave a singe stone unturned, even if there is little gain in the activity. I have seen lawyers who spend $10,000 of their clients' money chasing $1,000 in supposedly hidden assets. Find a lawyer who takes the long view of your interest and your life. Ask your lawyer if you can expect to still be on speaking terms with your wife when it's all over and whether she is committed to such an objective.

4. An assertive rather than an aggressive personality who can work with others without antagonizing them: By now you should be starting to get the picture. You want someone who is assertive rather than aggressive. An assertive lawyer supports your interest without antagonizing other lawyers or your spouse. Assertion is rational, but aggression is not. Nobody can be offended by the quiet assertion of a point. But most people are offended when the same point is made with anger and personal animus. Run away from angry lawyers, and run away from lawyers who brag about how they win all their fights in court. You want a lawyer who seldom has to fight in court because his style helps promote cooperative settlement. Before making a hiring decision, engage the lawyer in discussions about his style of practice and how he sees the world. Is he an optimist or a pessimist? Does he regard other people as essentially decent, or does he see the world as full of dangerous, duplicitous people. A lawyer's way of thinking about people will shape how he counsels you and how he relates to others. A suspicious, hostile, or depressed lawyer will serve you poorly and should be avoided like a disease.

5. An understanding of the needs of children: If you have children and if you and your wife have any disagreements about how parenting will be shared between you, then the advice of your lawyer in this area will be important. It is very useful if your lawyer has children of his own. Because most people like to talk about their kids, see if you can engage the lawyer for a few minutes on that subject. If the lawyer is a woman, find out what role her husband plays with the kids. If she is divorced, find out what kind of parenting arrangement exists between her and her ex-spouse. If the lawyer is a man, ask what role he plays with his kids. Find out how the lawyer views your role with your kids and whether that viewpoint is consistent with yours.

6. A willingness to support you in mediation: If you want to resolve your divorce through mediation, you will need a lawyer to consult with from time to time. If for some reason the mediation is unsuccessful or is only partially successful, you will want the lawyer to become more involved. Some lawyers dislike mediation, while others are ambivalent and may or may not sabotage the process. Still others think it is a good idea if it works and wholeheartedly support clients who are trying to mediate successfully. Those are the lawyers you want to find. But to find one, you have to ask the right questions. How many cases have they had in which clients have been successful in mediation? Mediation has been growing for the past 20 years, and an experienced lawyer who has not had numerous clients who have succeeded in mediation probably will not provide real support.

If either you or your wife has a lawyer who invariably wants to take over the mediation sessions, the ability of the clients to shape their own settlement quickly gets submerged in the competition between the lawyers. Lawyers who need to be central to every discussion and who have to take over for you are inconsistent with the objectives of mediation. It is also a very expensive process because three professionals are billing for each hour, and it is a nightmare to schedule because it is so difficult to find times when everyone is available. So don't be misled. Real divorce mediation reduces the role of lawyers to that of advisors only on matters of law.

Supporting you through mediation also requires the patience to fully explain legal and technical aspects of your case. When you go to a mediation session, you have to be prepared. If you are reasonably intelligent, there are no legal concepts so complicated that you cannot understand them as long as someone is willing to teach you. If the lawyer you are interviewing is condescending or impatient, or if he makes everything sound mysterious and complicated, keep looking.

7. Someone who does not counsel dirty tactics: If you interview a lawyer who counsels dirty tactics, run away from that lawyer. But don't regard your consult as a waste of time. Because you have had a professional consultation with that lawyer, he is now "conflicted out." This means that he cannot now represent your wife, because he has seen you. It is not unusual when you are in one of the smaller cities for someone to advise you to have consults with all the worst predator litigious lawyers in town. It may be costly, but it means that they will not be involved in your divorce.

The dirty tricks I am concerned with involve acts that begin the divorce on a note of bad faith. We have talked about raids on the bank accounts and safe deposit box as classic dirty tricks. Some lawyers will support a man who wants to use the threat of a custody fight to beat his wife into submission on economic issues. A divorce that begins with threats or unilateral grabbing of assets almost always goes sour. And lawyers who encourage or even support such tactics are to be avoided if you are to have any hopes of a good divorce.

8. Someone whose fees are reasonable: You can't get something for nothing. All divorce lawyers bill for their time, and the more successful the lawyer, the more she can charge. Most divorce lawyers have had many clients run up large bills that they could not or would not pay. Consequently, many lawyers want to get a substantial retainer, a payment in advance that they can bill against. Their retainer agreements usually provide that when the retainer runs out, you have to either stay current or make another payment in advance. A lawyer who thinks a case will take a lot of time is usually looking for a large retainer.

How much you pay in the end will depend on several factors. One is how demanding you are on your lawyer's time. If you are insecure and need daily reassurance or clarification from your lawyer, that daily phone call will soon add up to a lot of money. Many lawyers bill for every phone call, and most will charge you one-sixth of an hour as a minimum charge. So if your lawyer charges $300 an hour, every phone call will cost you $50. By the end of a long case, your phone calls alone could cost you several thousand dollars. Remember that the rate and how a lawyer's time is billed are also negotiable items.

The second factor that shapes your final bill is how well you and your wife negotiate between yourselves. If you can agree on parenting and division of property and only need the lawyers to get involved on a few issues, the cost will be lower than if you and your wife cannot agree on anything. If each lawyer charges for every phone call, then every time the two lawyers talk on the phone to each other will cost you and your wife at least a hundred dollars. Now add the cost of your call to your lawyer, his call back to you, your wife's call to her lawyer, and the call back, and the smallest issue delegated to the lawyers can cost you hundreds of dollars. The same applies every time the two lawyers correspond. And if you have them running back and forth to court, we're talking thousands of dollars every time.

The other factors have to do with the way your lawyer works. First, how much is the hourly rate? You should find out what the average hourly rate is where you live so you can tell if a lawyer proposes to charge more than other lawyers. But hourly rate is not the only important factor. It also matters how many hours the lawyer spends on each task and how much discovery the lawyer proposes to do on your case. Several lawyers I know insist on seeing every check you and your spouse have written in the past 5 years. That might be justified if you know you are going to trial, but to do that in every case just adds many unnecessary billable hours to the bill. If you are going to do discovery, you should get your lawyer to seek your consent every time she proposes to make a demand for depositions or experts' reports or to file a motion in the court. If you do this, you can at least exercise some control over costs. Although most divorce lawyers are not used to such accountability, it is completely commonplace in the corporate and commercial world.

I am unaware of any data that shows a correlation between the size of the legal fee and the results obtained for the client. Generally, the more you and your wife spend on legal fees, the more contact you have had with the courts, the angrier the divorce, and the worse the result. There is no winning in divorce court, only different degrees of losing. Every dollar you and your wife spend on legal fees constitutes the measure of your mutual failure to manage your divorce well. Don't be afraid to ask for references from other professionals a lawyer has worked with. He cannot divulge the names of other clients, but he can give you the names of other lawyers and accountants with whom he has worked. If ever *caveat emptor* applied, this is it. If you are determined to mediate, you should not pay a retainer. Tell the lawyer that you are in mediation and that you will pay her at the end of every consultation you seek. There is no risk to the lawyer in agreeing to this, and most responsible lawyers will so agree. For most middle-class divorces resolved in mediation, no more than 5 hours of consultation should be required, so big retainers are not justified. On the other hand, if the mediation is unsuccessful and you ask the lawyer to take over, be prepared to ante up for her retainer.

9. The gender of the lawyer does not matter: It is not unusual to hear people assume that if you are a man you should hire a male lawyer and if you are a woman you should hire a woman. Such an assumption is based on the premise that men are biased toward other men and women biased toward other women. However, in 25 years in the business, I have seen nothing that justifies such an assumption. Every skill (and every deficit) is equally distributed between men and women. So when you find a lawyer who you think can do a good job and who has a winning personality, the time for the case, a reasonable approach to legal fees, and a personality that you think you can work with, hire that person.

10. Someone who has time: Some lawyers who are just starting out may have a lot of time on their hands because they have no clients. And other lawyers may have too many clients and not enough time. Nothing is worse than having a lawyer who does not have time to give you what you need when you need it. Most very busy lawyers hire associates to do much of the work for them. In a well-managed practice, lawyers don't take on more than they can handle. But many practices are poorly managed, and many lawyers take on more than they can do well. These are the lawyers who take a week to respond to your call or to the call from your wife's lawyer. They are the lawyers who file court documents at the last moment or are forever seeking delays and adjournments because they have not had time to get to any but the most urgent tasks. At a minimum, this is the lawyer who will drag your case out forever and complete it only when the court deadlines make it absolutely necessary. You certainly do not want a lawyer who does not have enough time to do your case well and as quickly as it can be done. In litigation, delay begets delay and extends the time you and your family have to live in limbo. Remember, in almost every case there is going to be a settlement, and the sooner it happens the better off you are.

If your ego or your insecurity requires you to hire one of the "star" lawyers, in time this may be a problem for you. If your star lawyer is a good manager, you will find yourself pawned off on an associate who, your lawyer tells you, he is closely supervising. Because you have not chosen the associate, you may find yourself represented by someone without the experience you thought you were getting. And even though the associate's time is billed at a lower rate than that of the partner you hired, you get billed double every time they talk to each other. On the other hand, if your star lawyer is poor at time management, lacks organizational skills, and tries to do too much, you will find yourself fuming because you cannot get his attention when you need it. So take the time to inquire about the size of your prospective lawyer's caseload. Ask how long you can expect to wait until you receive a return phone call. Ask how long, on average, it takes for the lawyer to settle a case. While none of this guarantees you that you are hiring a responsive lawyer, it may help you weed out the bad ones.

Having dissected the legal culture and its destructive impact on couples and families going through divorce, it is time to turn our attention to the alternative—mediation—which we will discuss in chapter 7.

"I don't need time to think it over, Phillip—the answer is yes, I'll settle out of court with you."

Seven

MEDIATION

IN THE PAST 25 YEARS, MEDIATION HAS GROWN from a small reform movement into one of the most significant forces on the landscape of divorce. The legal profession has grudgingly accepted its existence while attempting to blunt its impact. When done well, mediation significantly reduces your contact with lawyers and the legal system, thus reducing the mischief caused by such contact.

What Is Mediation?

A mediator facilitates the discussions of the disputants. When people disagree, it is easy for their emotions to interfere with their ability to engage in constructive discussion and negotiation. The indignation that arises when one person feels wronged, wrongfully accused, or criticized results in an impulse to retaliate and punish. Unless people find a way to manage their feelings, discussion deteriorates into an exchange that is unpleasant and unproductive. When the discussion is guided and contained, however, most people can talk out the disagreement and find a mutually acceptable resolution. Guiding the discussion is traditionally the role of the mediator.

Having no personal agenda, the mediator's opinion has the inherent gravitas of impartiality and is harder to dismiss out of hand. The mediator provides a safe environment for discussion and imposes rules of conduct that ensure that the discussion stays on track and does not deteriorate into personal attacks. When necessary, the mediator establishes the agenda for the meeting and helps harness the creativity and knowledge of the parties in a search for amicable resolution. Mediation is a craft: part learned technique and part art. Good mediators have personal characteristics that command respect, establish rapport, and provide a calming influence. Mediators have no power other than the power to withdraw when a party to the dispute refuses to cooperate.

The divorce mediation movement has acquired momentum over the past 10 years. It began in the late 1970s when a group of reform-minded lawyers began to collaborate with psychologists and family therapists who were appalled by the carnage they were witnessing in the divorce courts. The premises were simple. Almost all divorces were resolved with a negotiated settlement, but the settlement came after years of litigation. With settlement as the incidental but nearly inevitable by-product of the preparation for trial, couples were put through a process that served as a meat grinder for whatever was left of family cooperation. So if the case was going to settle eventually, why not redesign the system to pursue settlement at the beginning of the divorce process rather than at the end? Instead of having the couple surrender all power to an adversarial process, why not keep the husband and wife in control and facilitate their own negotiation and settlement? That was the beginning of divorce mediation.

What came out of these discussions 25 years ago was a movement that today has thousands of practitioners around the country. Mediation was initially received with great hostility by the legal community. The notion that one professional could help two parties negotiate their own settlement conflicted with many tenets of the legal culture. Many lawyers painted vivid pictures in their minds of a horde of unqualified mediators promoting unfair settlements that robbed innocent people of their rights and produced unfair results. When I started offering divorce mediation in New Jersey in 1979, the bar association grumbled that I ought to be disbarred. Mediation, in their not-so-humble opinion, constituted a violation of the ethics rules of practice. It took a long time and great controversy within the profession to win a grudging acceptance for divorce mediation. Mediation not only violated the cultural norms of the legal profession, but also represented a serious economic threat. Divorce was the bread-and-butter income for many small law firms, and a process that could reduce legal fees by 90 percent was clearly unwelcome.

Today, mediation has become a permanent part of the divorce landscape. Lawyers as a group have not endorsed it, but mental health professionals have generally been enthusiastic. Most of the referrals to divorce mediators still come from therapists, although an increasing number of referrals come from satisfied clients. Therapists like it because it reduces the unintended consequences of divorce. It gets families reorganized at less emotional and financial cost, so it minimizes the impact of the divorce on couples and their children. Successfully done, mediation allows people to move on with their lives and curbs the type of chronic conflict that haunts many families who have endured conventional divorce.

Mediation and Risk

Divorce mediation is essentially a no-risk proposition. Nothing is binding until the agreement reached by the parties has been set forth in a contract prepared or reviewed by the parties' attorneys. You commit to mediation 1 hour at time and can withdraw if you believe it is not working for you. Most mediators charge as you go and do not collect retainers. So, if after three or four sessions you do not want to continue, you have lost very little time or money. You can always revert to a conventionally negotiated or litigated divorce. But if mediation does work for you, it can usually make the difference between a bad divorce and a good divorce. Mediation should be the first choice for almost all couples. If one of the spouses is violent, crazy, addicted, or so oppositional that cooperative discussion is impossible, mediation is not the answer. But for more than 90 percent of all couples, mediation is an appropriate choice. If you seek an amicable resolution, it is the only choice.

With or Without Lawyers?

Divorce mediation originally developed as a process that was done without the parties' lawyers in the room. The model of mediation that has been generally practiced is one in which the couple have advisory or consulting lawyers with whom they talk whenever they or the mediator feel that they need a consultation. We use lawyers as advisers and counselors rather than surrogates. Lawyers do not attend the sessions. As we discussed in the last chapter, it is too difficult to schedule meetings for three busy professionals— and it is too expensive because for each hour you are paying three professionals instead of one. The most important reason to leave your lawyers in their offices is that their presence usually negates the primary purpose of mediation, which is to keep the couple talking and in control of their own negotiation. In mediation, we want the couple to learn a new way of talking to each other so they can continue to communicate and cooperate around the children well after the divorce is final. When lawyers dominate the discussion, it defeats the integrity of the mediation process.

The only reason to have lawyers present in a mediation session is if one or both of the parties is too impaired to carry on a fruitful discussion. I have conducted cases this way when there have been allegations of domestic violence, addiction, or when one of the parties is too timid to fully participate. Lawyer-dominated mediation is preferable to litigation, but it is much less preferred to mediation in which the clients do the talking.

Court-Mandated Mediation

As mediation became more accepted, two things happened. Courts came under pressure to make the advantages of mediation available to litigants; and many lawyers sought a way to co-opt a process that reduced their centrality in the process of divorce. The result is court-annexed mediation that barely resembles the real thing. Many courts have set up programs that are called divorce mediation without really having any of its advantages. First, lawyers are usually present and do most of the talking. Second, the mediation is ordered late in the process of litigation when the parties have already been polarized by the adversarial process. Third, it is usually a one-time event that does not give the mediator much time to establish trust and rapport with the clients (something that could not be done in any event because the lawyers are doing the talking). Finally, the quality of the mediators is generally substandard because they are either unpaid volunteers or poorly trained, poorly qualified court personnel.

Because most cases settle anyhow as trial draws near, court-annexed mediation has often become a waste of time and money for the clients because it just creates another billing event for the lawyers and accomplishes little else. So if a lawyer tries to talk you out of real mediation on the grounds that you get it for free in the court system, hang on to your wallet and find another lawyer.

Choosing a Mediator

The task of choosing a mediator is complicated by the old adage "many are called, but few are chosen." For several reasons, there are too many ill-trained, inexperienced, and incompetent people holding themselves out as mediators. It will take some diligent effort to find the right mediator. They are there but must be ferreted out. Mediation has, over the years, attracted thousands of enthusiasts. Because mediation is multidisciplined, it is not limited to lawyers or therapists. Even if it were, that would not be of much help. There are many people who have earned a lot of money offering "training" seminars to would-be mediators. When the field was getting underway, there were almost no clients, and very few professionals had any experience as mediators. So training was a hit-or-miss affair. Most training opportunities were 5-day-long seminars during which enrollees practiced simulated or role-played mediation. Although such seminars can familiarize people with some aspects of mediation, they hardly qualify as training because training has always meant hands-on learning of a skill. Hundreds, if not thousands, of people took such programs and then labeled themselves mediators. I shudder to think of all the couples who have gone into mediation unaware that they were the mediator's first case.

One would have hoped that over the years the education of mediators would have matured with the field and that clinical training would have become the norm. But that has not happened. So many people have wanted to be certified as mediators, and so many mediators wanted to seek training profits, that the field became stuck and never evolved as it should have. To make matters worse, many state court systems eager to offer mediation set up programs that claimed to train and certify mediators. For example, in North Carolina, the state Supreme Court set up a program in which people are certified as mediators by the court after taking a 5-day seminar and observing a certified mediator conduct two cases. So in that state you can be certified as a mediator by the court even though you have never mediated a single case.

Because of the poor job the field has done in training and certification, you cannot rely on any of the formal credentials touted by mediators. Certification and completion of formal training programs are, for the most part, meaningless. This does not mean that you can't find a good mediator. It just means that you can't rely on the formal credentials. What you want to find is someone who has a lot of experience and comes highly recommended by other people, including therapists who have referred to this person before, lawyers who have represented clients who have been through mediation with this mediator, and, where possible, former clients themselves. You usually can get a number of referrals from mental health professionals. You can call divorce lawyers in your area and maybe get names from them. You can ask among your friends whether any have heard of others who have successfully used a mediator. You can also use the Internet to review the resumes of mediators in your area.

You are looking for an experienced mediator. I think that 50 completed cases would be the minimum number a mediator would have to have in order for you to be interested. It takes that many to really begin to develop the craft. Experience is the most important—but not the only—criterion. As mentioned in the previous chapter, one thing that is not important is the gender of the mediator. I have never believed that men or women are necessarily biased in the direction of their own gender. If all else works, gender makes no difference. So in the event that your wife insists on a woman mediator because she believes that a woman would be more sympathetic to her, you should readily agree. The more your wife commits to the process, the better off you are.

Another important issue is whether or not it is important for the mediator to be a lawyer. This has been a subject of considerable controversy over the years. About 40 percent of mediators are lawyers. Another 40 or 45 percent are mental health professionals of one persuasion or another. The rest are from other fields such as accounting, financial planning, and education. Although I do not believe that the profession of origin of the mediator is important in itself, I do believe that the knowledge and skill of the mediator is very important. A divorce mediator needs a basic knowledge base about divorce law, family finances, family dynamics, and the psychology of divorce. I have met psychologists, lawyers, and other professionals who, by virtue of their experience and study, are knowledgeable in all these things and quite able to do a creditable job of mediation. I also have met lawyers and accountants who are ignorant in matters of psychology and family dynamics, as I have met psychologists who are completely lost when it comes to the technical side of divorce. Anyone who is deficient in any of these areas is not fit to mediate divorces.

Here is a list of what you seek in a mediator.

▶ Expertise about divorce law and economics

▶ Expertise about family dynamics and the psychology of divorce

▶ Knowledge about the tax aspects of divorce

▶ Strong counseling skills

▶ A commanding presence

▶ At least 50 completed mediations

▶ References from other professionals who have been
involved in cases conducted by this mediator

How your mediator has acquired these skills and experience does not matter. Whether the person is a psychologist, lawyer, or accountant is not in itself very important. In a case that has great financial complexity, the probability of finding a psychologist with the requisite knowledge is very low. But most divorces are not very complicated from an economic perspective and do not require terribly sophisticated financial expertise. You have to analyze your own divorce and seek a mediator who has the background and skill appropriate to your problems.

Choosing and interviewing a mediator should be a joint activity of you and your wife. It is worth the time and money to interview two or three to get a good sense of what the mediator knows and how you and your wife relate to this person. The rapport you establish will be important. Is the mediator a calming presence? Does the mediator seem to know what she is talking about? Is the mediator's communication clear and concise? In the end, you both have to be comfortable. You are about to design very important and long-term plans, and a little extra effort is worth it to find the right person. Be prepared to pay for such consults. Professionals who give free samples are too hungry and probably not very experienced.

Styles of Mediation

Because mediation is a craft and depends so much on what the practitioner brings to it, mediators vary considerably in the way they mediate. As in several other aspects of this field, mediator style has been the subject of controversy. For example, some mediators will occasionally see each of you separately. Other mediators have been taught that such private caucuses are not desirable practice. Some mediators are more dominant and directive than others. They are more likely to make suggestions, provide active leadership, and suggest options and possible solutions when you are stuck. Other mediators are less directive and more facilitative. They tend to wait until you have worked it out and intervene less frequently, making fewer specific suggestions. Part of the difference is personal style, and part of the difference may be a purposely adopted strategy. However, among some mediators, there has developed a notion of "pure" mediation in which the mediator may only facilitate and never even offer an opinion. Such a mediator's ideology is based on a premise of absolute self-determination for clients, in which any intervention that introduces the mediator's perspective is regarded as wrong. I believe this view of mediation is so stringent as to be limiting.

I think you do best with a mediator who has significant expertise about what works and what doesn't work in divorce and who is willing to share that knowledge. The mediator should be prepared to do anything that the two of you request to help you reach settlement. What I enjoy most about this work is that it allows me to bring to bear almost everything I have ever learned about anything. Whatever knowledge I have is at the service of my clients, and the creative possibilities are unlimited. The mediator needs to have a vision of what a good divorce looks like and some sense of a map of how to get there. Some disciplines do not prepare people well to be mediators. I have been involved in training lawyers, psychotherapists, and others in mediation for 20 years and have worked with hundreds of students in a clinical program. We have found that psychotherapists who are trained to be passive in therapy and sit by while the client struggles for insight do not make good mediators because they are too reluctant to intervene when needed. Therapists who are trained in behavioral or cognitive therapies do better than therapists trained in psychoanalytic traditions.

As you interview prospective mediators, do not hesitate to ask if the mediator identifies with some particular style of mediation. Ask under what conditions the mediator will offer his opinion about what you should do. Ask about professional experience with divorce: In how many divorces has the mediator been involved? How much does he know about how families adapt to divorce? Also ask about his knowledge of financial matters that will be important in your divorce. If you have your own business, ask how the mediator will approach valuation and audit issues. A mediator should have the technical knowledge necessary to coordinate the work of the neutral economic experts who will participate in your divorce. Ask how many similar cases the mediator has done. And ask for references to lawyers who have represented clients who have been through mediation with this particular mediator. Avoid those who have a narrow scope of professional experience. This is one field in which gray hair (or no hair) may be an asset.

Finally, use the consultation to determine if you feel a sense of rapport with the mediator and, just as important, if your wife also feels a sense of rapport. It will do you no good to have your wife quit three sessions into the process because she believes the mediator does not understand her.

Using the Mediator

Now you have chosen a mediator and a lawyer and are ready to begin mediation. How do you do it well?

Setting the Agenda

One of the important jobs of the mediator is to set the agenda for discussion. Most mediators will move from parenting issues to support and then to property divisions. It makes sense to first establish the living pattern for the children before moving on to a discussion of economic issues. It is the mediator's job to help you organize the issues so your negotiation develops and flows in a logical and orderly fashion.

This is not to say that you should be passive in expressing your immediate concerns in mediation. Couples in the early throes of divorce are often very anxious and need guidance so that they do not bumble their way into a mess. The first session or two should settle several temporary issues. Here are the issues that must be addressed immediately.

MONEY MANAGEMENT: Divorcing couples receive much bad advice from well-meaning but ignorant friends and relatives, so couples often come into mediation worried that the other spouse will be irresponsible about spending or will withhold money as a power ploy. The mediator should probe to establish how you are managing money at present and then help you address the issues. Unless people are in immediate financial crisis, I encourage them to maintain the status quo until they have mutually decided on any changes. If you have been depositing your pay in a joint account, continue to do so. If your wife has been paying the bills, encourage her to continue until the two of you decide otherwise.

Sometimes people start out with money crises. The mortgage hasn't been paid for 3 months and the bank is threatening to foreclose. One spouse is running up credit card debt and the other is worried about getting stuck with the payments. These crises must be addressed immediately so that you can discuss your long-range issues without being in a state of panic.

The most common money problem that arises early is that couples who have recently separated into two households find themselves operating at a deficit. They had been living on 105 percent of net income in one household and now, having moved into two households, find themselves with a deficit of 30 to 40 percent. Developing budgets, agreeing on economic retrenchment, and exploring ways to increase income are the long-range tasks of the mediation. It is rarely possible to resolve these issues in a meeting or two. Nevertheless, the issues need to be addressed and an orderly use of money agreed to for the month or two that it will take to resolve the issues. Your mediator should help you address these immediate issues so you do not feel that you are in immediate financial peril.

It may take considerable restraint on your part, but you must not engage in the unilateral control of family money. If you do dumb things like closing the credit card accounts, you will frighten your wife out of mediation and into litigation. Use the mediator's influence to control the spending issues and reinforce rather than undermine the mediation process.

ACCESS TO CHILDREN: Although most couples come into mediation with some sense about how they will manage the children, some come in very anxious. Many men have heard horror stories about fathers being deprived of access to their children and seek immediate assurance that it won't happen to them. You may have a strong position that you should have equal custody with your wife and are worried that you might, in error, cede control to her. Heightened vigilance about parenting arrangements may be a hot issue from the beginning and again, it is the mediator's job to calm the parties so they can deliberate in an orderly manner. If you have already separated and do not have a parenting schedule in place that you find satisfactory, you may be very eager to get this resolved. But you must give the process some time to work and not insist on immediate results. If you are not yet separated but are skirmishing with your wife about child-related issues, let the mediator know so she can address them. It is important to immediately impose order so that the two of you do not make the situation worse. I generally ask that clients continue doing whatever they have been doing for a few weeks more, even though one of them is unhappy with the present arrangement. The immediate sense of crisis must be tamed before you can get into productive discussions.

Managing the Discussion

Follow the mediator's lead as she sets the agenda, and do not struggle for control with the mediator. It is the mediator's job to maintain a safe atmosphere in which you can explore the issues. The mediator is there to make it possible for you and your wife to have discussions that you probably cannot have on your own because of the state of your relationship. Let the mediator field the difficult emotions that you and your wife will inevitably express. A trained mediator will intervene and stop certain types of nonproductive discussion. If you or your wife launch a verbal attack on the other, expect the mediator to intervene. Remember my general rule for couples from chapters 3 and 4: "Don't attack and don't defend." That is, if you feel that your wife has attacked you or unfairly criticized you, do not defend yourself. Although it is instinctive to defend when criticized, that behavior just prolongs a tit-for-tat battle that escalates into general and abstract attacks on each other's character that derail the mediation. Instead of defending yourself, sit quietly and let the mediator correct the situation by reminding your wife that her comment is not helpful.

The mediator is there to monitor the discussion and to suppress the comments that accomplish nothing other than to distract you from your task. Clients frequently begin the mediation thinking that they have to counter everything that the other says about them. They worry that I will think poorly of them or be swayed by their spouse's criticism of them. I have to remind clients that I am not a judge and that in the end it doesn't matter what I think. They do not have to convince me of anything. But they do have to convince each other. So when verbal hostilities are exchanged, I will quietly ask the culprit to explain to me how what he or she just said would win the cooperation of the other spouse. If the comment just alienates the other, it is counterproductive to the reason the couple is in mediation.

Mediation offers you an opportunity to learn a new way of talking to each other. As mentioned in chapter 4, the model of communication you need here is the same as you would adopt in talking to a business colleague with whom you don't always agree. You do not use angry tones or words but maintain a civil tone at all times. You disagree on issues and ideas but do not make personal attacks. The mediator will guide you into this manner of discourse, so follow her lead and do not resist.

Reframing

Mediators often reframe things that you say to render them neutral rather than hostile. When you say, "I can't stand the way you waste money!" expect the mediator to say something along the lines of "So, you are concerned that the money be used wisely, is that correct?" Or when your wife says, "All you do with the children is let them watch television," the mediator may reframe the comment as "So you are concerned that the children use their time constructively. Is that correct?" Reframing is part of the mediator's job as translator, filter, hearing aid, megaphone, and bifocals. The mediator participates in the discussion to keep it task oriented and to help you hear each other and be open to each others' proposals. Again, follow the mediator's lead. Let him continually refocus the discussion so that it stays productive and doesn't get bogged down.

Reducing the Scope of Disagreement

One of the pitfalls of negotiation is that disputants often exaggerate their differences so that they think they are farther apart than they really are. The wife says, with great anger, "I have told him that I need $2,000 a month for the kids, and I will not accept any less just because he is selfish and tight." The husband replies, "Don't tell me about selfish! All you think about is yourself. I offered you $1,700 a month, and I will be damned if I'll give you a cent more!" To this hostile exchange I would expect a mediator to reply as follows: "Well, I am relieved to see that your positions are so close to each other. You are only $300 apart, and you are more in agreement than you think. Now how can we bridge the small gap that remains in your two viewpoints?" What the mediator has done is filtered out the hostile messages and the personal attacks, emphasized the commonality of position, and opened the way for compromise and negotiation. In time, we hope that couples will begin to adopt this more neutral way of addressing issues. Most couples settle down and begin to imitate this neutral, solution-oriented way of discussing issues. We teach mediators to look for ways that they can restate the differences of the couple to emphasize that they agree more than they disagree. The mediator in turn teaches this skill to the couple. This is one of the long-term benefits of mediation because it sets up a pattern for couples to be able to resolve disputes themselves after the divorce is final.

You can help the mediation succeed by adopting this stance as soon as possible. Before you disagree with your wife, reduce the scope of the disagreement to its smallest possible expression. People who are upset tend to "awfulize" a disagreement. That is, they present it as bigger and as more abstract than it really is. She says, "I am willing for the children to stay with you on weekends, but I want them to sleep in their home on school nights so I can be sure that they are ready for school the next day." This makes you angry, because you feel that it implies that you are not capable of taking care of your children and seeing them off to school prepared for the day. So your first impulse is to say something like, "I'm sick of your insinuations that I am not as good a parent as you are, and I'm tired of you trying to control everything and cut me out as a parent. I am not going to take it!"

Were you to say such a thing, you could expect the mediator to intervene with a neutrally reframed proposition such as, "I am glad to see that the two of you agree about the weekends. Now let's talk about how we ensure that both of you are involved with the children during the week as well." You can save the mediator the trouble by altering the way you respond to your wife: "I appreciate your concern that the children go to school prepared each day. But I can also help them do that. It is very important to me to have some overnight time with them during the week, so why don't we talk about how they can spend one or two nights with me during the week and how I can reassure you that I will have them ready for school in the morning?"

Note how this alternative manner of expressing your viewpoint is actually much more potent than your initial accusatory response. It maintains a tone of respect, acknowledges her legitimate fears, and seeks to reassure her at the same time it forcefully asserts your own legitimate needs. Study the way the mediator reframes the issues and try to imitate her.

Managing Anger

The expression of anger is a normal part of divorce discussions. But having recognized it as normal, we nevertheless seek less rather than more. You may be angry about issues related to the marriage and its ending, and you may be angry when your wife takes positions you find unfair or says things you regard as insensitive. But blowing up, yelling, or raging weakens you rather than strengthens you and slows the mediation process. It may also scare your wife right into the office of her lawyer. Available research on negotiation suggests that threats and attempts at intimidation almost never move the other side in the direction you wish and almost always polarize the dispute even more. If your wife gets angry and rages at you, you need to stay calm and cordial. Let the mediator calm her down or point out that her behavior is not helpful. Although mediators are trained to be impartial, you benefit and get the mediator working for you when you do not become the problem client.

Mediation is not the place to vent your anger or the other strong feelings associated with divorce. Divorce counseling may be useful and your therapist may be useful. But mediation is for negotiating, and negotiation objectives are not advanced by histrionics. If you begin to feel that you just cannot sit on your feelings anymore, ask the mediator for a brief caucus with each of you and use the opportunity to tell the mediator what you are feeling. That way you don't arouse your wife to further indignation and anger. A competent mediator will hear you out and help you to calm down so you can resume mediation. However, it is up to you to keep your anger on a tight leash.

Searching for Options

Mediation is a problem-solving approach to negotiation. The mediator will be trying to convert your issues into problems to be solved, and then try to help you develop the best options for solving those problems. The problems of parenting are posed as a series of questions. How do you develop a method of making decisions for the children? How do you create a schedule that meets the needs of each of you and the children? The economic issues are also restated as problems to be solved. How do you distribute family income so that all family members can thrive? How do you increase income and/or reduce expenses to balance expenses and income? In all these questions, there is neither a single answer nor are there infinite possibilities. The mediator will push you each to define a broad enough range of options so that you can find common ground. The mediator will also help you evaluate the options. Sometimes she will suggest that you consult outside experts on how well one option works as compared to another. For example, a child psychologist can help you evaluate how long a young child can go without seeing her mother or her father without suffering undue anxiety. Children's sense of time changes with age, and if the issue is how a child at a particular stage of development can manage a challenge, the expert will provide help in evaluating the alternatives.

Negotiation requires that needs be assessed and options developed and evaluated. Whether the issue is the psychological need of the child or how to manage a tax concern, the mediator will either have expertise of his own or will suggest an expert consultant. Most experienced mediators have developed their list of consultants over time, and it is a good idea to use those people when experts are required. You can get into protracted debate over whether to use Dr. Brown or Dr. Gray, whether to use John Doe, CPA, or Mary Smith, CPA. It moves things along to accept guidance from the mediator on such choices.

Past, Present, and Future

It is not uncommon for couples to waste a lot of time and energy arguing over what has happened in the past. If you want to litigate and fight, this is a useful pastime. Otherwise, it is self-defeating. Most disputes about what you did or she did in the past are about who is at fault for some problem, who should bear the blame, and who should suffer the consequences. Litigation is designed to determine wrongdoing, and if you are obsessed with fixing blame, go to court and don't waste your money or your time in mediation. With this in mind, you will not be surprised to discover that whenever you and your wife digress into futile arguments about the past, your mediator will intervene and try to move you into the future. You go to court to vindicate the past. You go to mediation to plan the future.

When I teach mediators, I emphasize that the cognitive shift from past to future is one of the critical strategic objectives of the mediator. Your disappointments with each other are rooted in the past. But the only further contact you will have with each other is in the future and that you can design for. So when the mediator tries to move you out of the past, do not resist. It is less important who did what as a parent in the past than it is who will do what in the future. It is less important how you spent money in the past than it is how you will manage money in the future. A future orientation is inherently cleaner, from an emotional perspective, than is an orientation to the past. One can project optimism into the future even if the past has been troubled. You will find that most good mediators serve as your cheerleaders and encourage you to shift from the troubled past to a more optimistic future. While we are not seeking a Pollyanna in a mediator, the mediator's optimism can serve as a healthy antidote to the pessimism that you and your wife may bring to the table.

Be Boring

When I teach mediators, I often encourage them to promote boring dialogue. More precisely, I teach them that it is always strategically useful to reframe abstract propositions as concrete problems. "You're spending too much on the children's clothes!" is reframed as "How much does a pair of sneakers cost?" "You are so lax and irresponsible that you let the children stay up to all hours!" is reframed as "What do you think the bedtime should be for the children?" "I won't take a cent less than half of the house equity!" is reframed as "How many dollars are at issue here?" In each case the mediator translates an abstract generalization by one spouse about the other into a practical, concrete question. You will note that in each case, the concrete question cannot generate anger, just inquiry. You can't get excited about the question about how much sneakers cost, but you can get very excited about whether you are irresponsible or a profligate spender. That is what I mean by being boring. State your viewpoints in the most neutral and concrete manner possible. It requires your negotiating partner to respond in kind and keeps you on track toward resolution. Although the mediator should reframe the issue for you when you become abstract, it is better if you do it for yourself. The more you can do this, the easier it is to get to agreement.

Keeping It within the Mediation

When people decide to resolve their divorce negotiations through mediation, I usually ask one thing of them. I ask them to agree that they will not get into disputes outside of my office and to commit to delaying any disagreement to the next mediation session. I ask this because I do not want to risk the goodwill that might remain between them on fights that leave them despairing. There is a special despair that I think couples whose marriages are failing can invoke in each other. It occurs at the moment when you are trying to be understood and you believe that the other person just cannot understand you and does not have enough empathy for you to resolve the dispute. You start to feel that dialogue with the other is hopeless and doomed to escalate into warfare. If you could do this on your own, you probably would not be getting divorced. You have chosen mediation because you want to work out your settlement without this intense struggle. So let the mediator do her job and avoid fights when you are not in the mediator's office. When couples do as I ask, they are able to live in relative peace between sessions, and that in itself helps to improve their sense of optimism and goodwill.

Do Your Homework

Because mediation is so fact-driven, it is important that you prepare the documentation that will be requested by the mediator. When discussing issues of alimony and child support, you will need budgets that accurately reflect the needs of both households, and you will need proof of income for yourself and your wife. When discussing the division of marital property, the mediator will request a statement of assets and liabilities reflecting everything that you own and everything that you owe. Each of these requests must be honored thoroughly.

The preparation of budgets is an important task. In your marriage, one of you may have been the primary bill payer. One of you may be more skillful than the other in financial calculations and balancing a checkbook. But it is important that each of you do your own. We want you to know what your financial needs and constraints are, and we want each of you to be able to manage your own household when the divorce is over. So you can ask each other for information, but you must each take responsibility for preparing your own budget.

You will also need to provide proof of your income. Today, many people who are employed receive only part of their compensation as salary. Commissions, bonuses, deferred compensation, stock options, and stock grants may all be part of the compensation package. It may not be possible to predict precisely what your income will be next year or the year after. But this is a common problem, and any experienced mediator knows how to help you manage the issue. It requires comprehensive information about your compensation. When in doubt, provide more rather than less information.

When you prepare documents, bring the original and two copies to the mediation so that you can provide a copy to your wife and one to the mediator. The copy must be legible. Your willingness to provide information without resistance or delay will go far to win the trust of your wife and the gratitude of the mediator. Some men resent being asked to prove what they say by providing supporting documents. But it is unfair to say, "trust me," and then to be indignant when asked to provide the documents. This is a business deal you are trying to strike, and you are not entitled to presume on the goodwill of your negotiating partner. In many divorces, this is a low point for trust in the relationship; an inadvertent failure to disclose information or a refusal to do so may provoke a great deal of unnecessary suspicion.

When preparing the statement of assets and liabilities, the same principles apply. Bring copies of all current account statements. If you believe that some of your assets are exempt from distribution, you will bring whatever documents are necessary to prove that assertion. Remember that even assets that are not marital must be disclosed. So err on the side of inclusiveness. Some of your assets may require appraisals. This can include real estate, pensions, professional practices, and family-owned businesses. Because mediation is an efficient process, it can move along quickly. Some appraisals, particularly business appraisals, take time to complete, so you want to get the appraisal process underway as soon as possible. You do not want to be ready to finish but faced with a long period of limbo because the appraisals are still underway. I suggest that you raise this question with the mediator early in the process so that the appraisals can be in process while you are resolving parenting and support issues.

From time to time your mediator will ask you to see your lawyer for a consultation about some particular topic. I usually request this of clients when they are having difficulty agreeing because one or both have unrealistic expectations. Reasonable and experienced attorneys can be very useful in providing a reality check and in helping clients to understand their alternatives if they do not reach agreement. Alimony is often a difficult issue, and you will need to understand what the settlement norms are in your locale. Your mediator can often provide information about this but may want you to also have the benefit of your lawyer's opinion as well. If asked to see your lawyer, do so in a timely manner so the mediation is not delayed. The mediator may also suggest consultations with other experts. Your cooperation with such requests will keep the mediation moving.

Why Not Try to Work It Out Ourselves without a Mediator?

In an ideal world, people would not need mediators. The norm for resolving most disputes in the world is that the disputants negotiate and talk themselves to some agreement or common ground. That is how most disputes are settled because if we needed outside intervention each time we disagreed with someone, we wouldn't have time for anything else. So if the norm is spontaneous and successful negotiation, the very fact that we need a mediator suggests that there is something not working quite right between the parties to the dispute. You can think about the mediator as someone who is there to help you bridge the gaps between you and your wife and to make it possible for you to negotiate successfully.

Think about why negotiations fail. They fail because of a lack of mutual trust, fear of the other, a failure of communication, and the inability to negotiate well. Many people do not negotiate well because they have never been taught. Limited negotiating ability is exacerbated by fear, ignorance, and worry.

When we ask divorcing couples to negotiate a divorce settlement, we are asking them to do something they can do only with help from an expert third party. That is why the mediator is there, to coach you so you can do what you otherwise might not. The mediator is a negotiation coach whose primary job is to make it possible for the two of you to negotiate effectively. She is there to help you avoid the stratagems and tactics that will mess up your negotiation. The mediator will monitor the dialogue and intervene when one or both of you engages in behavior that does not advance the resolution of your disagreements. All of the strategic interventions of the mediator are things you would do for yourself if you were more relaxed, knowledgeable about negotiation, and knowledgeable about the subject matter of divorce. Without the coach, you probably cannot do it. But with good coaching, you probably can succeed.

In chapter 8, I will look at things you can do to help you negotiate with your wife. Most of your settlement negotiation will occur in the presence of the mediator, but there will be numerous times when the two of you will have to resolve minor differences on your own. Whether you are before the mediator or just with your wife, how you negotiate will be the difference between success and despair.

"*Your wife's also asking that you rot in hell for eternity, but I think that's negotiable.*"

Eight

NEGOTIATING WITH YOUR WIFE

THROUGHOUT THE COURSE OF THE DIVORCE, you will need to negotiate with your wife. Some of these negotiations will occur directly between the two of you, and some will occur in the mediation process. The purpose of this chapter is to help you think about how to negotiate successfully.

In my experience, men and women tend to have different negotiation models. Women, for the most part, have learned to work toward consensual decision making and are socially more adept at seeking common ground. If you help to maintain a cordial tone, her natural instincts become a resource to the mediation.

Men are more of a mixed bag. Consensual decision making has been emphasized in modern management for three decades, and many men in corporate environments have learned to negotiate well. But there is still a popular negotiating model afoot, in which the man is a hard-boiled, tough-talking negotiator who never gives an inch until the last moment. This negotiator uses intimidation, threat, ridicule, and bombast to force the other to submit. He affects indifference to settlement because he claims he will win the fight, and he often presents himself as more than happy to go to trial or to war if he does not get his way. If your concept of negotiation is even flavored by this viewpoint, you will have a sad mess of a divorce. Divorce lawyers love it when the client on the other side behaves like this. It allows them to deploy that part of their repertoire that has them exhibiting their own tough-guy stuff, without even a hint of embarrassment. And it generates tons of billable hours. Adversary-as-hardliner evokes lawyer-as-hero helping the damsel in distress by slaying the evil ruthless dragon. That is not how you want to negotiate here.

Divorce settlement negotiation is probably unlike any negotiation you have done before. In business negotiation, you do not have an intimate connection with the negotiating partner. The deal is focused on money and on finding a mutually profitable solution. Even in litigation on contract matters or in personal injury litigation, there is minimal prior contact and no anticipated future contact. The focus is on the deal, not on the relationship. Divorce settlement negotiation is so different because there is a powerful history of a relationship and, if you have children, the certainty of a long future relationship. Even after the children are grown, there will be future contact at weddings, graduations, events related to grandchildren, and other family occasions. And if the children are younger, the relationship will be more involved, requiring weekly contact and coordination.

So the focus in divorce negotiation cannot be exclusively on the deal because the shape of the deal will have great consequence for the continuing relationship between you and your wife. How that relationship evolves will influence all your attempts to build satisfying new lives. In the negotiation of a business deal, if one side thinks they didn't get a good deal, after the fact, they will have regrets but limited recourse. If there is an ongoing business relationship, it may be strained by the "buyer's remorse" of one of the parties, but it will not affect the core of your life. It's the opposite in divorce. If you negotiate a deal that one of you regards as unfair, the dissatisfaction will reverberate through both your lives. Your resentment about paying too much support will color how you relate to her and even to your children. It will make you less likely to accommodate her when she seeks some help from you, and that in turn will affect her inclination to cooperate with you. If she feels that she did not get enough support, she will retaliate through the kids, who will show up at your house begging for a new pair of sneakers because "Mommy doesn't get enough child support to be able to buy us shoes." A residual sense of unfairness will invariably sour your ongoing relationship.

A consequence of this dilemma is that in divorce settlement negotiations you cannot focus on just the deal; you must also focus on how the deal will affect the relationship in the future. Sometimes it may pay to make concessions that you might otherwise not have to make. For example, your lawyer may advise you that the child support guidelines require you to pay $100 a week, even though the budget the two of you worked out would suggest $150 a week. You can stand on your rights and refuse to go beyond that. Or you can focus on your long-term interests and pay more. Standing on your rights is not helpful when the result is inconsistent with your needs and interests. Knowledge of your legal rights is an important element of background information, but it is less useful than many people think. It is far better for you to work toward achieving your interests, which are interwoven with the needs and interests of your wife and your children.

Finally, you must understand that the negotiation will shape more than just your agreement. If you and your wife will be raising children together, the negotiation is your mutual opportunity to develop the protocols necessary to living in peace. It is your opportunity to establish a cordial yet businesslike approach to solving problems and resolving the inevitable disputes that will arise in the future. The measure of the health of any relationship is its capacity to manage conflict. In the negotiation of your settlement, you will establish the precedents that will shape the conflict resolution capacity of the future relationship with your wife. So pay close attention to the tone you maintain during the negotiation because it will influence much more than the terms of settlement.

CASE STUDY: Bob and Anne

Bob and Anne are trying to resolve the equitable distribution issues of their divorce. The issue at the moment is that when the couple bought their house 15 years ago, Anne used $40,000 from her inheritance as the down payment. The house has appreciated a good deal, and the couple has paid off most of the original mortgage, so there is about $200,000 in equity. Bob believes that they should split the equity in the house 50-50 between them. But Anne believes that she should receive the $40,000 back plus interest before they divide the rest. "That was my inheritance," says Anne, *"and I will never get one again. When your mother dies, you will receive an inheritance that you will keep for yourself. Why should you walk off with half of my inheritance? I'm not going to give in to your bullying, and I am not going to let you get away with being selfish once again. If I have to fight for this, I intend to do it. My lawyer says that the judge will give this back to me before dividing what's left, and I intend to have it whether you like it or not."*

Bob does not see it that way at all. "For 15 years I supported this house. I made the mortgage payments. I renovated the kitchen, landscaped the yard, and built the deck. When the house needed painting, I did it. When repairs were needed, I used my free time to make them. I poured my sweat into this house. And while I was busting my butt working on the house you were out playing tennis or shopping or wasting your time with your buddies. Even considering your contribution to the down payment, I contributed much more than you did. I don't see how it's fair for you to get more than half after all these years. I know you don't give a damn about fairness but you are not going to get your way on this one. I spoke to my lawyer about this, and he told me that because you commingled your inheritance with the house, it is no longer exempt property and any judge will give me half. I am not accepting less than half."

Bob and Anne are off to a bad start here. They have different perspectives about how the contributions of each during the marriage should be reflected in the distribution of the equity of the house. But instead of asserting their interest in a respectful manner, each is wrapping the statement of the problem in a gratuitous personal attack and thus creating unnecessary resistance. If we return to the model of a business transaction, we can see how out of place this type of personal attack is when negotiating a business matter.

Divorce Negotiation as Paradox

One paradox of divorce negotiation is that each party often demands of the other the very behavior that was missing throughout the marriage. "If she had just been able to talk respectfully, we would never have needed to divorce. If he had just learned to communicate his concerns, we could have stayed married." It's tempting to say, "Damn it, you have been acting like an adolescent for 20 years. Now you're going to have to grow up!"

Bob and Anne are caught up in a symbolic replay of one of the struggles that was at the heart of their marital discord. They were never quite able to work out how much each would contribute to the marriage, and each always felt that the other was holding back and not contributing enough. Anne was resentful that Bob never acknowledged the contribution her family had made to their material comfort, and Bob had always resented the amount of time that Anne spent pursuing her hobbies and interests. Now they are being asked to communicate about these charged matters in a respectful and solution-oriented way.

The second paradox of divorce negotiation is that it requires you to behave reasonably when you don't feel reasonable. You feel angry, distrustful, betrayed, indignant, and even bitter. And if your behavior and demeanor in negotiation reflect your feelings, the negotiation will fail. Such feelings shape recrimination, personal attack, sarcasm, ridicule, and stonewalling. All of these behaviors will repel your wife in short order and bring your negotiation to a halt. They will also convince your wife that you want to injure her and seek revenge and that you are a hopeless candidate for a cooperative parenting arrangement. So the only viable alternative is to refrain from acting out your feelings during the negotiation. If you absolutely have to spout off and bemoan your fate, find someone other than your wife. You may have a friend or two who will listen to your lament, but even the best-meaning friend will soon wear out. A therapist, who is paid to listen, is the best bet. Your demeanor in negotiation with your wife must be businesslike and respectful.

Agreement versus Contract

There is more than a semantic difference between an agreement and a contract. Your lawyer wants to negotiate a contract—a formal signed exchange of promises to perform that is enforceable in court. But if all you negotiate is a contract, you may not have done enough. At least half of all couples that negotiate and sign contracts are back in court within 2 years, fighting over children and support payments. When one of you goes back to court, not only is it very expensive for the both of you, but it contributes to the steady deterioration of the relationship. It is really a testament to the failure of your negotiating effort.

In law school, we were taught that a contract requires a "meeting of the minds." That is, both parties have to have a mutual understanding of the terms of exchange. But a meeting of the minds does not necessarily mean that either party regards the contract as just or even workable. Contracts are often crafted out of grudging last-minute concessions made to avoid a fight or a trial. Contracts do not necessarily mean that either party is committed to the deal or that either party will honor it in spirit as well as legal detail. To be truly in agreement means that both of you will abide by the terms voluntarily because you regard the agreement as fair.

The truth of the matter is that going to court to enforce your contract does you little good. I have seen innumerable people get worn out trying to enforce a separation agreement when a recalcitrant ex-spouse continually resists. Unfortunately, a spouse who is hell-bent on sabotaging the agreement can get away with it because courts are reluctant to really punish those who default. Contracts cannot perform. Only people can perform. When you and your wife are divorced, you need to be able to rely on good-faith performance from her and not rely on the courts. Whatever your idea of a good divorce, a divorce in which people repeatedly go back to court is a bad divorce by any definition.

An agreement is not just a meeting of the minds; it is also a meeting of the hearts. You may still feel angry at each other when it is over, and each of you may be relieved to be divorced. But if you have a genuine agreement, you can get on with your life in a way that you can't if the two of you are still tearing at each other. It is for this reason that I urge you to know your rights but approach them with caution. Understand your rights in the context of a new relationship that serves your interests, and you will be able to work on genuine agreement.

Behavior, Not Feelings

Your task is to cooperate with a person who you may resent and toward whom you feel distrust and even dislike. How can you cooperate with such a person? The answer is that you must focus on your behavior rather than your feelings. There is little to gain by using the negotiation to vindicate your feelings. "You were the cause of this divorce, so you have to suffer the consequences, not me!" is a proposition driven by your feelings that will do nothing but alienate your negotiating partner. Accept this: There is no vindication available for the feelings that you have. There is only one measure of the usefulness of each statement that you make in negotiation: How well does it serve to recruit the cooperation of the other party? If it makes the other less likely to cooperate, it is self-defeating. If it evokes cooperation and trust, it is productive. A statement does not have to be conciliatory to be effective, and I am not suggesting that you surrender or cave in whenever there is a disagreement. However, it is important to express that disagreement in a productive manner.

By this time, you may be objecting that all this is well and good, but what do I do if my wife engages in these self-defeating behaviors? What if she is blaming me for everything and expressing her anger in ways that get me angry? The most effective way to shape the behavior of your wife is to provide the example. Do not retaliate or engage in the same behavior. Here is where you let the mediator help—any decent mediator will intervene and correct your wife's behavior. It doesn't usually take too long to extinguish nasty, demeaning, or blaming behavior if the attacked spouse follows the mediator's cue and doesn't retaliate or defend.

Self-Defeating Behaviors to Avoid

There are five types of behaviors that are almost always self-defeating in divorce negotiations because they antagonize without accomplishing anything. They often arise from the mistaken and macho misconception that you can intimidate a negotiating partner into submission. And even if they are occasionally successful in securing submission, submission is not agreement.

1. **SHAMING AND BLAMING.** "You are just no damn good! You lied about the affair. You are so greedy that I don't know how you can even show your face around here." Your critique of her character here is totally counterproductive and will induce nothing but hostility.

2. ACTING HELPLESS AND PASSIVE. "I didn't want this divorce. If you want it so much, you leave." Here you effectively deny any responsibility for the divorce, adopt a passive position, and demand that she absorb all the change and dislocation.

3. THREATENING AND INTIMIDATING. "Take it or leave it. But if you don't take it, I will fight you until you have nothing left." The research data suggest that threats almost always harden the negotiating partner's resistance and completely undermine your credibility.

4. MAKING PERSONAL ATTACKS. "You never did your share because you were too lazy and selfish to bother." Attacks on the character and personality of your wife underscore your unreliability as a negotiating partner, evoke defensiveness and counterattack, and frighten her into litigation.

5. CUTTING OFF COMMUNICATION. "I'm sick of your whining and bitching. From now on, let the lawyers do the talking." This effectively kills any chance of a cooperative divorce and speaks more to your lack of negotiating skill than to her behavior.

All of these statements are understandable in that they reflect feelings of hurt, anger, and frustration. Although it is difficult for you to sit on those feelings when you believe you are being provoked, your ability to succeed in your divorce depends on your ability to do so.

Behaviors That Help Negotiation Succeed

Invite Her to Negotiate through Mediation

Your wife may well take the lead and invite you to negotiate a settlement. If she does so, you should be gracious and accept. Express your appreciation that she has invited you and that she wants to shape an amicable settlement; take the opportunity to tell her that you share her desire for a fair and amicable resolution and that you wish her well. If she has not invited you, then you need to invite her. The reason I use the term "invite" here is that when we invite someone, we assume some responsibility for that person's comfort. We take the initiative to create the contact and implicitly express at least the spirit of solidarity. That is the spirit that we are trying to begin here. An invitation acknowledges the person's right to decline but expresses a hope that she will accept. It is an optimistic beginning.

If your wife is skeptical, don't try to talk her out of her skepticism. Rather, acknowledge it and the fears that go with it. Use the invitation as an opportunity to reassure and to express your own ambition to arrive at a mutually acceptable and workable resolution. When dealing with a skeptical partner, it is often better to suggest that you take the sessions one at a time. You are inviting her to sit down with you and a mediator to explore the issues. It is less threatening for the skeptic if you reassure her that the commitment is for only 1 hour at a time and that the two of you will mutually decide at the end of the first session if you want to schedule a second.

It is helpful if you have researched available mediators in advance of the invitation to mediate. If the two of you have discussed mediation before, you may both already have a mediator in mind. If not, you should inquire among the professionals you know to get a few names of mediators to check out. If the two of you are in couples counseling or have recently been in counseling, the counselor might be a good source of referrals because she has credibility with both of you. If your wife is not familiar with mediation, you should provide her with a book or article and can also refer her to some Web sites that discuss mediation. I have created a Web site—www.sammargulies.com—that will provide her with an overview of the process of mediation and answer her questions. Invite her to participate in the selection of a mediator and acknowledge that you may have to have initial sessions with more than one before you find a mediator with whom you are both comfortable. Throughout this discussion, take the opportunity to describe mediation as the vehicle not only to avoid litigation but also to achieve a cooperative postdivorce relationship.

Listen More Than You Talk

There is nothing like marital deadlock to induce despair. Each of you desperately wants to be heard and understood, and each of you thinks that everything the other has to say is something that you have heard before. So you interrupt each other, try to talk over each other, and before long the attempt to talk shuts down. It is for this reason that so many people think that they will never be able to negotiate with their spouses. It is also this pattern that requires a mediator to make it possible for the two of you to talk and understand each other. The mediator will serve as communications traffic cop and direct traffic to avoid a collision. Follow the mediator's lead.

But even with the help of the mediator, you will not be heard if you do not follow some simple procedures. First, you will be heard and understood only in proportion to the extent that you listen and understand. The key to being heard is listening. And I don't mean the kind of listening in which you are just biding your time, waiting for your chance to talk, or thinking of what you want to say next. You must be an active listener.

Active listening is twofold. The first element is paying attention to the content of the message. "I don't think it's good for the children to stay overnight with you on school nights." This part is straightforward and involves nothing more than registering the facts of what is being said. The second aspect of active listening is hearing the emotional message and noting the affect with which the message is delivered. "When the children are away, I worry about them and I miss them terribly." If this is delivered with a worried expression it is important that you try to understand what feelings accompany the statement. Active listening means taking steps to assure the other person that you have heard both the message and the emotional content. The easiest way to do this is a simple summary of what you have heard, highlighting what you think matters most to her. "So as I understand it, you are worried that if the children stay overnight with me they will not get their homework done and you will miss them. Do I understand correctly?" If you have missed something, she will correct your understanding. But when she is done, she will know that you have both heard and understand.

Now two things will happen. First, because she knows that you have heard and understood, she doesn't feel the need to repeat herself. And second, she is very likely to imitate the behavior that you have modeled. With the help of the mediator and some active listening skills, you will be able to have a dialogue that you have not been able to have until now.

Affirm Conciliatory Gestures

In the course of your negotiations, there will be many issues on which you disagree, some big and some small. Your mediator should set the agenda and will move you away from issues on which you get stuck, seeking agreement on other issues and returning to the hard ones later. In the course of the process, it is likely that you and your wife will each make concessions to each other. She may change her viewpoint about a parenting issue and agree to the children spending more time with you than she initially wanted. You may agree to move to an apartment or to stay close to the children rather than moving closer to your work. She will make concessions on property issues and support issues, as will you.

When your wife agrees to something that you seek, it is important that you affirm her for doing so. Even though you are getting divorced, you are still connected emotionally to each other in many ways and you each continue to desire the approval of the other. It is very discouraging when someone makes a concession in negotiation but gets no acknowledgment for it. Failure to acknowledge conveys the feeling that you believe you were entitled to the concession or that you take for granted that she would modify her position to reach agreement with you. If you reinforce her concession or conciliatory gesture, it makes her more likely to do it again. If you act as if her gesture is a victory for you or a defeat for her, it will reduce the chance of further concessions from her and raise her fear that you are taking advantage of her. This does not mean that every concession has to evoke a counter-concession from you. But it costs you nothing to say, "I really appreciate that you have agreed to that because it means so much to me. I am very encouraged by the progress we are making and I hope you feel that way too." Conciliation begets conciliation.

Pay Attention to Your Tone

As relationships deteriorate, people tend to disagree in an increasingly unpleasant manner. You become more and more frustrated with each other, and the frustration is reflected in the tone of voice that you use when talking to each other. Tone, independent of the words used, can convey not just frustration but also anger, complaining, contempt, and ridicule. So two things may be happening. First, you may each become allergic to the tone of the other. "When she starts that whining, I just lose it." Or, "When he starts using that angry condescending tone of his, it just totally turns me off." So tone can independently derail what would have otherwise been a completely reasonable message. If this applies to you, you will know it because you will have had many discussions in which she complained that the tone of voice that you used was offensive. By tone alone you can make her feel intimidated, demeaned, and put down. None of those feelings will help her cooperate with you or be able to hear your legitimate needs.

If this has been a problem, there are several ways to monitor your own tone of voice. First, you lose nothing by acknowledging that your tone may, on occasion, be offensive. "Sometimes I get carried away because I'm frustrated, and I know it's wrong. Please tell me when it happens, so I can fix it." You can also request that the mediator cue you if she thinks that your tone is getting in your way. If you do these things, you will be quickly aware and can modify the way you are speaking before you unnecessarily create difficulty for yourself.

Don't Take the Bait

Throughout this book I have focused on your behavior rather than your wife's behavior. You may begin to believe that I am unaware that your wife can be obnoxious, stubborn, or vindictive. Divorce engenders fear, and people who are afraid often act in ways that are unpleasant and offensive. So what happens if you are following my advice, watching your tone, listening carefully, and trying to understand her needs and, while you are doing this, she is being a total pain in the ass? What happens if she keeps attacking you, makes sarcastic remarks, and does all the things that I am admonishing you to avoid? Are you supposed to just take it without striking back? The answer is *yes*.

You are not a trout, and you do not have to rise to every piece of bait that appears on the surface. You do not have to defend yourself from her attacks, nor can you be harmed by them—they are only words. Part of what is going on may be related to routines of attack and counterattack that many couples evolve and then follow as if they were following a script. She attacks you for being insensitive; you attack her for being picky. You may have developed a complex choreography of mutual accusations and put-downs, as if you were rehearsing for a performance on stage. So her attack cues your counterattack. Her indictment evokes your defense of *not guilty*.

But why bother responding to her unproductive provocation? The mediator is not a judge, and you do not have to convince the mediator that you are being maligned. Your angry defense to her attack just makes the mediator's job harder. Most mediators do what they do because they get professional satisfaction from helping people reach agreement. Mediators do not like personal attacks and are generally more concerned with the tone and behavior than they are with the content of the message. Don't worry that your wife will turn the mediator against you. Your calm demeanor and your refusal to be drawn into unproductive verbal sparring will actually win the mediator's sympathy for you. I repeat my central dictum: Don't attack. And when attacked, don't defend. In time she will get the message.

Acknowledge Convergent Interests

One of the problems with an adversarial relationship is that it tends to focus us on areas of disagreement rather than on areas of agreement. Divorcing couples have many interests in common, and it is helpful if you spend some time in negotiation identifying convergent interests. Certainly the obvious area of convergent interests is the welfare of your children. You may have some disagreements about how the well-being of the children can be best achieved, but the common objective is worth reiterating. You also have parallel interests. You each have an interest in building new lives, and it is in each of your interests that the children obtain the permission of each of you to like the new partners you may choose in the future. It is in the interest of each of you that the other thrive because your children will thrive only if both of you do. The review of convergent interests is a good exercise when you are stuck on some issue, because it maintains perspective and reduces the gloom that arises when you momentarily despair of ever reaching a comprehensive agreement.

The second aspect here is a focus on minimizing differences instead of exaggerating them. She is demanding $1,000 a week in child support while you believe that $800 is more than enough. It is true that you are $200 apart in your views. But it is also true that you are 80 percent in agreement and that your positions are much closer than they are disparate. "Look, we are only $200 apart. What can we do to compromise so that we both end up with something closer to what we believe is right? If I were able to stretch to $900, do you think that you could live with that?" I have often had couples come to see me after they have been engaged in litigation for years. When I explore with each of them what they need to resolve the matter, I discover that they are within 5 percent of each other's positions but are unaware that they are so close. Because the communication between lawyers and their clients is so inefficient, couples may live in limbo for months or even years when they are, in fact, within easy reach of a settlement.

The adversarial culture is a pessimistic culture in which it is easy to become riveted on differences and miss the degree of real underlying agreement. So try to state your position in terms of convergence rather than divergence. "I have heard your viewpoint, and I think that we are very close and believe that we could reach agreement with relatively minor modifications" is much better than, "I don't care what you say; I am not going to budge a dollar over $800 a week."

Think Future, Not Past

I touched on this in the previous chapter, but it is important enough to reiterate here because it is one of the most common roadblocks to successful negotiation between divorcing couples. When I teach mediation techniques to professionals, one of the strategic interventions I urge on them is to keep the couple focused on the future and not the past. I routinely tell couples that in over 3,000 cases, I have never succeeded in helping a couple reconcile their conflicting versions of history. Perhaps, if I had unlimited time, unlimited polygraphs, and the ability to assemble witnesses, I might be able to get a couple to come to a common agreement on their history together. But even if I had these unlimited resources, what would be the point? People have different histories because they have had such different experiences. You have lived the last 20 years with your wife and she has lived with you. You have had radically different experiences and have come away from those experiences with very different beliefs about what happened and what it meant. It is not only a waste of time to wrangle over what happened or who was wrong, it is destructive because it just generates more pessimism.

Most arguments about history have two themes. First is the struggle over who was right and who was wrong. About this you seldom agree. But then there is the inevitable attempt to link the other's wrong behavior to the proposed distribution of resources. "You were so neglectful of the marriage that you don't deserve half the assets. While you sat around and did nothing, I was working to earn us a good living. Because you did so much less, you should get less." "It's outrageous that you even think such a thing. I did everything for this family. All you did was go to work and then come home and expect to be served like a king. Don't tell me that I deserve less than you do." History almost always is a reprise of blame, vindication, and just desserts. It is a waste of time and energy in divorce negotiations, and although I would hope your mediator would intervene and refocus you on the future, it is better that you avoid the endeavor yourself.

Your past may be troubled and irreconcilable, but your future is quite different. The different ways the two of you experienced the same events contaminates the past, but not the future. It is much easier to decide what will happen in the future than it is to decide what happened in the past. Historical references by each of you only trigger defensiveness and resistance. So don't make statements about your history, particularly the statement that serves as a premise about why you should get more. As soon as she hears it coming, her resistance rises, and instead of working on solving problems, she is preparing to defend against an attack. And following the admonition against taking the bait, the easiest way to defuse her comments about history is to say, "I can understand that you may feel strongly about that, but I don't believe it will help us reach agreement if I respond. So I am going to respect your thoughts about that, but I am not going to talk to you about what you think." This is a respectful response that acknowledges her but declines to engage in a discussion that can't lead anywhere useful.

Plan and Prepare

Good negotiation requires planning and preparation. Although you cannot predict everything that your wife will do or say, you can be prepared to provide needed information, and you can think through many of the likely scenarios.

The first task is to prepare the necessary information. Each issue requires its own preparation. If the two of you need to negotiate about parenting schedules, you can come prepared with your own proposed schedule showing where the children would be each night over a 2-week period. Even though she may not be in agreement, the schedule facilitates a focus on the areas of agreement and disagreement and facilitates discussion. And remember; always bring three copies: one for you, one for your wife, and one for the mediator. When you get to financial issues, preparation is vital. You are going to need the following, so you might as well assemble the package now.

▶ Three years' tax returns

▶ All current statements for bank accounts, brokerage accounts, and retirement accounts

▶ Any appraisal of real estate

▶ A completed statement of assets and liabilities

▶ A copy of the plan document if you have a defined benefits pension plan

▶ A current statement showing all debt, including mortgage, home equity loan, credit card accounts, or other debt

▶ A completed budget

If you assemble your package early, you and your wife will not have to interrupt a discussion because you are speculating about the value of some asset. The mediator will be grateful because it allows him to move you along without unnecessary delays. Obtaining information is a collaborative venture. Do not hesitate to ask your wife for help if she has easier access to some documents or accounts. It does not matter who gets the information, only that you have it when you need it.

The second aspect of planning is a strategic analysis of the issues. Think through how you can solve both your problems and those of your wife. An issue is resolved only when both of you regard the solution as workable and fair, so trying to see it from her perspective is as important as seeing it from your own. Try to think through budgetary issues from both points of view. What are your most vital needs and requirements? What are hers? If you anticipate that the two of you will disagree about how long she can stay in the house, prepare a flow analysis for each possible housing scenario. Then at the meeting you can show her the analysis and ask her to help figure out how to solve the problem. Written budgets and proposals move things along more efficiently than verbal descriptions.

Use Neutral Language

You and your wife are trying to discuss difficult issues in the context of a difficult past. It is very easy for each of you to use language that offends the other. All of the feelings we have discussed in this book may be with each of you at any moment, and it is almost natural to slip into the mutually antagonistic dialogue of the past. It's also very counterproductive. Insults, put-downs, sarcasm, negativism, condemnation, guilt, and blame are understandable but set you back. For this reason, it is important to monitor your choice of words all the time. The more difficult and tense the topic, the more important this becomes.

Using neutral language is a critical negotiating technique. Neutral language conveys information but limits the effect attached to the message. "It will be a cold day in hell before I ever accept a harebrained proposal like that!" is a self-defeating way to say no. Even if you are offended, respond without the offense. "I don't think that would work for me because it doesn't leave me enough money to pay rent." "I don't think that is something to which I can agree." "That doesn't sound like something that will work for me, but let me reflect on it for a while." You can also use neutral language to disarm an attack. "I understand you are upset and frightened, but when you call me names it makes it hard for me to agree with you."

Neutral language avoids characterizing the other person or her behavior in harsh terms. It can acknowledge that something is difficult or unpleasant but chooses the least colorful and least dramatic words available. It emphasizes "I" statements but minimizes "you" statements. Think back to our discussion about personal attack and defense. Whenever you begin a statement with the equivalent of "You did something bad," or, "You are bad," or anything loosely similar to that, you trigger her impulse to defend and counterattack. So even when provoked and indignant, use neutral language because it lowers the heat and helps to keep it down.

Four Strategic Elements of Negotiation

In a now-classic book on negotiation, *Getting to Yes*, Roger Fischer and William Ury of the Harvard Negotiation Project have provided an invaluable four-step process for successful negotiation. This little book can be read in an evening or two, and you should read it before you start your mediation. While you are at it, pick up a copy for your wife and give it to her.

1. Attack Problems, Not People

The central concept to principled negotiation is the reframing of struggles from battles to be won to problems to be solved. A good divorce agreement does not allow for dominance and submission. It won't work if it is nothing but a collection of grudging concessions. So winning the argument will invariably mean that you lose something later. The measure of resolution must be mutuality. It is for this reason that the adversarial process, geared to victory and defeat, is so ineffective. So it is important to continually restate the issue until you have a problem that you can solve.

Here is an example of a couple where one was engaging in personal attack, while the other maintained the determination to attack the problem, not the partner.

Will: "You want the divorce, so you ought to leave. I don't see why I have to uproot myself and go. This is all your fault, and you are the one who is betraying me. You want to live without me, you move."

Maya: "It's no longer an issue of who did what. With your travel schedule, you have to admit that I need to live with the kids most of the time, and it makes no sense to have me and the kids move to an apartment while you stay in the house. You are only here half the time."

Will: "But it's not fair. You are the guilty party. Why does my life have to be ruined? You screwed up. You suffer."

Maya: "But Will, the problem now is how to organize housing for the entire family: you, me, and the kids. Why don't we focus on that instead of rehashing the divorce? How do you think we can best solve the problem of housing?"

Will: "How is it that it just works out that you get your way? You are so selfish. Where do you get off telling me to move?"

Maya: "Well, maybe your moving isn't the best idea. Why don't we look at all the alternatives, and maybe we can find one that will work for all of us."

Note how Maya keeps restating the issue as a problem to be solved. They have to separate and somebody has to move. So even in the face of continued provocation by Will, Maya keeps bringing the subject back to the problem and reiterates how there must be an answer. She refuses to take the bait and continually seeks resolution. In time, Will can drop the personal attack because it is not getting a response and can join the search for a solution to the problem. Although Will wants to obtain an amicable resolution of the divorce, he backslides now and then and engages in self-defeating behavior. But in this case, Maya helps to keep the negotiation moving forward. You can do this too by quietly translating each angry proposition into a problem to be solved. How can we best house the children? How can we best ensure that they get what they need? How can we distribute our assets so we can both get a fresh start? How can we solve my problem for capital and your desire to stay in the house?

2. Define the Problem by Defining Interests

Earlier in the book we discussed the good divorce and suggested a number of characteristics of a good postdivorce relationship. They included a mutual sense of economic justice, the ability of the children to have robust relationships with both parents and their new mates, and the ability to resolve disputes without rancor. The reason I emphasize these objectives is that they provide you with a sense of your own interests as they relate to the parenting and economic issues. A common problem for divorcing couples is housing. The wife wants to retain the house with the kids and may believe that you should take an inexpensive apartment so that she can afford to stay in the house. Although it appears to solve the cash flow problem, it conflicts with a number of your important interests.

▶ You need a dwelling that is reasonably comfortable for you and the children when they are with you.

▶ You need a home that you find welcoming at the end of the day.

▶ You need to find a dwelling that is in close proximity to the children.

▶ You need a monthly housing cost that leaves enough money for other things as well.

You should also consider your wife's interests.

▶ She needs to minimize transition in the short run.

▶ She wants to allay the emotional tear of "losing" her home.

▶ She needs comfortable housing for herself and the children.

▶ She needs a mortgage that she can afford.

Your wife will undoubtedly have her own additions to make to your list of needs. But you take a large step forward when you offer the following: "I have tried to write down my housing needs here, and I have also tried to write down some of yours. Why don't you add any that I have missed and then let's try to find a solution that addresses them all?" You and your wife will have to embrace many changes in the course of adapting to the divorce. It is in both your interests to embrace those changes so you can control them and maximize your choices rather than to adopt a posture of trying to maintain the status quo. As you define your interests, some of the things that you find onerous about the divorce may seem less so. For example, you may anticipate having to spend every other weekend without your kids as a terrible thing. If it's terrible, it's to be resisted, so you might try to fight for more weekends with the children. But if you understand your long-term interests, your view of weekends may change. You need time off from your children if you are to build a new social life. Talking your wife into letting the kids spend every weekend with you could leave you without the time to date new women and without the solitude everyone needs when building a new life. Defining your interests requires that you take the long view rather than just trying to minimize what you see as the damage of divorce.

3. Develop All the Options

After you have engaged your wife in a process of defining problems to be solved and framing those problems as the management of your and her interests, you will be on your way to productive negotiation. Now it's time to identify the options. Let's return to the problem of housing. How do you satisfy the needs both of you have identified as bearing on the problem?

There is usually more than one possible way to solve the problem. Consider the following:

▶ Sell this house, divide the money, and buy two smaller houses in the same or a nearby neighborhood.

▶ Have her buy out your interest in the house using other assets, the proceeds of refinancing, or a combination of those. You can hold a partial mortgage for some agreed period of time.

▶ Maintain the status quo. She stays in the house until the kids grow up, and then the two of you sell the house and split the proceeds.

▶ Maintain the status quo for a year (or 2 or 3 years) and then sell the house and split the money.

▶ Continue in joint ownership, but refinance to liberate at least part of your equity so you can buy a small house nearby.

Depending on other factors, such as income and the local real estate market, there may be several other options. Not every option is the same; some will better achieve your joint interests than others. But your wife may find the process threatening and worry that if she explores other options that she is conceding something that she fears. Now what do you do?

Again, your own preparation can move you forward. Having prepared a list of options, you can also do much of the research to help you explore how each option relates to the interests that the two of you have defined. So if refinancing the house is one option, you can explore the cost of doing so and calculate the monthly cost of the new mortgage. If it turns out that number is within the budget, it helps her consider it. If you want to explore whether it is feasible to sell this house and buy two smaller ones, you can research the market with a realtor, calculate the costs and cash flow, and help determine whether it is a viable possibility. There are no general formulas here because it depends on so many personal financial factors. But if you do the homework, you enrich the discussion and help keep it on track to resolution.

At this point you may be asking, "Why should I have to do all the work?" Ideally, your wife will be assuming a fair share of the tasks. But she may not be able or willing to do so. Finances, for example, may be mystifying to her, and she might be completely unable to research an issue that comes easily to you. This is not the time to worry about a fair division of labor. Define what needs to be done and if she can't or won't do it, then you do it. The more work you do here, the easier and more productive the ultimate settlement will be.

4. Work Until You Develop a Mutually Acceptable Solution

Negotiation can be tiring. And your divorce negotiation occurs at a time when the decision to divorce and all the stress associated with it have already left you spent. So it is easy for you to feel worn down as negotiations seem to drag on and it becomes tempting either to use ultimatums to obtain agreement or to just give in. Neither is a good idea.

It is okay to just give in on something small for which you will not have lasting regrets, but that does not apply to major issues. The premise of mediation is that you struggle with alternatives until both of you think the result is fair.

Let's return to the example of the marital home, which she wants to keep and you want to sell. Keep generating alternative scenarios. A useful variable to consider in such cases is time. What is not acceptable today may be acceptable 2 years from now. There are many benchmarks in the history of the family that can ease a move. A child graduates from high school or middle school, which means that a change of schools will take place anyhow. Your wife finishes her masters degree and is ready to start a career that will change her cash flow and allow her to refinance. Engage your wife in a discussion in which she helps find an alternative that meets at least the minimal needs of both of you. And be very slow to declare an impasse. The fact that there is disagreement today does not mean that there will be disagreement tomorrow. If you are stuck on an issue, table it. "Let's think about this some more and come back to it next time. Maybe one of us will think of another possibility by then. Let's move on to the next topic." Your mediator should also be helpful here by steering the discussion to more productive subjects so you can accumulate some success before returning to the hard issues.

Impasse

There may come a time when you are so frustrated that you just want to walk out and hand the matter over to lawyers. You should never be the one to threaten such a move. My advice is never to quit. Never be the one to walk out, and don't be the one to declare an impasse. It is tempting in a moment of frustration to threaten to end the mediation unless your wife agrees to something you want. I regard that as a mistake. In the unlikely event that you are so stuck that there is no point of continuing, let the mediator make that decision. If a couple has been stuck for a long time and has been unable to find common ground, I will tell them that I see little point in continuing. There are some couples who cannot reach agreement in mediation, but even those couples will end up negotiating a settlement through lawyers. Remember, the case has a 99 percent probability of settlement, so the failure of mediation does not mean the end of a negotiation process. Don't poison the water as you exit. Let the mediator call the halt so that your wife does not perceive that you have quit. I have seen many couples return to mediation and successfully complete an agreement after a mediator declared an impasse and suggested some time out.

Time can be very helpful in breaking an impasse. It is not unusual that one member of the couple is not ready to accept some proposed change such as moving to another home, taking a child out of private school, or some other budget-cutting measure. If you force the issue now, you may end up in a fight, when you could have had an amicable resolution had you only waited a few weeks. Paradoxically, the most effective way to slow things down is to turn the matter over to lawyers for litigation. I have seldom seen a process accelerated by lawyers. Be patient and let time work for you. Your wife is as eager for resolution and closure as you are but may just not be ready today to resolve the difficult issues. Impasse does not mean that you have failed, but only that you have not finished.

"*Actually, I was assigned to Heaven, but it would have meant spending eternity with my first wife.*"

Nine

SHOULD I MOVE OUT?

ONE OF THE SIMPLEST BUT MOST DIFFICULT REALITIES of divorce is that someone has to move. Two people who are divorcing cannot stay very long in the same house without increasing bitterness and rancor. Because both you and your wife are so stressed, each of you needs a peaceful place to live, but neither of you gets peace as long as you live together. It's almost impossible to maintain the same routines that you had before the decision to divorce. Family meals, if even possible, become tense affairs with stilted dialogue or uncomfortable silences. It is difficult to negotiate new protocols for managing the chores. Does she do his laundry or cook his dinner? Does he continue to deposit his paycheck into the joint accounts? Do they continue to see other couples socially? What do they tell family and friends? How do they divide the responsibility for managing the children? It is difficult to work these things out living in the same house because there is so much confusion on both sides. Married couples are used to turning to each other as friends, but the friendship is now in tatters. There is little definition of what you and your wife can expect from each other, so misunderstandings accumulate and anger often intensifies.

As each of you begins trying to figure out the future, each may consult with friends and relatives and, as discussed earlier, receive some very bad advice. Mutual suspicion grows as each partner is fed alarming fears by amateur advisers. Most couples inevitably find themselves trying to get reassurance from each other, only to be disappointed when the other reveals that he or she sees the future very differently. Some couples can resolve many issues, but others cannot agree on much of anything without professional assistance.

Tension can accelerate until each one feels that he or she cannot take it anymore and just wishes that the other would leave. But who leaves frequently becomes the first battle of the divorce.

Who Leaves?

In about 80 percent of divorces, it is the husband who moves out and establishes a new residence. The reason is that in about 80 percent of divorces, it is the mother who will be the primary residential parent. Even though more fathers are getting custody than they were 20 years ago, most divorces still end with a fairly traditional division of labor in which the mother continues to do most of the parenting tasks and the children live with her the majority of the time. In most cases, it is this way because both parents want it to be. In some cases the father gives in because he doesn't see any alternative way and can't convince his wife to try something new. An increasing number of fathers struggle to get equal time with the children, and some of them succeed. But even when this happens, chances are good that the mother will continue to stay in the marital home, at least for a while, and the father will move out.

So even though in the end, 80 percent of husbands move, many endure a lengthy struggle before they do. There are several reasons this happens. One reason men are reluctant to move is that they fear that such a move will be used to their legal disadvantage later. Many laypeople believe that if they move, their spouse will be able to accuse them of abandonment and use this accusation to punish them in court. This is untrue, for the simple fact that almost no cases ever go to trial and in the few that do, judges are aware that once a marriage is over, someone has to move. So the fear of being accused of abandonment and desertion can be easily allayed. Your wife is probably desperate for you to move. Ask her to write a letter to you in which she acknowledges that she is asking you to move in the interests of the mental health of the family. With such a letter in hand, you are completely protected against subsequent accusations of abandonment.

A second fear often reinforced by your army of amateur advisors is that by moving you forfeit your property rights in the house. This is also completely untrue. If you and your wife own the house together, you will continue to maintain your ownership interest after you leave and the settlement will eventually have to detail how you get your money out of the house. Some men worry that once they move out, they will not be allowed back in if they change their minds. This may be true because courts will be reluctant to risk the conflict that may develop if you try to reoccupy the house after a lengthy period of separate residence. You may be able to reduce this risk by asking your wife to include in her letter a statement that you are entitled to reoccupy the house at any time if you so choose. Of course, why you would want to do such a thing is another matter.

A third obstacle to moving is the bad advice many lawyers give to their male clients about moving. Most lawyers tell their clients not to move because they fear that such a move will weaken their negotiating position. Many men are hoping that their wives will agree to sell the house and move to smaller quarters. They also fear that their wives will withhold the children or insist on more support than they can afford. Because the husband's continued presence in the house is an irritant to the wife, his lawyer believes that the very discomfort caused to the wife by her husband's staying will provide incentive for her to make other concessions just to get him out. Many lawyers also worry that by moving out and leaving the wife in place with the children, the male client will inadvertently establish a status quo that will later be continued by a court even if the man cannot afford it.

I cannot say that such a ploy will not work, as it may indeed induce concessions from the wife on occasion. But more often it does not work and results in rising tensions and ever-increasing bitterness. As mentioned in chapter 6, one of the greatest limitations of lawyers is their woeful ignorance of the psychological consequences of the advice they give their clients. Lawyers do not have to live with the emotional consequences of their advice. Nor are they conscious of how long it takes to get to resolution once the couple hunkers down into angry deadlock.

Finally, many men refuse to leave because they do not know how they will be able to afford decent housing for themselves while continuing to pay the bills for the existing household. Many middle-class couples live right at or just beyond the financial edge. They have little in the way of reserves and live paycheck to paycheck. So the cost of another residence looms as an insurmountable financial obstacle and they fear that moving will plunge them further into debt.

Why You Should Leave Sooner Rather Than Later

Notwithstanding all the reasons you may come up with for not leaving, I still believe that it is in your interest and the interest of your children for you to go sooner rather than later. And even assuming that your departure may give your wife some hypothetical tactical advantage, you should go now if in fact you are going to be the one to leave eventually.

To explain fully, I have to take you back to the distinctions made in chapter 2 between a good and a bad divorce. The essential features of a good divorce involve the retention of enough goodwill to facilitate cooperative parenting and a mutual sense of fairness. The objective of a good divorce is the efficient rebuilding of new lives that the stuff left over from the first marriage is not forever sabotaging. None of these things are served by a long period of holy deadlock while two divorcing people continue to live in the same house. The refusal to leave when it is apparent or logical that you will leave eventually helps to destroy whatever residual trust there might be between you. It suggests that you are willing to engage in a war of attrition to get your way. It also delays the period of healing and adjustment that you all need, a period that does not begin until you actually separate. Until you separate, you cannot begin to establish new lives. You do not feel comfortable having friends visit. In fact, it is nearly impossible to feel comfortable at all in a home you are occupying under duress. This means that at one of the most stressful times in your family's life, there is little safety in being home, something that just aggravates the stress you are already feeling. And if you get into a struggle in court, the period of limbo can last for several years. These are years that you and your wife and kids could have been finding peace and rebuilding social and emotional lives.

Living together in a state of deadlock with your wife is also very bad for your children. In fact, living with divorcing parents is one of the leading causes of depression in children. They feel the tension even if there are no outward displays of anger. And when there is overt hostility between the parents, children find it frightening. The situation prolongs the grieving and mourning that inevitably accompany divorce. It proves to the kids that their parents are unable to cooperate in their children's interests and may leave them feeling that there is no one in charge. It also establishes that their parents will be unable to resolve disputes in the future. All this just adds to the insecurity caused by divorce.

Solving the Problems of Moving Out

Negotiating and executing a decent separation is one of the last important tasks of the marriage. Although it may strike you as ironic, you and your wife have a strong mutual interest in achieving a rapid and cooperative separation. For the most part, the things you worry about—kids and money— have to be resolved cooperatively. And if you don't poison the atmosphere with a lot of rage and bickering, you should be able to recruit your wife's cooperation in achieving a move. In the 70 percent of divorces initiated by women, wives are eager for you to go. So when you ask her to help you move out easily, she will be motivated to help. If you are the initiator and she is resisting the divorce, she may dread your departure and be less willing to cooperate. In that case, you should simply wait a while if you can until she is able to accept the inevitability of the divorce and begin to think about what she needs in order to have a good divorce.

If we put aside the bad advice you get from amateur advisers and lawyers, the chief problems that remain are children and money. Most fathers are reluctant to move out until there is some agreement about their access to the children. Second—and we will discuss this at length in chapter 11—economic retrenchment is a necessary part of every middle-class divorce. The second household generally represents an increase of about 30 percent in overall spending. This means that either the family must cut spending, increase income, invade savings, or do some combination of these. But deficit spending can only take you so far and then you have to come to grips with balancing a budget.

You may not be able to resolve all these issues completely before moving out, but you can make a beginning by involving your wife in the problem-solving process. What you want to say is some version of the following:

"I think it would be a good idea for me to move and I know that you think so too. But I am worried about two things, and I need your help to solve the problems. As soon as we begin to get a grip on these, I will move. First, I am worried about how I will get enough time with the children if I move out, and I need some reassurance from you about that. Second, I do not know where the money will come from to pay for this, and I need your help to figure out how we will pay for both households."

Note two things about the statements above, because they illustrate the principles discussed in chapters 7 and 8. First, they are stated in neutral language. They state a problem to be solved. There is no accusation and there is no hostility. If you were to say something similar to, "If you want me to move, then you better quit spending so much money and go out and get a job and stop expecting me to do everything for you," then you will undoubtedly inspire an angry and defensive response. Remember that neutral language focuses on "I" statements rather than "you" statements. And it never includes blame or accusation. "I need to move out for all our sakes" is a neutral statement. And "I don't know how we can afford the second household" is a neutral statement. "Can you help me solve it?" is an invitation to cooperate that is difficult to resist.

The second important thing is that you do not begin with a position about how to solve the problem. For men, this is an important lesson because we tend to be problem-solving oriented and often fail to understand that women frequently process difficult problems differently than we do. They need to wrestle with the emotional implications for longer than we do, and they need men to be patient while they do it.

Invariably, your move is going to require that your wife accept some changes that she finds unpleasant and scary. Budget cutting in a society as materialistic as ours is painful for most people. If she has been in a home-making role for a long time, she may resist the need to get a job and provide income for herself. She may be worried that the children need her full attention more than ever and that this is no time to have their mother absent when they get home from school. She may be worried that selling the house and moving to smaller quarters will be bad for the children because they won't be able to assimilate all that change so quickly. The fact that some or all of these changes will be necessary does not distract her from her initial resistance to them. So when you begin by telling her what you believe to be obvious—that you must sell the house, that she must get a job, and that you both must cut spending—you create resistance and an un-necessary struggle. But by inviting her to join you in solving these problems, you pay her the courtesy of allowing her to come to emotional terms with these difficult changes before she actually concludes that indeed, the house must be sold or a new job found. When people are permitted the safe space necessary to solve their own problems, they get to the solution much more quickly and with far less stress. That is the key to securing her help rather than her resistance.

This is not to say that these problems will be resolved easily and without struggle. But the critical thing at this stage is for you to help maintain a tone of cooperation instead of confrontation. Both of you are frightened, and you are getting counsel from others that you should each attempt to shift as much change as possible to the other. It is very easy at this point to slip into blame and recrimination for the divorce as a way to justify why the other spouse is responsible for the trouble and therefore should bear the burden of the solution. This is why neutral language is so important and why an insistence on joint problem solving is so critical. It is possible that your wife may meet your initial attempts with skepticism. She may greet your statements with anger and resistance, and she may even be provoca-tive in return. But patience on your part and your refusal to be drawn into a tit-for-tat exchange of accusations will pay off if you can exercise the willpower not to retaliate. "I understand that you are angry and scared, but I also believe that we will never fully agree on history. Why don't we see if we can come to agreement on the future?" This is a far more productive way to create an atmosphere of negotiation than telling her that "This divorce is as much your fault as mine, and if you had been more affectionate, you might have received what you wanted from me!" Accusation inevitably causes defense and counterattack. Don't attack, and when attacked, don't defend. It is the best way to arrest the slow deterioration into a war of attrition.

The same approach that applies to the money applies to the children. "I am concerned that the children get to spend enough time with me to maintain our relationship and I want to do my fair share of parenting so we can both get on with our lives. What are your thoughts on how we manage this?" Again note that you are not beginning with a position such as "I insist that I get equal time with the kids, and I won't settle for anything less than 50-50!" Positions such as these are bound to induce resistance and need to be avoided. Neutral language and an invitation to solve problems are your posture and your tone. "I know we need to separate and want to move out as soon as we can solve this" is neutral. "I'm not going anywhere until you agree to my proposed schedule" is provocative. Although both say essentially the same thing, namely that your move is connected to agreement about the children, the latter evokes resistance while the former does not. This is not just semantics; it is your key to keeping the discussion constructive.

Financial Implications of Your Move

Whether they can afford to keep the house or whether they have to sell it is one of the most wrenching decisions for many divorcing couples. How this decision is made may often decide the tone of the entire divorce. Typically, it is the husband who wants the house sold and it is the wife who is arguing to keep it. As it is the husband who most frequently is moving out, he has already accepted that he can no longer live in the house. But the wife is reluctant to give it up. Once you accept that you have to move, the house becomes just a house. But if you are struggling with the transitions of divorce, giving up your *home* takes on an additional emotional coloring.

The woman who is to continue as primary parent worries not only about her own loss of home, but also about the children's ability to assimilate so much change. So she may resist and may use the welfare of the children to justify why she should stay in the house.

There are two financial aspects to the decision whether to retain or keep the marital home. The first is cash flow, and the second is a matter of capital. Cash flow is a matter of deciding if your income is sufficient to pay the mortgage and taxes on the house at the same time that you are paying rent or another mortgage on a second home. Conventional mortgage underwriting principles suggest that no more than 30 percent of gross household income should be used for rent or for mortgage, taxes, and insurance. If the two of you bought the house 2 years ago on the assumption that you would spend 30 percent of your combined incomes on housing, keeping the house is going to be a major stretch. I have seen couples who buy new houses and pay 40 or 45 percent of their combined incomes for mortgage and taxes. The only way this couple can keep the house if they get divorced is for the one who moves out to accept very cheap and generally inadequate housing. The long-term consequences of this are not good. If you want an indicator of whether you can afford to keep the house, estimate the household income of each household after alimony and child support are paid. Now, take 35 percent of each household income as the maximum payment for housing. The cost for housing should not exceed that number. For example:

Fred is an engineer earning $70,000 per year. Jill is a nurse earning $32,000 a year. They have agreed that they will have joint parenting, with the children spending equal time in both households, and they also have agreed that Fred will pay Jill alimony and child support necessary to equalize the income in both households. So each will have total household income of $51,000 per year or $4,250 per month before taxes. If we take 35 percent of that, we get $1,487 as the maximum amount each can spend on housing and still be able to afford all the other items in their budgets.

The couple bought their house 4 years ago for $200,000, putting $50,000 down and taking a mortgage of $150,000. They have annual taxes of $3,600 and a monthly mortgage payment of $1,200 for interest and principal with a 15-year mortgage term. Homeowners insurance is $75 a month *for a total housing cost of $1,575—slightly more than Jill's monthly maximum of $1,487. They may be able to keep the house.*

But there is a second issue as well. The husband wants to get his equity out of the house so he can make a down payment on a small house of his own or just to have some cash reserves available. How and when he gets access to his equity can become a controversial issue. Frequently, lawyers and some judges will argue that the husband's equity in the house should be left there until the last child graduates high school and the house is sold. Although this makes it easier on the wife financially, it can be unfair to the husband if it means that he gets no access to his equity for 10 or 15 years. Generally, continued co-ownership of the house for a long time after the divorce is not a good idea because it keeps the couple bound together when they should have separate economic lives. This breeds acute resentment on the part of the husband and makes him feel unfairly treated, something that may cause him to feel that he has no further reason to be fair in his treatment of his wife. Let's return to Fred and Jill.

Fred is willing to have Jill stay in the house if she buys him out. The house is now worth $220,000, and the mortgage balance has been reduced to $146,000, so the equity in the house is now $64,000. The couple is in agreement that the assets of the marriage should be divided equally, so Fred would be entitled to $32,000 for his share of the house. If there are other assets of equal or greater value, Jill may be able to use her share of those to buy out Fred's interest. But if the only other assets are tax-deferred retirement assets, this may not work because it would leave Fred with either no available cash or the necessity of cashing in retirement assets at a significant loss to taxes and penalty. So what are the alternatives? Jill may still be able to buy Fred out. Maybe she can pay him part in retirement assets and part in cash derived by refinancing the house. If interest has come down since they bought the house, she may be able to refinance, take a 30-year mortgage instead of a 15-year mortgage, and still be able to afford it. As this book is written, mortgage interest rates are about 6 percent. With a 30-year mortgage at 6 percent, a $175,000 mortgage would require about $1,100 a month—a figure that is $100 lower than the present mortgage payment. So Jill can afford to give Fred about $30,000 for his interest in the house and still lower her monthly payment. In this case it turns out fine for everybody.

But of course it doesn't always happen this way. If their house was worth $300,000 and Jill needed another $50,000 to buy Fred's interest, she could not afford to do it. Then she would have a choice of selling the house or insisting that Fred keep most of his equity in the house. Or if Jill was not employed and the couple had $30,000 less income, she would also have a big problem trying to stay in the house. It is easy to see how the house issue can shape so many others, such as support and custody issues. I am convinced that most custody fights involve men who are the noninitiators of the divorce who are holding onto the custody issue in the hope of also getting occupancy of the house. When this happens, everyone in the family loses big.

The decision about whether to sell the house and, if so, when to sell it, is complex and needs to be approached with subtlety. The decision must be viewed as an emotional process as well as a financial decision, and the importance of using neutral language and problem solving cannot be overemphasized. "What are your thoughts on how we can both afford adequate housing?" will take you further than "We must sell the house right away!" In the end, the numbers will tell. But your wife's willingness to explore options will be shaped by how you approach the subject. If you are too anxious and push too hard and too fast, it's easy for her to get stuck. Even if the house has to be sold, it may be possible to put it off for a while and sell it next year or in 2 years. Your willingness to explore all the options with your wife will shape her willingness to explore them with you.

Note that the decision whether to sell the house is not necessarily connected to whether and when you will move out. If it is clear that you will move out whether your wife moves or stays, then you should move as soon as the two of you can resolve initial issues of your access to the children and the management of finances. The timing of your move has its own logic and should occur when the family is ready for you to move.

What About the Kids?

A common objection to selling the house is that the move will be so disruptive for the children that it should be avoided at all costs. "The children are upset enough about the divorce as it is. To ask them to move on top of all this change is just asking them too much." There may be some truth to this assertion, but usually not as much as people think. The assertion alone should not serve as a conversation stopper.

Children do not like moving and do not like change. But families who are not divorcing move frequently without worrying that the change will set back their children's development. People move to bigger and better houses, and people move because job transfers and career opportunities beckon. So outside of the context of divorce, moving is generally not regarded as so traumatic for the kids that the family never moves.

A second consideration is that not all moves are the same. If you move to a new town and a new school, your children have to start all over again building a new social network. This is challenging for all kids and genuinely scary for some, particularly children who may be shy or retiring. On the other hand, if you move to a smaller house in the same school district, it may constitute nothing more than a change of bedrooms and have no impact on a child's daily life or social network. So not all moves are equal, and moving should not be an unexamined taboo subject if the finances of the family require it.

Still another consideration is the timing of a move. A move may be a big problem this year but not so bad next year or the year after. It is rarely a requirement that the house be sold immediately, and in the face of a need to sell the house, a delay of a year or two may make an otherwise objectionable move somewhat more palatable. If reaching agreement requires a financial stretch for a year, that will not be as onerous as a stretch for 10 years. So you must take a posture that is not rigid and does not require your wife to do immediately something she fears is harmful to the children. By discussing a move as one possibility among others and being open to compromise about where and when, you may avoid a bitter standoff.

Where Do I Go?

Whether you are going to buy a house or rent an apartment, you still have to resolve the question of where to relocate. Many men's initial impulse is to move closer to where they work in order to reduce their commuting time.

Other men are eager to move to a more urban area because the social opportunities for single people are better. Both of these are legitimate reasons for choosing where to live. But if you have children and you hope to have your children spend much time with you, you will need to consider what factors facilitate your children's willingness to come and spend time where you live.

Will and Joan separated 5 months ago. Joan and the children continue to reside in the marital home located in a New Jersey suburb. Will wanted to reduce his daily hour-long commute to work, so he moved to an apartment 20 minutes from his office and in an apartment complex right in the center of the social action. He was very pleased with the move. But Will's children were not so pleased. Marie, age 12, and John, age 9, complained whenever they had to go to their father's for the weekend. Will and Joan, like most couples, had agreed to alternate weekends with the children, and Will had also committed to spending Wednesday evenings with the children. Because it was impractical to drive the kids 40 minutes each way on a weekday evening, Will would drive to Joan's house to take the kids out for dinner. This only worked sometimes. Often one or both children claimed that they had too much homework to go out for dinner. They wanted Will to spend the evening in the house with them so he could visit and help with homework at the same time. Will had tried this numerous times but felt increasingly uncomfortable being in what had become Joan's house. And Joan, who had been eager to see Will move out, did not welcome the invasion of her privacy. So Wednesday evenings were not particularly satisfactory to anyone.

Weekends were not much fun, either. John was a dedicated athlete. He played soccer in the fall and baseball in the spring. He had practice almost every afternoon and games almost every weekend. So when he spent a weekend at his dad's place, it meant that John would have to miss a game or that Will would have to spend the weekend driving back and forth. Sometimes John would skip the weekend to stay with his mother. Marie also had her problems with the weekends. Marie was in junior high school and was a popular child with a large circle of friends. Her friends usually met for parties or a movie at least one evening of the weekend, and Marie resented having to miss the fun to go to her dad's house. Marie also played soccer and sang in the school chorus; both activities required attendance at weekend events. All this put Will in a difficult position. Either he spent the entire weekend driving back and forth, or he refused and told the children they would have to spend the weekend in Hoboken with him. When this happened, he found himself going crazy trying to entertain two sullen and disgruntled kids. Increasingly he found that one or both children would plead to be allowed to skip a weekend and this created tension with Joan because she wanted some time to herself and was resentful when she had to give up her weekend off because the children didn't want to go to Will's place.

Will's dilemma is a common one. But the consequences can be serious because they can ruin the ability of the family to adjust well to the divorce. A successful parenting schedule is one in which children can share their parent's lives without undue disruption of their own. So it comes down to this: If you expect to maintain a robust relationship with your children, you need to live within their social orbit. Once you move beyond that boundary, you will probably have problems. The problems will arise with all children but will be particularly acute with teenagers. Adolescence is a period in which the developmental task of children is to begin to separate from their parents. Their peers become much-preferred companions and teens don't particularly want to hang out with their parents, whom they increasingly regard as a source of embarrassment. So when a teenage child spends the weekend with you, she may actually be with you for only a few hours as she spends most of her waking hours with friends and in activities apart from you. If you interpose yourself in this process and insist that she hang out with you, I promise you nothing but a grumpy kid. You move away at the expense of an easy relationship with your children.

Do I Buy or Rent?

Assuming that buying a house of your own is financially feasible, you still face the question of whether to buy or rent. For many people, owning a house is a major indicator of life success and having to live in a rental may be seen as a big step down in life. So I see many men who assume from the beginning that the thing to do is to buy a house. The impulse is understandable, particularly for men who like to work in the yard or need a workshop in the basement for their hobbies. Certainly home ownership has advantages over renting. But it also has a downside that should be considered.

Divorce is a time of change. After you have separated, you are very likely to date and find a new mate within a few years. Your wife may herself choose to move, or you may have negotiated a settlement in which the house is sold after 1 or 2 years so that she must move. So retaining some flexibility is a great advantage. If you have purchased a house, you may find yourself stuck with it or having to absorb a loss in order to sell it after only a year or two. You may want to live with the woman you are dating, and the house you have bought does not work for any of several possible reasons. Most rentals have 1-year leases and so allow you a lower-cost move after a year. Retaining this flexibility for a year or two may turn out to be a great advantage.

Another advantage of renting rather than buying at first is that it makes for a much easier transition. It takes time and energy to find and buy a house. It takes time to obtain a mortgage and it can take time, money, and energy to decorate or redecorate a house. It is not unusual for the process to take 6 months or more depending on real estate market conditions. To find a rental and move takes a month, or 2 months at most. It brings on the separation sooner rather than later and shortens the period that the two of you need to live together. When it comes to moving out, sooner is much better than later. Overall, I generally encourage men to rent for a year rather than buying. The cost of a second move is easily offset by the advantages of flexibility and speed of separation.

The Need for a Real Home

When money is tight and the pressure is on to get separated, it may be tempting to settle for the smallest, least-expensive apartment you can find. This is a mistake and to be avoided. For both your own welfare and the welfare of your children, you need a real home. You are too old to resume the life of an undergraduate. You need someplace to come home to at the end of the day that is comfortable and aesthetically pleasing. You need enough space to accommodate your children for overnights and to have a little privacy when they are there. Sleeping bags on the floor may seem like fun at first, but it gets old quickly. Your children need their own room and possibly two rooms, depending on their ages. It is not reasonable to ask a teenage daughter to share a room with her 10-year-old brother, and if you do, you will find her resisting staying with you.

Setting up a real home requires some time, energy, and skill. Some men have these, while others are clueless. You will need to shop for furniture to supplement whatever you take from the marital home. There is plenty of inexpensive but attractive furniture on the market, and you should seek consultation among your friends to find someone who knows how to help you. There are a multitude of interior designers seeking work, but you should hire only someone who comes well recommended and who will commit to a fixed budget. But there is more to setting up a home than just buying furniture. You need sheets and towels, bedding, pillows, and placemats for the table. Equipping a kitchen is more demanding than meets the eye, as it requires pots, utensils, dishes, glassware, flatware, condiments, and spices. A single trip or two to a good department store can be all that is needed to fully equip your apartment, but it has to be planned, and if it's all new to you, you probably need some assistance.

Setting up a home is something you do once, but running a home is something you have to do all the time. If you are someone who can't cook, buy some simple cookbooks and start to learn simple dishes. Anyone with at least six fingers and an IQ exceeding two digits can learn to cook basic, appetizing meals. You will have to attend to cleaning or hire someone to clean your house. Either figure out how and where to wash your clothes or find a good laundry to do it for you. All of this can and should be done within the first month. It may seem daunting at first, but it is far more manageable than would appear and within a couple of months, you can have a fully equipped, smoothly functioning home that is appetizing and inviting for your children, for you, and—one day—for the women you date as well.

Financial Implications

Setting up a proper home costs money, and you are probably feeling strapped right now. Nevertheless, the need for a real home is not just a matter of material comfort. It is also a matter of mental health for you and your children. You will need to have some discussions with your wife to secure her support and cooperation. If the two of you have savings, now is the time to spend some of it. Depending on how much furniture you already have, furnishing a two-bedroom apartment should be possible for $3,000 to $8,000. This assumes you are not going to go crazy spending on high-end electronics and custom-made furniture. Setting up a kitchen costs between $2,500 and $3,000, depending on what you already own. So about $10,000 in round numbers should do the job well. Additionally, you will need to pay a security deposit that will be 1 or 2 month's rent; depending on where you live, you may also have to pay a broker's fee that typically runs about 1 month's rent. To find and rent a two-bedroom apartment, again depending on local markets, can cost from $1,200 to $2,500. So while vast sums are not needed to set up a real home, $10,000 to $15,000 is a realistic range and requires you and your wife to do some planning to make it happen. Avoid the logic that says that you just move out and find anyplace to live, whether suitable or not. That is a sure path to depression and trouble with your kids.

Who Pays?

Some couples faced with this situation get into wrangles over how the cost of the move will be distributed between them. Typically, she wants him to absorb the cost from his share of the marital assets, and he wants her to share in at least part of the transition costs of the move. More often than not, the move will occur before the financial settlement has been worked out, and we don't want the move to aggravate insecurities about the settlement. I have several recommendations here. The portion of the expenses that are strictly transition costs should be shared. The broker's fee and the cost of moving are transition costs. But the expenses that are incurred to acquire things that will be your property should be paid for out of your assets. The security deposit is property belonging to you. Furniture and equipment are your property. These things should be paid from your share of the marital assets. Later I will tell you how you should go about dividing the household goods. It is not a good idea to argue that all the existing furnishings should stay in the house while you buy new furniture paid for by the two of you. The disagreements over valuing the existing furniture invariably create problems neither of you need. Generally, if you have difficulty coming to agreement on how to apportion the costs, I suggest that you agree that the expenses incurred are "without prejudice" and will be worked out later when you resolve the rest of the property issues.

The important thing is to achieve a move quickly and amicably into a dwelling that serves the needs of the family, and disagreements over the relatively small amounts of capital involved should not be permitted to create a deadlock. Although I generally discourage credit card spending, this is one of the few times that I would suggest use of debt, if necessary, to facilitate the move. If you need to take a small home equity line to accomplish the move, you should do it. The debt will be managed as part of the overall settlement, and as long as you stay within reasonable cost parameters, the debt will not cause a problem.

What If You Are Staying in the House and She Is Leaving?

Although it is the husband who moves out in most cases, there are some divorces in which the wife moves out and the husband stays. In some cases the wife moves out in desperation because the husband has absolutely refused to budge and conditions in the home have become poisonous. When the wife is the primary source of parenting for the children, she moves with the children, leaving the husband by himself in the house. These cases are typically ones that are intensely litigated. The wife moves out to a rental that is expensive because she needs separate bedrooms for each child and sues the husband to provide support necessary to pay her rent and other expenses. He ends up paying high support to her as well as shouldering all the expenses of the marital home. Unless there is a lot of income, this situation usually precipitates a financial deterioration of the family.

There are several conditions in which the husband staying in the house occurs as part of a constructive settlement. When children are grown or almost grown, the decision of who stays in the house becomes more a matter of lifestyle and economic choices, with fewer consequences than when younger children are involved. Husband and wife are parting. After spending many years raising the kids, she wants to live in a smaller and simpler house. He wants to stay in the old house, and the economics are not a problem. Given this profile, there is nothing remarkable about the husband staying in the house. The second condition that keeps the husband in the house is one in which he is the primary parent. As we will explore later, when we look at parenting, it is very difficult and unlikely that a woman can voluntarily surrender a primary parenting role without feeling acute social stigma and loss of identity. But there are some cases, usually involving older teenagers, where the wife happily lets the husband take his turn caring for the children while she seeks to build a new career. For one couple whose divorce I mediated, the wife had decided at the age of 48 that she wanted to go to law school. The children were 15 and 17, and the husband was competent as parent and homemaker. She moved out to concentrate on her studies and spent weekends with the children. She was also available when they needed her to take them places or help with homework.

A similar situation may occur in couples who decide to share parenting responsibilities equally and the wife prefers a smaller home while the husband stays in the marital home. This may also be conditioned by the fact that the husband earns considerably more than the wife and even with alimony, she would be rent-poor if she stayed in the house. Because true joint parenting requires close physical proximity, the wife will usually find a smaller house nearby so the couple can easily coordinate joint parenting.

So except for the disastrous cases in which the husband has simply dug in his heels and the wife and children move out, most cases where the husband stays in the house are marked by a high degree of cooperation between the partners.

If you aspire to staying in the house under similar circumstances, your ability to manage constructive negotiation with your wife is critical. If she is to move out leaving you with an equal or primary parenting role, you must be aware of the criticism and stigma that may attach to any woman seen as "abandoning" her children. Your job is to promote a public posture among friends and family that she is a great and responsible mother, that she will continue to be vitally involved in the lives of the children, and that your new arrangement is designed to help her achieve some worthwhile and valued goal. Instead of permitting the story that you are staying because you are the superior parent, you need to proclaim that you are just stepping up to the plate to do your share and that she has earned your assistance by her years of dedication. If you do this well, you provide your wife with the social approval she needs to make this transition.

A Bad Idea

Before leaving this chapter, I need to attend to a bad idea that often appeals to couples whose primary concern is avoiding change for the children. At some point in the early discussions, one partner proposes that the children stay in the house and the parents alternate living in the house with the kids. For example, one couple I saw recently proposed that the parents would each occupy the house every other week while the children stayed in the house. There are many reasons that this is a very bad idea. First, it is expensive. It requires three dwellings instead of two, as each parent needs his or her own apartment in addition to the house. If they get one apartment and share it as well as the house, they are now sharing two dwellings and in effect never really separate. The second reason is that this arrangement keeps them tied financially. They have to continually coordinate expenses in the house, and if they also share an apartment, they have to coordinate expenses for that. As a consequence, they have no privacy with respect to each other.

But the most important reason not to do this is that it will fall apart in a short time. As each parent starts to build a new social life, the strains of this arrangement will begin to show. No new girlfriend or boyfriend will tolerate sleeping in the same bed vacated just yesterday by the ex-spouse. And no new significant other will tolerate for long moving between two residences. It also falls apart because the complications for the parents of moving between two residences and constantly coordinating with their ex-

spouses are just too great. The arrangement prevents either from really settling into a new home and starting a new life. I have never seen this work
for more than a few months. The arrangement also reflects confusion about
the organization of the needs of parents and adults. The desire to protect
children from change and the willingness of the parents to accept any price
that results from that posture is illusory at best. If you wear yourself out
trying to protect your children from the reality of the divorce, you won't be
of much use to the kids. Everyone in the family must accept a degree of
change in order for the family to adapt well. To subordinate all of your
needs to those of the kids will mean that nobody will thrive over time. The
needs of all family members are equally important.

"My dad was too much of a babe magnet for the marriage to have worked."

Ten

FATHERS AND CHILDREN

IT IS UNFORTUNATE that the popular media has made such a mess of the subject of custody. Perhaps the subject is just so appealing to soap opera fans that the images of children being torn away from one parent are just too sensational not to use. We have had numerous movies, television programs, and bad novels in which one parent struggles to take a child away from the other parent because of some allegation that the other is a bad or unfit parent. Although it may make good drama, it creates unnecessary fears in the minds of parents who are about to be divorced. I find that many people come to see me scared to death that they are about to "lose" their children. Fortunately it usually does not take long to calm them down because the realities are very different from the fictional depictions of custody fights.

Although there are indeed too many custody fights in the courts, they represent a small percentage of all divorce cases. Remember that only 1 or 2 percent of all divorces ever go to trial and that in most of these, the issue is custody of the money, not custody of the kids. Although there are few custody trials, there are many threatened custody fights, and the damage is about the same. I have come to regard most custody fights as the product of lawyer failure. Because these battles are based on ignorance and fear, I fault the lawyers for not educating their clients and calming their fears. In the last 1,000 divorces I have mediated, only one deteriorated into a custody fight. That is not because I am a magician, but because my mission is to put out rather than stoke the fires of fear.

The truth about custody issues is far from what most laypeople believe. If approached gently and intelligently, the subject of how to parent the children is almost always resolved without a struggle. Most of the issues that arise are based on fear and on honest disagreement that lends itself to enlightened discussion and negotiation. In this chapter, I want to show you how to do that.

An Overview of the Law of Custody

I will talk about custody in this section and then abandon the term for the rest of the book. Custody has become a poisoned concept. It connotes that one parent "wins" the kids and the other parent "loses" the kids. Custody is, at its very essence, an adversarial concept and many states are substituting "parenting" for the term custody. I applaud the change and have adopted it in my own discussions.

Traditionally, custody was awarded to the parent who "won" the divorce. In the post–World War II era, modern psychology began to influence the courts to award custody based not on marital fault but on the best interests of the child. This, coupled with the assumption that women were better connected emotionally to the children, meant that the mother usually was designated as the custodial parent. But the courts also recognized that children needed contact with both parents in order to develop correctly and so usually "awarded" the noncustodial parent visitation rights. If the father lived within a reasonable distance, he was usually awarded alternate weekends with the children. Increasingly, he was also awarded some access during the week and on holidays. So by the early 1970s, the routine and classic custody arrangement was one in which the mother had custody and the father saw the children every other weekend and on Wednesday nights.

Beginning in the 1970s, we began to see yet another shift that favored fathers. As the movement for women's rights and sexual equality gained steam, more fathers began to assert the right to equal treatment and fought against the assumption that sole custody by the mother was the best thing for the children. Fathers fought against the sense of disenfranchisement that came with the designation of noncustodial parent and bitterly resented their designation as visitors in the lives of their children. By the late 1970s, many couples were negotiating joint custody agreements in which the children would typically spend 1 week or 1 month with the mother and then spend 1 week or 1 month with the father. Although this worked well for many couples, it worked poorly for many others. We will explore why a little later.

Joint Legal Custody

By the 1980s, scholars and judges were looking much more critically at the issue of joint custody, and lawyers started looking for alternatives. The question was how to avoid the sense of disenfranchisement of the noncustodial parent while constructing a parenting system that gave greater continuity to the children. The answer was some old wine in new bottles; the concept of joint legal custody with one parent, typically the mother, being designated as parent of primary residence. What this concept does is make explicit that by having joint legal custody the parents will make all important decisions affecting the health and welfare of the children consensually. Each parent has equal access to school and health records and reports, and each has equal rights to attend meetings and conferences involving the children. And instead of talking about visitation rights, we talk about parenting schedules that delineate the time the children will spend with each parent.

Joint legal custody with one parent designated as the parent of primary residence has become the most common form of parenting in American divorce. Although it often looks similar to the old pattern of having the mother in charge and having the father spend alternate weekends and Wednesday nights with the children, it does provide at least symbolic recognition of the important place the father occupies in the life of the child. The specific parenting schedules that most people use will be described shortly.

Guardianship and Decision Making

Think about what it involves to be a parent. First, you have to nurture the child by providing basics such as food, clothing, shelter, and love. You also have to teach the child how to get along in the world and provide educational opportunities and recreation. In other words, you have to take care of the child so that he or she thrives and develops. So nurturing includes not only making decisions for the child but also teaching the child how to make good decisions. You decide where the child goes to school, who will provide medical care, and what activities are acceptable. We generally distinguish between decision making and nurturing, although the two are closely related.

When a couple divorces, they have to divide the responsibility for raising children in some workable and reasonable manner. They have to decide how they will take care of the child and how decisions will be made and by whom. If they are unable to decide, the court will decide for them. Usually the court will declare that one of the parents is in charge and that the other parent will play a secondary role. Generally, we do not want the court to decide because it cannot do a very good job.

The two aspects of the parenting agreement, then, are the decision-making protocol and the parenting schedule. When we call the parenting arrangement "joint legal custody," we require the parents to make important decisions consensually. When we call the arrangement "sole custody," we say that the custodial parent has unilateral decision-making authority. The schedule specifies what days of the week the child will spend with each parent and with whom the children will spend which vacations and holidays.

The Fears of Fathers

Many fathers approach divorce with the fear that they will be effectively cut out of their child's life. Fathers fear that their wishes and preferences will be ignored, that they will lose the opportunity to share the child's life in any meaningful way, and in many cases they fear being replaced as the father by the wife's next husband. In short, fathers fear losing their place in their children's lives.

Two questions arise here. First, how well-founded are these fears; and second, what do you need to do to allay such fears? The statistics on fathers are not encouraging at first glance. About half of divorced fathers default on their child support payments or pay later and less than they are supposed to. Many fathers drift away from their children, and many fathers spend much less time with their children than they otherwise could. Whether this is because they are not interested and committed, or whether this is because mothers sabotage fathers' relationships can be debated at length. But the statistics include many couples who had children out of wedlock and at a very young age. They do not provide an accurate picture of middle-class, educated couples. Among educated couples, continued and robust engagement by fathers is the norm rather than the exception. Poor teenage parents suffer from so much disorganization in their lives that it is a minor miracle when they can pull off successful parenting. So I suggest that you ignore the gloomy statistics.

The way to allay your fears is by asserting an active interest in your role as parent and insisting that the parenting agreement you will negotiate with your wife will help to maintain full relationships between the children and both of you. As I will explain as we proceed, I suspect that your wife will be cooperative because it is in her interest to do so unless the two of you get involved in a rancorous divorce.

What Parenting Arrangement Do You Seek?

A few of the divorcing men that I see come in seeking sole custody of their children. In very few cases, there is compelling justification. If the mother is mentally ill to the point of being unable to take care of the children—that is, if she is incapacitated—such a goal may make sense. But such incapacitation is rare. Just because your wife is suffering from depression doesn't mean she is unable to take care of children. Her depression may be caused in large part by the failing relationship and will improve once things settle down. In a few cases, I have seen very destructive and abusive mothers. In such cases, the father is right to insist on sole custody. But these cases are very rare. It is very unlikely that your wife is an unfit or abusive parent, and it is therefore unlikely that you seeking a traditional sole custody arrangement with you as the custodial parent makes much sense.

Gender and Family Roles

Although your family structure may deviate from the norm, in most families we still see traditional gender-based roles. It is true that 70 percent of mothers are employed at least part time. But in addition to that employment, they also tend to administer the lives of the children. It is mostly mothers who will be found in the waiting rooms of pediatricians and scheduling playdates and extracurricular activities, at parent-teacher conferences, at home when a child stays home sick, and at the wheel as the chauffeur of the kids as they go here and there. This is not to suggest that fathers don't do these things, but the ones we see there most often are the mothers—not because of an anti-male conspiracy, but because both partners want it that way.

The truth is that it is women who are most often in charge of the emotional life of the family. It is typically the wife who schedules not only the children's social lives but also the couple's social life. It is not unusual to find that it is the wife who maintains contact with the friends and relatives, including in many cases the husband's own family. The emotional maintenance of the family is a role that more often than not falls to the wife. Whether this is a result of cultural influence, genetics, or both is not important here. What is important is the recognition that it applies or doesn't apply in your family. It is important to assess because if it does apply and you want to seek an equal parenting role in the divorce, you will need to acknowledge both to yourself and your wife that you will have to learn some new tricks with the kids. There is nothing wrong with joint custody, and when it works well it's a good arrangement for everyone. But many men who are outraged that their wives resist joint custody fail to comprehend that they are proposing a new emotional arrangement with the children.

At the risk of political incorrectness, it is necessary to recognize that in most cases mothers are closer emotionally to the children than are fathers. That is not to dismiss the critical importance or vitality of your role as father. But there is a difference in the emotional connection between mothers and children that is related to pregnancy, nursing, and caring for babies and little children. In most families it is the wife who spends more time with the children, especially when the children are small. I have seen a few two-career couples in which everything has been done equally and both parents have spent equal time with the children beginning in infancy. If this applies to you, I expect it will continue into the divorce and that parenting schedules will not be an issue. But if you and your wife have had a more traditional arrangement in which you were the primary breadwinner and she was the primary parent, you must acknowledge that fact now or risk alienating her beyond easy reconciliation.

Despite lip service paid to equality of the sexes by lawyers and judges, there is still a presumption that the mother is more involved with the children and that her emotional connection to them is stronger than the father's. There is also an assumption on the part of many people that—post-divorce—a woman who does not have the primary parenting role has been found to be a less than good mother. Your wife, like most mothers, is eager to have the children closely connected to you as long as you acknowledge her primacy. You can probably give her what she seeks without sacrificing your own goals for you and the children.

CASE STUDY: **John and Maria**

John and Maria were divorcing after 15 years of marriage. They had two children—Becky, age 11, and Jeb, age 8. John was a successful CPA and partner in an accounting firm. He had routinely worked 60 hours a week for many years, but the couple had a nice home and some money in the bank to show for the hard work. Maria was employed as a teacher in the public schools and had chosen that job in order to be out of school at the same time the kids were. Maria routinely attended to the children while John put in long hours and earned the money needed by the family. Maria earned $30,000 a year, and John earned $200,000.

The couple's relationship had been struggling for many years and they had had several unfruitful rounds of marriage counseling. Although both had given up on the relationship, they had been held together for years by inertia and a mutual concern for the children. But when Maria found out that John had had a brief affair at a convention, she was livid. She told John that she wanted a divorce and that she wanted him to leave. John was relieved in some ways that the marriage was finally over but was anxious about the children and about his relationship to them. Like many couples, John and Maria had some initial discussions to feel each other out about what the divorce would look like. Maria told John that she expected to stay in the house with the kids and that she would agree that he could see them frequently as long as they lived with her.

"That's not good enough," said John. "I want joint custody. I want the kids to live with me half time. I'm not going to become some visiting father without any rights. I'm just as good a parent as you, and there is no reason for me to be a second-class parent!"

Maria was incredulous when she heard this. "Where have you been all these years while I've been doing everything for these children? You are rarely home in time for supper. You almost never supervise their homework. You don't take them on errands, and on weekends you say you need to go unwind and play golf. How do you expect to be an equal parent now when you never have been before? Forget about joint custody because I'm not agreeing to it."

Now John was angry. "Well, I'm not moving out of this house until you agree to joint custody. I'm not just going to leave my house and my kids and everything I worked so hard for and send you a fat check every month. Until you change your mind, I'm not going anywhere. And if the only way I can get a fair shake with the kids is to sue you for custody, I will do so."

John and Maria settled into an angry state of deadlock. They were in separate bedrooms and barely talking. Maria consulted with her friends and was encouraged to hold her ground. She saw several lawyers who told her that few judges would order joint custody under the circumstances and that no judge would give John sole custody considering the history of the family. John also consulted friends and cronies. Several of them told him to stick to his guns and fight for his rights because they knew too many men who had gotten "taken" by their wives. John sought a lawyer who told him that the odds were against him in a custody fight but that he might get joint custody, depending on which judge heard the case.

John and Maria each asked their lawyers how much it would cost to take *the case to trial. Well, Maria's lawyer opined, it would depend on how sour the other economic issues became. In his experience, if custody is contested, everything is contested, and if that happened the cost to her could approach $100,000. John's lawyer told him something similar. As neither one was willing to commit to that much money, each just hunkered down to see if the other would give in. Six months passed and nothing happened. The atmosphere became ever more tense at home and the children became gloomy and depressed.*

One day Maria received a call from Becky's guidance counselor at school. The counselor told her that Becky was not doing well in school and that several teachers had noted that she seemed listless and irritable in class. Her grades had fallen, and a child that had been an excellent student was suddenly missing homework assignments and flunking quizzes. The counselor suggested that Maria come in for a consultation and suggested that John attend as well.

John and Maria are similar to many couples I have seen. John fears being cut out as a parent. Maria fears that John is seeking something he does not deserve and something that would not be good for the children. But neither is looking ahead at what the family needs, and neither is attending to what the children need right now. Living with divorcing parents can cause depression in children. But neither parent understands how to break the stalemate that is preventing all four of them from healing and moving forward. They get encouragement from others to fight but are intimidated by the cost. They are not willing to go to court but they don't know how to resolve the issue.

John and Maria attended the session with the counselor a few days after the phone call. After reviewing the teachers' comments with them, the counselor asked if anything was going on at home that might explain Becky's sudden poor performance in school. When Maria told her that they were on the verge of divorce but couldn't agree on custody, the counselor suggested that there was a probable connection between their struggles and Becky's problems. She said that she had seen this many times and that the problem would resolve if they could get their own issues resolved. She said that she thought it was very important that John and Maria figure out how to cooperate as parents very soon before Becky got into long-lasting trouble. The counselor suggested that they consider mediation and said that she had seen it work in similar cases. They asked for a referral and the counselor referred them to me.

John and Maria came to see me about a week later. They both appeared to be pleasant and essentially reasonable people who were caught up in the fears that often dominate a divorce. Although they brought all their economic issues as well as their parenting issues to mediation, I will comment here only on the parenting discussions.

John and Maria summarized their viewpoints. Maria had always been the primary parenting figure and saw no reason to give up that role now. She said that John's role with the children had always been played within a framework maintained by her. John saw the kids as he came and left the house. He might see them at breakfast, but it was she who was preparing their breakfasts. The same applied to dinner when he was home, which he frequently was not, particularly during tax season. Although John often attended the children's sports events, it was based on whether it was convenient for him, and it was assumed that whenever it did not suit his purpose she would be there to take care of the kids.

John agreed that Maria's depiction of history was more or less accurate. But he believed that the divorce meant that many things would have to change. For one thing, he was tired of killing himself at work. Last year one of his colleagues had a heart attack, and he wasn't going to have that happen to him. And it was precisely because his contact with the kids had been based on the assumption that Maria would cover for him that he would need to take more time off from work to spend with the children. He was not about to become peripheral to their lives.

A second thing that was obvious to him was that Maria was going to have to get a job that paid more money. Maria had an MBA and had earned twice the salary of a teacher before the kids were born. So if this happened, Maria would have to work more and would have less time to spend with the kids, time that John would have to cover. That was why he wanted a full joint custody arrangement.

What Each Parent Needs

Although John and Maria appear to be at loggerheads, they have more in-terests in common than they realize. At the moment, they are struggling to hold on to what they have in the marriage. They will solve their problems when they move to organizing their lives for the future.

Each parent needs two things with respect to the kids. First, each needs to spend significant time nurturing the children and enjoying their company. As we raise children, they become integral to our identity as a person in that our role as parent becomes an important part of our sense of self. Any parenting agreement has to attend to the need of each parent to spend time with the children. A second need of each parent, frequently over-looked by women, is the need for substantial time off from the children. Most people divorce hoping to meet someone new and, in time, connect with a new mate. You will be dating and trying to build a relationship. To do this, you each need time without your children. When you are dating, your children are a liability, not an asset. If you become involved with a woman she will, at best, tolerate your children; she will not welcome them. So if you are available only with your kids in tow, few potential girlfriends will stick around for long.

The ability to understand the need for time off from the children often depends on whether one is the initiator or the noninitiator of the divorce. I find that those who do not want the divorce and have not yet made peace with the fact of divorce have also not yet figured out that they are going to have lives in the future. I can recall several couples in which the noninitiating wife fought every overnight that the husband sought with his kids. She came up with one far-fetched reason after an-other until he was totally frustrated. Finally, I asked her if she had much of a support system in friends and family. She replied that she did not. So I asked her who provided her with companionship and support, and she answered that it was the kids. Then I asked how she felt when she did not have a child at home, and she answered that she felt devastated and lonely. Only then were we able to talk about other ways not to feel devastated and lonely so she would not have to clutch the children so hard.

As you think through your need for an emotional life independent of your children, your need for time off from them will become apparent. If your wife does not yet feel a similar need, give her time. She will probably change her thinking as she becomes more engaged in building a new life for herself.

What the Children Need

Children need time with both parents. As we have emphasized elsewhere in this book, children need to share each of your lives and to have each of you share their lives. They need for both of you to care for them and love them and for both of you to be involved, at least to some extent, with their activities. But what children need most of all is for the two of you to be able to cooperate around issues affecting them. They need you to cooperate around financial matters so they don't end up in the middle when you disagree about money. They need you to be pleasant to each other when they move between households and they need you to be reasonable with each other in accommodating to changing schedules. They need encouragement to be comfortable in both households. And when one of you identifies a new significant other, they need the permission of the other parent to like the new person.

Most scholars who study divorce agree that the level of cooperation between the parents is the most powerful predictor of how well children will adapt to the divorce. There are data that suggest that the level of psychological problems is no greater in children of divorce so long as there is a high level of cooperation between the parents. It does not really matter what you call the custody arrangement, and the specific schedule is not that important so long as each parent gets significant time with the children and the parents have a cooperative arrangement.

In my discussions with John and Maria, I began to introduce these ideas. I suggested to John that he needed to validate Maria's claim that she had been the primary source of nurturing for the children. Only then would she be able to stop trying to prove that she had indeed played a primary role. In time he was able to do so. With a little coaching, here is what he finally said to Maria: "I am sorry that I ever questioned your role as the kids' mother.

Of course, you have done most of the work, and you have done a wonderful job helping the children to be successful. I hope you will work with me to create an arrangement in which I can now have an expanded role. I think they need a full and rich relationship with both of us, and I will help you any way I can."

John's statement to Maria helped her to relax and not feel so acutely that her identity and role of mother was being threatened. Now Maria could exhibit some grace toward John. *She said to him, "I appreciate how hard you have worked to provide for me and the children, and I know that you have not always had as much time with them as both of us would have wanted. I will work with you to keep you central to their lives."*

This small shift in the way the two of them framed the issue set the stage for a cooperative resolution.

Parenting Schedules and Joint Custody

The struggle over definitions is seldom productive. It really doesn't matter if we call it joint legal custody or joint physical custody. In the end, those designations will not facilitate the achievement of your goals for your children or yourself. A few key concepts help lower the temperature of the debate over schedules.

First, almost everyone alternates weekends. The exception occurs in families in which one or both spouses work on weekends. This could be police officers, airline pilots, medical personnel, or shift workers in factories. In these families, every other weekend does not work well. But for most couples, alternate weekends are the rule because they accomplish several things. First, they give each parent half of the time when the children are off from school and you are off from work. Thus the largest block of available time is shared equally. Of equal importance, weekends are the time that most people date, and you can count on being free every other weekend to pursue your social life. It is interesting to note that alternate weekends are almost universal even in situations where a judge has awarded sole custody to one parent after a custody fight. Alternate weekends are almost a foregone conclusion in most divorces. So that leaves the question of school nights.

Weeknights are usually the subject that causes the most stress in parenting negotiations. Listen to Maria.

"It's fine with me if the children spend weekends with you, but I think they should spend school nights with me. I think the confusion of moving back and forth like bouncing balls will be bad for their schoolwork. They're used to me doing homework with them, and I am afraid that they won't get their homework done or that they won't get enough sleep. I think they should be in their home on school nights. You can come have dinner with them and do homework anytime you want, but they should stay in my house"

To this John responded with great frustration, "It's just not good enough for you to tell me that I should have the kids only four nights a month. How can you say that you want them to have a rich relationship with me when I would have them so few nights? I won't accept that."

Maria's objection to the children having overnight stays with John during the week is uninformed and unfortunate. It is important that John not overreact and that he let the mediator do his job of educating Maria. When you divorce, it means that your children have two parents in two houses and need to spend time with each parent in each house. It does introduce a measure of disorganization, and one might as well acknowledge that. It's easier to live in one home than two. But in divorce, the choices are limited. Either the children spend significant time in both households and learn to manage a degree of disorganization or they spend all their time in one house and in effect lose significant contact with one parent. In the latter case, the loss is too significant.

There are several issues here. First is the issue of who helps the children with homework. When I was a child, my parents expected me to do my homework. If I didn't do it, I caught hell from my teachers and received bad grades. Then my parents would be angry and life would be unpleasant for a while. But it was my problem and my homework. On occasion, if I was stumped by something, I could ask my father for help and he would help. But I had to take the initiative. There was nothing unusual about my parent's approach and it was no different than that taken by my friends' parents. Today we seem to live in a much more child-centered world, in which too many parents inject themselves as integral to their children's homework. The result is children who cannot sit down and do their homework without a parent hovering by.

Part of the solution depends on how you and your wife have handled this in the past. If she has been the one who has always done homework with the children while you did something else, you will have to ease your way into the role. Certainly, fathers can help kids with homework as well as mothers can. Of course you may want to have a discussion with your wife about letting the children become a little more independent and take responsibility for their own work. The easiest way to institute any change is to try it as a pilot program. So here is what John was coached to say.

"I don't fully agree with you about how much we should be helping the kids with their homework, but I am willing to cooperate. Let's have an experiment for a month. I will help them every other week and you help them the rest of the time and let's see how it works out."

By framing his proposal as an experiment, John avoids a fight and secures Maria's agreement to try the arrangement. Over time, John may be able to get Maria to relax about the homework issue. But this should not determine if the children stay overnight with their father during the week.

The second issue raised by Maria is the "bouncing ball" complaint. She assumes that if the kids move between two households that they will literally be bouncing and therefore be too confused to function. Again, in an ideal world it would not be necessary to move kids back and forth. But in the world of divorce, some movement between homes is unavoidable. We move them back and forth on weekends. If the two of you are cooperating, some movement during the week will not hurt. The objective is to have the kids spend sufficient time with each parent to achieve the needs that parents and children have for each other. But we want to do so in such a way as to minimize the transitions.

If John were to seek the children two nights a week and wanted them on Monday and Wednesday nights, that would be a poor schedule because it has the children moving almost every day. But if he sought to have them on

Monday and Tuesday nights, it would reduce the number of moves to a minimum. That is the strategy I urge on my clients.

Long Weekends

One good way to increase the time children spend with each of you is to extend weekends from Friday evening through Monday morning when you would see them off to school. This increases the amount of time you have them without any additional transitions. They are already located at your home for the weekend, so they just stay over another night. I find that this is easy for women to agree to, and it is appealing because it gives them a bigger block of time off from the children.

Consecutive Nights

If you make weekends three nights, all that is left is Monday through Thursday nights. If the children were to spend every Monday night with you it would mean that you have them 5 out of 14 nights. If you were now to add Tuesday nights, you would have them 7 out of every 14 nights, or precisely half-time. But in either case, we connect the weeknights to the weekends so that the children only make two transitions each week. In the first case, what I call a 5/9 schedule, you have them four nights one week and one night the alternate week. In the second illustration, what I call a 7/7 schedule, you have them five nights one week and two nights the next week. I have found that either of these schedules reduces confusion to a minimum.

The Issue of Equality

We have been raised to believe that equal and fair are nearly synonymous. Equality is so deeply ingrained in political discourse that we almost automatically assume that if it is less than equal it is unfair and unjust. I find that for many men, equality of time with their children becomes the symbolic test of whether they are being treated fairly and often becomes more important than the larger question of what works. For men who seek joint custody in the face of resistance from their wives, the divorce may come down to a choice between the equal joint custody and an arrangement in which the children spend less than half their time with you but enough time to accomplish your objectives. I submit that the issue may, in the end, prove more symbolic than substantive.

Let's return to John and Maria.

When I started working with Maria, I found that she could shift her position on things as long as she was allowed to think about new proposals. I began by proposing to her that it would not work well for the children to spend only every other weekend with John. My first reason was that such a schedule did not give her enough time to herself, time that she needed and deserved. It also did not give John enough time with the children to feel he was fully involved. Finally, it wasn't enough time for the children to fully develop a relationship with their father. What did she think might be done to increase the children's time with their dad?

"Why can't he come over during the week, do their homework with them, and see them to bed? Then I could go out at least for part of the evening," she replied. "How will you feel having John in your house several evenings a week after you have separated? Won't you feel a need for more privacy?" I asked. "Well, I might," she replied. I told her that in my experience, people are not comfortable having an ex-spouse in their homes and the ex-spouse rapidly becomes uncomfortable being in his former home. What was her objective in doing it that way? "I want to avoid having the children leave their home. If he takes them to his house, then they would have to come home at the end of the evening, and that's too much for them." "Well, why do they have to come home? If they are at his house already, why not have them stay over once or twice a week?" She repeated that she was afraid that it would cause too much confusion. We talked a while about the lesser of two evils and we ended the session.

The next week when she came, she said that she would be willing for the children to spend one overnight during the school week with John. She was open to them spending more time with him during vacations, but one night during the week was enough. I then turned to John and asked him for his thoughts. "That won't do it. If she can't do better, I'm going to fight. I don't want a battle, but I'm not going to be pushed out as the kids' father. Every other weekend and one night a week isn't even close to half time. I want half time." I asked John what was important about half time. "It's only fair," he said. "Fair means equal."

I asked John what an equal pattern would mean. He said he didn't care as long as the number of nights was the same in each household. I asked them to look at a 2-week schedule. Maria was proposing that the children spend 4 out of 14 nights with John. John was proposing that the children spend 7 out of 14 nights with him. Their disagreement was about three nights every 2 weeks, or one and a half nights a week. I described a schedule to them that I have seen work hundreds of times. If we expanded the weekend to include Sunday night, the children would be with John every other Friday through Monday morning. That added two nights a month. Now, as Maria had already agreed to one night a week, and if we made that night Monday, then the children, already at John's house through Monday, would now stay through Tuesday morning. On the off week for John, he would have them Monday night. Now he would have them 5 nights out of 14, which was only two nights a week less than the half time he had sought. This would also address Maria's concern about moving the children back and forth too frequently.

John said that he would think about it, but was still upset because it wasn't equal. I observed that by adding Tuesday night, the schedule would become equal, because he would have them 7 nights out of 14. Then I asked John to tell me what time he came home at night and when the children went to bed. "I come home at 6:30, and the kids go to bed at 9:30," he said. "So," I asked, "are you telling me that you are willing to spend $50,000 and make a mess of the divorce over 3 hours a week?"

After thinking about it, John replied that maybe it might work if Maria would let him have the kids more during the summer. I asked Maria if she would consider having the kids at John's another night during the summer and if she could accept the 5/9 schedule I had described. She agreed to the schedule during the school year and agreed that the children would also spend Tuesday nights with John during the summer. The matter of parenting was resolved.

John didn't get his equal time arrangement. Is this unfair? Maybe. Fair is such an abstract concept that it is not very useful when we talk about divorce and children. The more important question is whether the schedule agreed to by the couple works for all of them. With his 5/9 schedule during the school year and 7/7 schedule during the summer, John has enough time to maintain the full, rich, and robust relationship he seeks with the children. Maria retains, at least in her mind, her primary role but gets enough time off from parenting to build a new life. The children get the time they need with both parents.

This family has done about as well as it could. If Maria had been comfortable with an equal schedule, that would have also worked well, but frankly, the specific schedule is not that important as long as it meets the needs of the entire family. The range of possibility is not unlimited. Four or five nights every 2 weeks are enough to maintain your place in the children's lives. If you have six or seven or even eight, that is also workable. I have seen few court battles over this subject that made sense in terms of cost-benefit or gains and losses.

Household Rules

John and Maria separated and began to live with the schedule they had negotiated. About 2 months later, I received a call from a distraught Maria. "This isn't working. John is doing stuff with the children that I can't approve of, and either he has to stop or I will fight him in court." I asked her to tell me about the problem. "Well, there is more than one. First, John refuses to give Jeb his Ritalin when the child is with him because he says he doesn't believe in giving such medicine to children if they don't need it. So on weekends he says he won't give the medicine to Jeb. The doctor never told us to skip weekends, and Jeb comes home too wound up after he has been with John. I also found out that John lets the children stay up past their bedtimes, and the kids need sleep." Is there anything else?" I asked. "Yes, it gets even worse," she said. "John took the kids snowmobiling and didn't have them wear helmets. He also took Jeb for a ride on his motorcycle, when he knows that I am deathly afraid of motorcycles. When I told him that was irresponsible, he just told me to quit telling him what to do and that he would decide what was best when the children were with him. And worst of all, I found out that John's new girlfriend spent the night with John when the kids were there, and I absolutely won't tolerate exposing

the kids to that immoral behavior." I suggested that she invoke the media-
tion clause in their agreement and come in for an appointment with John.

It is seldom that a divorced couple agrees on all the rules that should
apply when the children are in residence with the other parent. People
differ on many aspects of childrearing, from how to discipline, what
to feed them, when to put them to bed, what lessons to give them, and
what risks to allow them to take. Some parents forbid TV; others allow
unlimited TV access. Some indulge their children, and some believe
the children should live more Spartan lives. When children live in separate households, there is an unlimited opportunity for parents to get
into conflicts. And as in most of the conflicts arising from divorce,
most are not worth fighting in that the transaction cost of the conflict
usually exceeds the importance of what the dispute is about. Transaction
cost refers to the secondary costs of hurt feelings and accumulated re-
sentments that arise whenever harsh words are spoken or one of you
criticizes the other.

There are a few rules that I urge on people. The first, and perhaps the
most difficult for many mothers, is to mind your own business when the
children are in the other household. You cannot expect your ex-spouse to do
everything the same way that you do. It will not happen, and if you push it
too hard, it will just sour your parenting relationship. Most issues are not
worth the struggle.

Although it is preferable for the regimens in both households to be similar, children will not be injured if the two of you feed them differently or if
one of you is more lenient than the other. Children quickly figure out that
their parents are different and have different expectations and styles. If the
father lets them stay up later than the mother, they might be sleepy once in
a while, but it's not going to ruin their lives. The same applies to some of
the other issues that seem to occupy people. Food faddists and alternative
medicine devotees may get worked up about what the child eats or what the
doctor prescribes, but it's really not going to shape the children's lives in
important ways. What will shape the children's lives is perpetual battles between the parents. My rule, therefore, is to bite your tongue until it bleeds.
Don't precipitate a conflict unless the life and limb of a child is truly endan-

gered. Stupid and reckless behavior that exposes the child to great risk is worth discussing. For example, it is very stupid to let kids ride bikes or inline skate without helmets and protective gear. It is not acceptable to violate such principles, and you are not breaking the rule when you object to such a thing happening when the child is with the other parent, but if you're upset because your spouse took the kids to a movie of which you disapprove, you would be better advised to hold (or, if necessary, bite) your tongue.

How do you know the difference? The biggest part is common sense. There is a difference between your ex doing something you don't like with the kids and doing something that by objective standards is dangerous. When in doubt, let it go. But there is another side to this as well. If your ex-wife asks you to abide by some rule or regimen and you don't think that she is right, when should you comply, and when should you refuse? Here is where we return to the concept of transaction cost. In each instance, ask if it is worth it to assert your autonomy. Sometimes you should give in only because she feels strongly about a thing. If she does and you don't, it's not worth the fight. Sometimes we comply with the wishes of others for no reason other than to please, indulge, or even humor them. Its called getting along. Men often have exaggerated autonomy needs that cause them to get angry whenever they think someone is trying to tell them what to do. Most women have trouble understanding this and think that men are just being unreasonable. But this is not a book about gender behavior. It is a book about how to live in peace with your former wife. So pick your fights carefully. Try to change her parenting only when you think the welfare of the children is genuinely endangered. And defend your own parenting only when it's really worth it and not just when you worry that she is telling you what to do. Let's see how some of the issues played out when I saw John and Maria next.

John and Maria came to their appointment angry. John was indignant. "She's always trying to tell me what to do. It was bad enough when we were together. It's intolerable now, and she'd better learn to mind her own business!" Maria is equally indignant. "I'm sick and tired of his insensitive adolescent behavior. This is just what I was worried about, and if John can't be a more responsible parent, I will go to court and reduce the amount of time the kids spend with him."

I asked them both to calm down. I also asked Maria to tell me which of her issues she regarded as the least important and that we would take that one up first. "They are all important, but if I have to pick the least impor-tant, I would say the bedtime issue." "What are the kids' bedtimes and what do you know about their bedtimes at John's house?" She answered that she enforced a 9:30 bedtime and seldom made exceptions. She said that Becky had told her that on weekends, John let them stay up as long as they wanted and that on weekdays, he let them go to bed as late as 10:30. "That's not true!" said John. " On weekdays, I try to get them to bed by 9:30. Every now and then, I let them stay up for something special, but it's only once in a while. And on weekends I'm not even willing to discuss it. They can sleep late in the morning and there is nothing wrong with it." They argued for a short time, and then I asked if there was any rule John might agree to with respect to bedtime. He replied that he would be willing to try to adhere to a 9:30 bedtime during the week but not on weekends. I asked Maria if she could live with that, and she said yes, even though she would have reservations. I said okay, let's move on to the next topic. She said the next issue was the Ritalin.

Medical Treatment

Most parents agree about medical treatment for their children. They choose a physician, take the child when he is sick or needs a checkup, and do what the doctor tells them to do. But occasionally we see people who are deeply invested in a particular viewpoint. I had a case with a chiro-practor who was strongly against children receiving vaccinations. His wife had gone reluctantly along with him while they were married, but now wanted the children to be vaccinated. This caused intense conflict because both genuinely believed that they were fighting for the health of the chil-dren. I strongly encourage people to identify a pediatrician acceptable to both and to abide by the doctor's advice. If a doctor prescribes medicine, each parent is obliged to carry through. I have seen too many court battles caused by one parent deviating from medical advice because that parent had decided that his expertise exceeded that of the doctor. I strongly discourage such behavior. I find that even when one or both of the parents are devotees of "alternative medicine," they can usually find a physician upon who they can agree.

I asked John what was happening with the Ritalin and Jeb. "I have never said that I won't give him the medicine, but the doctor never said to use it when Jeb is not in school. In general, I don't think it's a good thing to give these medications unless it's absolutely necessary." "Have you asked the doctor?" "No, I haven't. Maria always takes Jeb to the doctor, and I've never met him." I asked him whether he would abide by the doctor's judgment, and he agreed that he would. I asked Maria if that was acceptable to her and so we moved on.

We then took up the motorcycle and the snowmobile issues. I asked them if they could agree that the children would always wear generally acceptable protective gear when riding bikes, horses, inline skates, skateboards, or any other vehicle in which they were exposed to injury. John said that he would. "Well, why didn't they have helmets on when they were on the snowmobile?" asked Maria. "That was a one-time exception that won't happen again. We had an opportunity to try three snowmobiles one day, and we didn't have helmets with us. I felt the conditions were not too dangerous, so I made an exception for the few minutes that the ride lasted. I have no intention of letting it happen again," answered John.

So far I felt that we were doing well. But then Maria raised the question of the motorcycle, and John became angry. "You have never liked motorcycles, but they are an important part of what I like to do, and you're not going to stop me from sharing that with the kids. There is nothing wrong with riding motorcycles if you are careful, and I have never had an accident because I am careful." But Maria was adamant. "Motorcycles are 20 times more likely to get you killed than cars. It doesn't matter how careful you are, if some crazy driver comes along, you're dead. If you want to kill yourself, that's up to you, but you are not taking the kids with you!"

Risk Tolerance

Men are generally more risk tolerant than women are and are more insistent that their children should be able to take greater risks. Risk taking, autonomy, independence, and mastery are more important to most men's identity than they are to the identity of women. And if the child is a boy, many men worry lest the child turn out to be a "wuss." So it is not uncommon that fathers and mothers disagree about what is and is not safe. Although there are some women who are physically bolder than their husbands, the issue of physical safety for the children is more likely to be asserted by mothers than by fathers. So when Maria and John square off about the child riding on John's motorcycle, that is the script that is being played out. If this happens to you, what should you do? Again I urge you to consider the transaction cost. What is it worth to you? And what does it cost her?

I asked John how central was riding the motorcycle to him. "Well, it's not the most important thing in the world, but I find it thrilling, and I want to share it with Jeb." I asked him whether he understood how frightened it made Maria. "She's always been frightened about the bike, and I've never been able to get her to come with me." So I asked him if, given that history, he believed that Maria's resistance to Jeb being on the motorcycle was caused by real distress or whether she was just trying to thwart him. "No, she has always been scared of the bike, and this is nothing new." I asked him if he could conceive of keeping Jeb off the motorcycle, not because Maria was right, but because she was so frightened that it wasn't worth causing her that much grief over what was simply an enjoyable pastime. "But what about the principle of the thing? Does this mean that every time she doesn't like what I'm doing she can tell me what to do?" I turned to Maria and asked her if this meant that she was trying to tell John what to do. "No John," she said, "I am really terrified about this. If you could accommodate me, I would really be grateful." In the end, John agreed that Jeb would not be invited to ride on the motorcycle until he was 15 years old. His agreement to so refrain was framed as an accommodation to Maria's fears, rather than a submission to her will.

Just because you are getting divorced does not mean that you can give up your humanity with respect to your wife. When there is an agreement on something related to risk tolerance, the degree of distress caused to her is a legitimate factor for you to consider without worrying whether you are allowing her to dominate and control you. That does not mean that you should always agree to do it her way, but that her feelings are still an appropriate basis of your own cost-benefit analysis. The payoff is that it works both ways and that you can expect her to reciprocate when your strong feelings are at stake. This is not a matter of rights. It is a matter of retaining a working relationship in which both of you feel respected. This is a goal you can achieve.

"Marsha, I can't take the kids—I've got my mutual funds this weekend."

Eleven

BUDGETS AS PLANNING TOOLS FOR SUPPORT DISCUSSIONS

SUPPORT NEGOTIATIONS BETWEEN YOUR WIFE and you can be a struggle to see who gets more and who gets less. Or it can be a mutual investigation to look at how to solve the problem of allocating scarce income to support two households. The former tests your relative power and ability to tolerate stress. It is, in short, a war of attrition. The latter is the only way to do it if you seek a good and decent divorce. The instrument that facilitates this discussion is the household budget that each of you will prepare and use to generate agreement on how much each of you will spend and on how the households will be funded.

Preparing your budgets is a vital task, and it is important that you and your wife agree to do this in good faith. The usefulness of budget preparation can be ruined if you use it simply to justify why you should get more and she should get less. I have been privy to too many negotiations between lawyers who have encouraged their clients to put every conceivable expense in the budget in order to stake out an aggressive bargaining position. The resulting budgets are not only an exaggerated statement of need but also a living demonstration of cynicism and indifference to fairness. Each of you will prepare a budget that reflects your current estimate of what you need in your separate households. Your historical pattern of spending is a useful guide to what you will need in the future but is not necessarily, or even possibly, the standard of spending you will have in the future.

Fiscally, there are two types of American middle-class families. The first is a calamity, a family that spends 105 percent of net income supporting one household. The second type is one that is frugal and that spends less than its monthly earnings. When we analyze those families' finances we find a minimum of short-term debt, a significant portion of income routinely saved and conservatively invested, and a real safety net that has been accumulated by saving. Unfortunately, these families are in the minority, but if you are among them, you will have an easier time in the divorce. The majority of couples I see fall into the first category. They have almost no savings other than their pension programs and have $10,000 to $15,000 in credit card debt and car loans on at least one car. They have routinely financed their annual deficit by refinancing their homes every couple of years to tap the increase in equity occasioned by a rising real estate market. If this describes you and your wife, you have a more difficult task in front of you, and the budgeting process is the only orderly way to go about it.

For you, the divorce is a double whammy. First, you will need to bring spending into line with income. This requires the end of deficit spending. Second, you will have to curb spending in order to absorb the 30 to 40 percent increase in expenses caused by having two households instead of one. So for many families, divorce requires a 30 to 50 percent reduction in monthly spending. If you don't approach this with a commitment to both equity and pragmatism, your discussions will quickly degenerate into an adversarial divorce. Middle-class divorce is about budget cutting, a painful exercise in a society that so frequently measures a sense of well-being by how much is consumed. This is a critical task for the divorce, so do it well.

The Budget Form

I have provided you with a budget form that I have found useful in the past. Some other forms available are less comprehensive and others are more comprehensive. I think this one strikes a good balance and recommend that you use it.

About the Budget Form

You will note that the budget is divided into three parts: Schedule A (shelter), Schedule B (transportation), and Schedule C (personal expenses). Schedule C includes a category of "other" for you to use when you have recurrent expenses not otherwise listed in the budget.

You will also note that there are two columns labeled 1 and 2. I will discuss the use of the second column later. For now, just concentrate on column 1.

Your assignment is to complete the budget as a proposed budget for your separate household over the next few years. If you have not yet separated, if you have moved into temporary housing but anticipate a move into larger quarters in the near future, or if you anticipate selling the current family home and buying new houses, then budget for the projected future. If you are not sure what housing you will occupy, budget for two or more alternatives. The budget is a planning tool and can help you decide which alternative makes the most sense.

By the time you are preparing the budgets you will, I hope, have a pretty good sense of what your parenting pattern will be. You will know what kind of accommodations you will need to have for the children when they are staying with you. If the children will be with you half the time because you are doing full joint parenting, you will need a separate bedroom for each child. If the children can share a room, that should also be reflected. We are seeking the budget that most closely reflects how you propose to live after the divorce is negotiated.

Doing the Budget

Expenses of the children should be reflected in the budget of the household that will bear the expense. For example, if it is your pattern that your wife buys the clothes for the children, then the cost for that clothing should be reflected in her household budget. If the children will spend half of each month with each of you, then the cost for food in each household should reflect what will actually be consumed.

You will undoubtedly come across some items where you do not know how much they will cost. If you have not been used to shopping for

(continued on page 230)

BUDGET FORM

MONTHLY EXPENSES

SCHEDULE A: SHELTER	1	2
TENANT		
Rent		
Heat		
Utilities		
Tenant insurance		
Other		
HOMEOWNER		
Mortgage		
Real estate taxes		
Homeowners insurance		
Heat		
Utilities		
Other		
TENANT OR HOMEOWNER		
Telephone		
Cable TV		
Other		
TOTAL SHELTER COSTS		
SCHEDULE B: TRANSPORTATION		
Auto payment		
Auto insurance		
Maintenance		
Fuel		
Commuting expenses		
TOTAL TRANSPORTATION EXPENSE		

SCHEDULE C: PERSONAL EXPENSES	1	2
Food at home and household supplies		
Restaurants		
Nonprescription drugs, cosmetics, etc.		
Clothing		
Hair care		
Entertainment, sports, and hobbies		
Gifts and contributions		
Newspapers and periodicals		
Life insurance		
Medical insurance		
Unreimbursed medical and dental		
Psychotherapy/counseling		
Prescription drugs		
Payments to nonchild dependents		
Prior family child support		
Adult educational expense		
Monthly debt service		
Domestic help		
Orthodontics		
Children's private school costs		
Day care expense		
Children's lessons		
Children's tutoring		
Summer camp		
Babysitting		
Other		
TOTAL PERSONAL EXPENSES		
TOTAL BUDGET (SCHEDULES A+B+C)		

groceries, you may not have enough experience to know what they cost. To some extent, you can ask your wife and rely on her estimate. But the preferred way is for you to make a grocery list and go to the supermarket to find out what you need to spend. Whenever you can obtain actual costs, it is preferred to estimates. If you are just moving into an apartment, you can call the utility company to get an estimate of expenses for heat, gas, and electricity. The more precise your figures, the better the budget will be. It is really worth the time to do this right.

Some Tricky Issues

Some expenses are straightforward and obvious. Auto insurance, for example, costs what it costs. But many other expenses fall into a more discretionary category, and as you begin to complete the budget you will also be able to anticipate where you can reduce spending. For example, you can buy a dress shirt for $25 at most department stores. You can also spend $60 for a dress shirt or even $120 for one that is custom-made. Clothing, restaurants, vacations, luxury cars, and entertainment are all items that are essentially discretionary. You and your wife will be having some discussions about cost cutting, so use your own budgeting exercise to note what aspects of your own spending are discretionary. When the two of you begin to review the expenses for the children, the same issues will apply. You can buy kids' clothing at Sears or at Bloomingdale's. You can send the kids to day camp in the summer or to expensive sleep-away camps. And once you decide on private schools for your children, costs soar. The budgeting exercise is designed to give you a systematic way to evaluate your family's approach to spending.

CASE STUDY: Will and Liz

Will and Liz are trying to negotiate their divorce settlement after 17 years of marriage. Will, 46, is the CFO of a small software company. He has a salary of $110,000 a year and expects an annual bonus of somewhere between $20,000 and $70,000—depending on how well the company does each year. Liz is employed part time as a programmer and earns $22 per hour for 20 hours a week. The couple has two children, Maggie, 14, and Max, 9. Liz worked full-time before Maggie was born, did not hold a job for 10 years, and then returned to part-time work a year ago.

The relationship between Will and Liz is civil but tense. The couple has had marital conflict for about 6 years and has had several rounds of counseling. About 6 months ago, Will felt that he was at his wits' end and could no longer take the tension. He told Liz that he wanted a divorce. She was surprised by Will's news and was angry at first because she believed that if he had worked harder in therapy they could have made it. She is resigned to the divorce but worried about the future.

The couple has always lived on the financial edge. Although Will earns a good salary, they lived in an expensive suburb and always lived pretty well even when they could not afford it. They have little savings and have accumulated about $30,000 of short-term debt over the past 5 years. Although Liz is resigned to the divorce, she is determined that the children not be dislocated. She has been reading a lot of divorce books and read that you should minimize the changes inflicted on the children. She is determined that the children and she stay in the house and that she continue to be available to the children after school.

Will recently signed a lease for an apartment 2 miles from the house. He and Liz are in agreement that the children will spend every other weekend with him and that he will have Maggie overnight on Monday nights and Max overnight on Tuesday nights. He leased a two-bedroom apartment and expected to share a room with Max on the nights that both children were with him. The couple did not have any difficulty agreeing on parenting issues but were not sure it would be easy to agree on monthly support. At the direction of their mediator, they each prepared a monthly budget.

(continued on page 236)

BUDGET FORM

MONTHLY EXPENSES FOR LIZ

SCHEDULE A: SHELTER	1	2 (Revised)
TENANT		
Rent		
Heat		
Utilities		
Tenant insurance		
Other		
HOMEOWNER		
Mortgage	1330	1320
Real estate taxes	350	350
Homeowners insurance	75	75
Heat	125	125
Utilities	125	125
Other (home equity loan)	350	
TENANT OR HOMEOWNER		
Telephone	75	75
Cable TV	60	60
Other (cell phone)	50	50
TOTAL SHELTER COSTS	**2540**	**2180**
SCHEDULE B: TRANSPORTATION		
Auto payment	425	425
Auto insurance	100	100
Maintenance	50	50
Fuel	100	100
Commuting expenses		
TOTAL TRANSPORTATION EXPENSE	**675**	**675**

SCHEDULE C: PERSONAL EXPENSES	1	2 (Revised)
Food at home and household supplies	600	600
Restaurants	200	100
Nonprescription drugs, cosmetics, etc.	100	100
Clothing	350	175
Hair care	50	50
Entertainment, sports, and hobbies	150	75
Gifts and contributions	100	50
Newspapers and periodicals	30	30
Life insurance		
Medical insurance	350	
Unreimbursed medical and dental	150	150
Psychotherapy/counseling	250	125
Prescription drugs	80	80
Payments to nonchild dependents		
Prior family child support		
Adult educational expense		
Monthly debt service	220	
Domestic help	240	120
Orthodontics	100	100
Children's private school costs		
Day care expense		
Children's lessons	160	160
Children's tutoring	200	100
Summer camp	180	180
Babysitting	100	100
Other (vacation)	250	125
TOTAL PERSONAL EXPENSES	**3860**	**2420**
TOTAL BUDGET (SCHEDULES A+B+C=)	**7075**	**5275**

BUDGET FORM

MONTHLY EXPENSES FOR WILL

SCHEDULE A: SHELTER	1	2 (Revised)
TENANT		
Rent	1200	1200
Heat		
Utilities	100	100
Tenant insurance	30	30
Other		
HOMEOWNER		
Mortgage		
Real estate taxes		
Homeowners insurance		
Heat		
Utilities		
Other		
TENANT OR HOMEOWNER		
Telephone	60	60
Cable TV	60	60
Other (cell phone)	40	40
TOTAL SHELTER COSTS	**1490**	**1490**
SCHEDULE B: TRANSPORTATION		
Auto payment	480	320
Auto insurance	100	100
Maintenance	40	40
Fuel	150	150
Commuting expenses	50	50
TOTAL TRANSPORTATION EXPENSE	**820**	**660**

SCHEDULE C: PERSONAL EXPENSES	1	2 (Revised)
Food at home and household supplies	300	300
Restaurants	300	150
Nonprescription drugs, cosmetics, etc.	30	30
Clothing	200	100
Hair care	20	20
Entertainment, sports, and hobbies	250	125
Gifts and contributions	50	50
Newspapers and periodicals	50	50
Life insurance	150	
Medical insurance		
Unreimbursed medical and dental	45	45
Psychotherapy/counseling		
Prescription drugs	40	40
Payments to nonchild dependents		
Prior family child support		
Adult educational expense		
Monthly debt service	100	
Domestic help	240	120
Orthodontics		
Children's private school costs		
Day care expense		
Children's lessons		
Children's tutoring		
Summer camp		
Babysitting	30	30
Other (vacation)	300	150
TOTAL PERSONAL EXPENSES	**2105**	**1210**
TOTAL BUDGET (SCHEDULES A+B+C)	**4415**	**3360**

The budgets prepared by Will and Liz reflect the way they have been living and also show why their debts have been increasing. Consider the following:

Liz's budget total	$7,065
Will's budget total	$4,415
TOTAL EXPENSES	**$11,480**

These expenses are net after tax, meaning that Will and Liz must earn more money, pay taxes, and then meet their expenses from what is left. Consider their take-home pay.

Will's monthly net pay	$5,996 (salary)
Liz's monthly net pay	$1,551
TOTAL FROM SALARIES	**$7,547**

Additionally, Will expects to receive a bonus at the end of the year of between $20,000 and $70,000. If we assume that 30 percent of the bonus will go to taxes, his net bonus will be between $14,000 and $49,000 or, on a monthly basis, $1,167 to $4,083. If he receives the maximum bonus, the couple will have net income equal to their net proposed expenses. But if his bonus is anything less than the maximum, they will be operating at a deficit. So, if Will receives the maximum bonus and is willing to finance Liz's entire budget deficit, the couple will balance their budgets. This is what it would look like.

Liz's Budget	**$7,065**	**Will's Budget**	**$4,415**
Liz's net pay	1,551	Will's take home pay	5,996
		Will's maximum bonus	4,083
Liz's deficit	$5,554	Will's surplus	$5,681
ALIMONY AND CHILD SUPPORT $5,554			**($5,554)**

When Will sees these figures, he is upset. "There is no way we can as-sume that I will get that bonus any year, much less every year. We have not been having a good year, and the economy isn't going to do much better for at least 2 or 3 years. I am more likely to get a bonus of $20,000 than $70,000, and if the bonus is on the lower end, there is going to be a deficit of $3,000 a month. I cannot and will not give you that much support. I don't have to, and I am entitled to keep enough of my salary so that I can live a decent life. I don't expect to be living in an apartment forever, and I want to be able to buy a house of my own. This budget is strictly tempo-rary, and I'm not going to accept that I can never have my own house again."

Liz agrees that they have a problem, but reiterates her determination to be able to stay home with the kids. "I do not want to move and do not want to go to work full time. Just because Will wants out of the marriage doesn't mean that the kids have to suffer."

Liz and Will are typical upper-middle-class people with typical prob-lems. Even though they have a significant deficit, we have trouble feeling sorry for them. If Will gets his minimum bonus, he and Liz together earn more than $150,000 a year, which puts them in the upper 10 percent of all families in the country. From any objective perspective, we have to con-clude that they have enough money to live well as a divorced family. After all, if they can't do it, who can? They have choices to make that they would prefer not to make. All of us would find it pleasant to be able to spend more, and all of us have a long list of things we would like to have. But that does not mean it's tragic when we can't have all of those things. Liz and Will now have to start bringing their desires into line with their re-sources.

After the mediator has reviewed the couple's budgets with them, he asks them what they plan to do about this looming deficit. Liz and Will have four options: First, they can increase their incomes to balance their bud-gets; second, they can reduce their expenses to match their incomes; third, they can engage in deficit spending and reduce their savings over time; or fourth, they can use some combination of these solutions.

An investigation of the options should look both at ways to reduce spending and ways to increase income. Let's analyze the budgets to see where reductions might be made with minimal pain.

Refinance Debt

Liz and Will bought their house about 10 years ago for $250,000. They took a $200,000 mortgage at 7 percent and have been making their payments ever since. When their credit card debt got too high, they took a home equity loan to consolidate their other short-term debt. Since then, they have accumulated yet another $10,000 in credit card debt between them. Short-term debt is usually more expensive than long-term debt, and interest rates on credit cards are extremely high, sometimes as high as 24 percent. Short-term debt also assumes a shorter period of amortization than long-term debt so that each month you are expected to pay off more of the principal. Paying off principal is good, but if you have a cash-flow problem, it may not be so great. Let's look at this couple's debt payments.

Monthly Payment

Mortgage (7 percent, balance outstanding is $180,000)	1,330
Home equity (balance outstanding $26,000)	350
His credit cards (balance $2,500) minimum payment	120
Her credit cards (balance $8,000) minimum payment	220
TOTAL MONTHLY DEBT PAYMENT	**$2,000**

If the couple were to refinance their mortgage at current rates of 6 percent and borrow enough to consolidate all their debt, they would need a new mortgage of $216,500. And if they also borrowed the closing costs, they would have a new mortgage of $220,000. At 6 percent for a 30-year mortgage, their payments would be $1,320 per month, as shown in column 2 of Liz's budget form. By refinancing, they would reduce their monthly expenses by $680 per month. Although not everyone can do this successfully, it is something you should look at in case it works for you.

Analyzing Discretionary Spending

Let's look at what this family proposes to spend on categories we can label discretionary, in that they could be reduced without eliminating anything vital for survival.

	Liz's budget	Will's budget
Restaurants	200	300
Clothing	350	200
Entertainment	150	250
Gifts	100	50
Psychotherapy	250	
Domestic help	240	240
Vacation	250	300
TOTAL DISCRETIONARY SPENDING	**$1,400** +	**$1,340** = **$2,740**

If discretionary spending were to be reduced by one-half, the saving to the family would be $1,370 per month.

Other Possible Reductions

Life Insurance

Will has a universal life insurance policy that has a modest cash accumulation. The problem with such coverage is that it costs more each month. A term policy pays only if you die, but the same amount of coverage would be $600 a year, for a savings of $100 per month over the universal life policy.

Medical Insurance

Although Liz does not want to go to work full time, if she did get full-time employment, her employer would provide her with medical insurance with a savings to her of $350 per month.

Tutoring

Max goes to a math tutor once a week. If the parents spend more time working with Max, this expense might be reduced by half, for a savings of $100 per month.

Car Lease

Will's car lease is about to expire. He can lease another Saab for $480 per month, or he can lease a Honda Accord for $320 per month. If he leased the Honda, he would save $160 per month.

Summary of Possible Savings

Let's look at the possible areas for saving, beginning with the least painful.

Monthly Savings

Refinance	680
Change life insurance	100
Change car	160
Reduce discretionary spending by half	1,370
Tutoring	100
Medical insurance	350
TOTAL POTENTIAL REDUCTIONS	**$2,760**

Note that the monthly deficit, depending on the size of Will's bonus, varies from no deficit to $3,000.

Three Rounds of Reductions

Another way to reduce your budgets is to make three rounds of reductions. First, you go through your budget and reduce the total by 10 percent. Then you go through it a second time and reduce it by another

10 percent. Finally, you go through it a third time and reduce it by another 10 percent. What you have accomplished by doing three rounds of cuts is you have established your priorities. The things that are easiest to forgo are reduced first, and the things that are dearer to your heart are reduced last.

Increasing Income

Liz wants to continue to work half time so she can take care of the children after school and take them to their appointments and activities. The couple may decide that she should indeed not return yet to full-time employment. But they do need to understand what it would mean if she did. In Liz's case, a full-time job would provide her with an annual salary of $50,000 per year plus benefits. Her net take-home pay would be $3,200 a month, an increase of $1,700 per month. But from this the couple would have to pay increased costs for after-school care for the kids. Liz researches this and finds that anything that would be at all acceptable to her would cost $800 a month. So her net increase in available cash would be $900 per month.

Will has been looking at the job market for some time and says that there are no opportunities at present for him to change jobs and get a significant increase. It may be possible in a few years, but not for now.

For this couple, we now know that there is the possibility to increase their monthly cash flow by at least $3,600 with full-time employment for Liz and budget reductions as indicated. This does not necessarily mean that these are the cuts they ought to make or that there are not other reductions that should be considered. It means that they have many choices to negotiate and that their problems are not at all insurmountable. How they distribute reductions in spending or how they increase their incomes will require considerable negotiation that will, undoubtedly, touch on many emotional issues. But before they begin to negotiate they must first have their facts established, and preparation of budgets is the best way to be prepared.

Allocating for the Children

To determine what your children actually cost, you and your wife need to review your budgets one more time. For each category of expense you will write down in column 2 that part that you attribute to the children. Some expenses, such as children's lessons, are 100 percent allocated to the children. Most of the expenses in Schedule C will be like this. Other expenses are household expenses and need a bit more reflection. When you shop for food, you cannot separate what you spend on food for the children from that which you spend on food that you will eat. So here, a pro rata share is appropriate for the children if they live with you most of the time and somewhat less if they are not primarily in residence with you. So if you look at the budget forms that follow showing Liz's and Will's expenses for the children, you'll see what they have done. Liz allocated one-half of her household food budget to the children and Will allocated one-third of his food budget to the kids. Each also has allocated part of such items as gifts, vacations, and entertainment to the children.

Housing and transportation costs are different. In principle, you allocate to the children only that portion of the expenses that you would not incur if you did not have children with you at all. For example, both Liz and Will have allocated very little of their transportation expenses to the children because both would sustain the complete expense for a car even if there were no children. Will has allocated $200 of his $1,200 rent to the children because that is the difference between what a one-bedroom and a two-bedroom apartment would cost. Liz has allocated the difference between her mortgage and taxes on the house and what she believes she would spend to rent an apartment if she had no children. She also has allocated a small part of her utilities to the children.

By allocating the children's budgets carefully, Liz and Will have determined that the total monthly cost of their children are $2,045 in Liz's home and $545 in Will's home, for a total cost for the children of $2,580. Now the couple can begin to systematically discuss how to fund the children's budgets between them. They can also separate what Liz is proposing to spend on the children from what she proposes to spend on herself.

Although the couple may have some challenging negotiation ahead, they have done their homework and can discuss both alimony and child support from a concrete and factual perspective, in which lifestyle issues and standard of living can be discussed with specificity rather than vague generalizations.

In chapter 12, we will look at the application of the budget to the negotiation of support.

BUDGET FORM

LIZ'S EXPENSES FOR THE CHILDREN

SCHEDULE A: SHELTER	1	2 (Children)
TENANT		
Rent		
Heat		
Utilities		
Tenant insurance		
Other		
HOMEOWNER		
Mortgage	1330	600
Real estate taxes	350	
Homeowners insurance	75	
Heat	125	25
Utilities	125	25
Other (home equity loan)	350	
TENANT OR HOMEOWNER		
Telephone	75	25
Cable TV	60	
Other (cell phone)	50	
TOTAL SHELTER COSTS	**2540**	**675**
SCHEDULE B: TRANSPORTATION		
Auto payment	425	
Auto insurance	100	
Maintenance	50	
Fuel	100	20
Commuting expenses		
TOTAL TRANSPORTATION EXPENSE	**675**	**20**

SCHEDULE C: PERSONAL EXPENSES	1	2 (Children)
Food at home and household supplies	600	300
Restaurants	100	50
Nonprescription drugs, cosmetics, etc.	100	30
Clothing	80	
Hair care	50	25
Entertainment, sports, and hobbies	75	50
Gifts and contributions	50	40
Newspapers and periodicals	30	
Life insurance		
Medical insurance	350	
Unreimbursed medical and dental	150	50
Psychotherapy/counseling	125	
Prescription drugs	80	30
Payments to nonchild dependents		
Prior family child support		
Adult educational expense		
Monthly debt service		
Domestic help	120	60
Orthodontics	100	100
Children's private school costs		
Day care expense		
Children's lessons	160	160
Children's tutoring	100	100
Summer camp	180	180
Babysitting	100	100
Other (vacation)	125	75
TOTAL PERSONAL EXPENSES	**2675**	**1350**
TOTAL BUDGET (SCHEDULES A+B+C)	**5890**	**2045**

BUDGET FORM

WILL'S EXPENSES FOR THE CHILDREN

SCHEDULE A: SHELTER	1	2 (Children)
TENANT		
Rent	1200	200
Heat		
Utilities	100	25
Tenant insurance	30	
Other		
HOMEOWNER		
Mortgage		
Real estate taxes		
Homeowners insurance		
Heat		
Utilities		
Other		
TENANT OR HOMEOWNER		
Telephone	60	10
Cable TV	60	
Other (cell phone)	40	
TOTAL SHELTER COSTS	**1490**	**235**
SCHEDULE B: TRANSPORTATION		
Auto payment	320	
Auto insurance	100	
Maintenance	40	
Fuel	150	
Commuting expenses	50	
TOTAL TRANSPORTATION EXPENSE	**660**	**—**

SCHEDULE C: PERSONAL EXPENSES	1	2 (Children)
Food at home and household supplies	300	100
Restaurants	150	50
Nonprescription drugs, cosmetics, etc.	30	
Clothing	100	
Hair care	20	
Entertainment, sports, and hobbies	125	50
Gifts and contributions	50	30
Newspapers and periodicals	50	
Life insurance	50	
Medical insurance		
Unreimbursed medical and dental	45	
Psychotherapy/counseling		
Prescription drugs	40	
Payments to nonchild dependents		
Prior family child support		
Adult educational expense		
Monthly debt service		
Domestic help	120	
Orthodontics		
Children's private school costs		
Day care expense		
Children's lessons		
Children's tutoring		
Summer camp		
Babysitting	30	30
Other (vacation)	300	50
TOTAL PERSONAL EXPENSES	**1210**	**310**
TOTAL BUDGET (SCHEDULE A+B+C)	**3360**	**545**

"This is just like you, Beverly. We're supposed to meet
alone and you bring your attorney."

Twelve

NEGOTIATING SUPPORT

CHILD SUPPORT AND ALIMONY are the two most complex issues of divorce. For a few wealthy couples, property division is the most difficult issue. But most middle-class couples do not have so much property that dividing it causes much controversy. For these couples, it is ongoing support issues that are the most difficult to negotiate. And of the two, alimony is one that gives men the hardest time. In this chapter, I want to help you think about your approach to these subjects and to suggest ways to make your deliberations easier. First we will look at the basic definition of each.

Child Support Defined

Child support is paid by one spouse to the other to help pay the expenses of the children. Supporting children until they are grown—emancipated—is the responsibility of both parents. All states have some scheme to apportion the expenses of the children between mother and father in proportion to their incomes. But there is significant variation from state to state, and few of the state guidelines for child support are wholly adequate. Child support is generally paid to the parent of primary residence by the other parent. So if the children are living principally with the mother, we would expect to find the father paying child support to her. If the children are living primarily with the father, we would expect to find the mother paying child support. Although that happens on occasion, the most common scenario is that the father pays child support. Child support is paid with after-tax dollars: You earn the money, pay your taxes, and then pay child support from what is left.

Child support is paid until emancipation, but emancipation is defined differently in different states. All states will consider a child emancipated at age 18 or graduation from high school, but some states will extend child support if the child goes to college.

Child Support—How Much Should I Pay?

There are two ways to think about how much child support should be paid. The first is to follow the child support guidelines of your state. About 15 years ago, the Federal Government required all states to establish minimum mandated guidelines for state courts to follow when awarding child support. The legislation was a response to the problem caused by judges who ordered ridiculously low child support and left the primary parent struggling to support the children. The legislation did not establish the same guidelines for all states, but left it to each state to construct its own guidelines. So state courts appointed committees, typically composed of lawyers, to recommend guidelines to the court. In most states the guidelines apply up to some defined, maximum level of family income and then discretion reverts to the court beyond that level of income. The guidelines establish *minimum* levels of support based on the relative incomes of the parties. Judges are not supposed to permit lower levels of support unless the couple can provide compelling justification.

There are several problems inherent in the application of child support guidelines. The first is that the standard of living established by the guidelines is politically established. It depends on the values and training of the lawyers who constitute the committees. Few lawyers are trained in economics or in statistics. They are also sensitive to the various constituencies such as women's groups and father's rights groups that campaign for higher or lower standards. The result is that the amount of child support that would be paid at particular levels of income varies considerably from state to state. And the amount of support that your state guidelines require you to pay for your children may be woefully inadequate to meet their needs. And even though guidelines are supposed to establish minimum standards, most lawyers and judges are too lazy to inquire whether the application of the guidelines in a particular case provides enough support. So for many lawyers, the minimum guidelines also become the maximum guidelines, and they are disinclined to go beyond what the guidelines require.

A second problem with the guidelines is that the way these guidelines have evolved in many states actually promotes conflict between the parents. In the early years of guidelines, formulas were simple. Once the needs of the children were calculated, child support was determined as a fixed percent of the payer's income or was determined by applying a straight ratio of the husband's income to the wife's income. So if he earned $1,000 a week and she earned $500 a week, he would pay two-thirds of the amount determined to be the need of the children. Although there were some conceptual inconsistencies in these formulas, they were at least simple, and anyone could calculate them in a few seconds.

In later versions of the guidelines, the committees charged with formulating them got fancy. In particular, they responded to the lobbying of father's rights groups who wanted support standards reduced in general and more specifically sought a reduction in support when children spent more time with their fathers. Conceptually, the argument had some merit. If children spend more time with fathers, it should lower the costs of the mothers and raise some costs of the fathers and therefore require adjustment of the support. So far, so good. But then several problems arose. To calculate the adjustments that were due required formulas so complex that computer programs were needed to calculate child support. After all, how do you really calculate the impact on household expenses when a child spends one more night a week at the father's house and one less at the mother's house? How do you calculate the change in utilities or food bills? Many expenses are fixed and do not vary, while others vary with time spent. So the result was a set of guidelines that are extremely complex, require more lawyer time, and produce higher legal fees and not much else.

But the biggest problem with the new guidelines is that they link the amount of support a woman receives and a man pays to the amount of time the child spends with the father. So if the mother is the parent of primary residence, she gets less support if the child spends two nights a week with the father than she does if the child spends one night a week with the father. So now mothers became suspicious that the only reason fathers were seeking more time with the kids was because they wanted to pay less support, and the fathers became cynical that the mothers were trying to withhold the children because they wanted more support. Linking the amount of time the child spends with the father to the amount of support paid has been a minor disaster in the courts. It promotes cynicism and leads lawyers to suggest to their clients that the other parent is motivated only by money rather than by the needs of the child. Some lawyers counsel clients to seek more or less time with children simply as a bargaining ploy to minimize or maximize child support. This change has served lawyers well but divorcing families very poorly. It simply has made it more difficult to resolve divorces smoothly, prolonged litigation, and enriched lawyers.

Finally, the guidelines may have little to do with the way you and your wife have chosen to raise your children. Suppose that you have children on whom you spend $1,000 a month, and the child support guidelines say that based on your family income, the children should cost $700 per month. If you insist that your support obligation should be based on the guidelines, then you will, by definition, not pay sufficient support. You will also delegate to your wife the entire burden of deciding how the expenses of the children should be reduced. It is difficult to take such a position and then turn around and claim an equal role in decision making for the children. Child support guidelines were intended as mandatory minimums for people who cannot agree. They assume an adversarial relationship between you and your wife and often result in a bad divorce.

There is a second way to look at how much child support you should pay—as the product of a joint decision-making process between you and your wife, based on the particular needs of your own family.

Alternatives to Child Support Guidelines— Budget-Based Child Support

In the last chapter, I encouraged you to use budgets to determine the needs of your children. I encouraged you to determine the needs of both households and then to separate the expenses for the children. If you have done this diligently, you will have a pretty accurate assessment of what the children cost for each household. I believe that your own assessment is much more accurate than the statistically and politically derived standards depicted in the child support guidelines. Your calculations should be the basis of your child support discussions. That way, you are not simply relying on arbitrary standards that may apply poorly in your case.

CASE STUDY: Craig and Brenda

Craig and Brenda have two children, ages 9 and 6. Craig is an airline pilot who earns $110,000 a year flying for a small commuter airline. Brenda is employed as a claims adjuster for a local insurance company and earns $55,000 a year. The couple have decided to divorce and that the children will live primarily with Brenda because Craig travels so frequently. They have agreed on their respective budgets as follows:

	Brenda's house	Craig's house
Total monthly expenses	$5,700	$3,400
Children's expenses	$2,700	$400
PARENTS' EXPENSES	**$3,000**	**$3,000**
Brenda's take-home pay: $3,575		
Craig's take-home pay: $6,700		
BRENDA'S MONTHLY DEFICIT: ($2,125)		
CRAIG'S MONTHLY SURPLUS: $3,300		

Let's look at the different ways Craig and Brenda can calculate child support. Brenda does not seek alimony, so that is not an issue.

Child Support Guidelines

Craig and Brenda consult the guidelines and find that for two children in families with total income of $165,000 a year, guidelines project the total cost of $2,200. The guidelines allocate the cost proportionate to income, and as Craig earns two-thirds of the total family income, his projected child support would be two-thirds of $2,200, or $1,467 per month. His lawyer has told him that he does not have to pay more than that if he does not want to. So if Craig pays the guidelines support of $1,467, Brenda will be left with a deficit each month of $651. Note that Brenda and Craig have each calculated their individual costs at $3,000 per month.

Where is Brenda to make up her deficit? She will have to reduce her own standard of living, reduce the children's standard of living, or both. And where will this leave Craig? He has a budget surplus of $3,300 from which he pays $1,467, leaving what is now a monthly surplus of $1,833. His budget is fully funded, while the budgets for Brenda and the children are reduced approximately 11 percent.

Real Costs of the Children with Pro-Rata Allocation

The first alternative is to calculate support based on the actual cost of the children and apply the ratio of income earned by each party. The total cost of the children has been calculated at $3,100, of which $2,700 is incurred in Brenda's house and $400 is incurred in Craig's house. If Craig should pay two-thirds of this, he should pay a total of $2,067, of which he is already paying $400 in his own house. So he should pay Brenda the difference of $1,667. Now Brenda will have a deficit of $448 a month, while Craig has a surplus of $1,623. Again Brenda has a difficult choice. If she is to spend the $3,000 on herself that she and Craig each calculated as their own personal expenses, then she must manage her $448 per month deficit by unilaterally reducing the children's standard of living. Or, if she is unwilling to cut the children's consumption, she will have to cut her own consumption by $448 each month and in effect give that to the children. In either case, she will be resentful watching Craig enjoy a surplus while she absorbs what she regards as a disproportionate share of the children's expenses.

Real Costs of the Children
with Pro-Rata Allocation Based on Income

The real problem with the way lawyers allocate child support is that they assume that it is fair to allocate support based on proportion of earnings. Thus, if a wife earns one-quarter of the income, she should pay one-quarter of the support. But why is this fair? The assumption made by the lawyers is that people should pay relative to their ability to pay and that by allocating based on percent of family income earned, we are allocating based on ability to pay. But when we look at how this applies to Brenda and Craig, we are left with some troubling inconsistencies. If Brenda and Craig each need $3,000 for themselves, what is really their capacity to contribute to the children? Brenda only brings home $3,575 a month and needs $3,000 for herself. If we tell her to pay one-third of the children's costs, which is $1,033, how does that relate to her ability to pay? In fact, it does not; and our system leaves Brenda with a deficit, while it leaves Craig with a surplus.

To be really fair, we would measure ability to contribute to the children by what is left over after each has paid essential costs—in other words, from their discretionary income. After paying $3,000 for herself, Brenda has $575 left each month. After paying $3,000 for himself, Craig has $3,700 left each month. What happens if we base our allocation on the percent of discretionary income?

Craig's discretionary income per month	$3,700
Brenda's discretionary income per month	$575
TOTAL DISCRETIONARY INCOME	**$4,275**
CRAIG'S PERCENT OF DISCRETIONARY INCOME	**86.5%**
BRENDA'S PERCENT OF DISCRETIONARY INCOME	**13.5%**

Now, let's apply this to the couple's budgets and see what we get. Total cost of the children is $3,100, of which Craig should pay 86.5 percent or $2,681. He is already paying $400 in his own house, so his payment to Brenda is $2,261.

	Brenda's Budget	Craig's Budget
	$5,700	$3,400
Income	$3,575	$6,700
Child support	$2,261	($2,261)
SURPLUS	**$136**	**$1,039**

With this allocation, the children's budgets are fully funded in each household. Craig and Brenda's needs are fully funded. Brenda has a small budget surplus of $136, while Craig has a larger budget surplus of $1,039. Craig is still wealthier than Brenda, a reflection of his greater income. We have not made them equal. But we have allocated child support fairly between them.

The method of equitable child support allocation described here is not reflected in any of the child support guidelines of which I am aware. I know of few lawyers who use this approach. But it is the only way to do this if what you seek is fairness. Your lawyer will not encourage you to use this method, nor would a judge use this method if you were in court. So you don't have to do it. Nevertheless I believe that a good divorce—one that is fair to everyone and that thus breeds cooperation rather than competition—requires this type of analysis, and I recommend it to you.

Other Child Support Issues

Health and Life Insurance

Most child support agreements specify which parent will provide health insurance for the children. Most couples have at least one partner who is employed and who can cover the children through an employer's group health insurance at reasonable cost. When that is possible, it is preferred because it saves money and usually provides better coverage than is available through individual plans. The extra cost of the children's premium is a negotiable item. The agreement should also provide how you and your wife will pay for uninsured medical and dental expenses. For the most part, that is limited to copayments for medical treatment but can involve considerable expense for dental needs such as orthodontia, or for psychological counseling. These expenses should be apportioned between you and your wife, based on ability to pay, in a manner similar to how the two of you decide to allocate child support.

You should also agree on life insurance to provide for the children if one of you dies. I encourage people to estimate the total projected support to be paid until the child is emancipated and to provide an amount of term insurance to cover that. Ideally, both parents will provide life insurance for the benefit of the children. The surviving parent should be designated as trustee. If you die, the children will be solely reliant on their mother, and she should not have to go, hat in hand, seeking money from former in-laws every time she needs to spend on the children. Unless she is overtly incompetent with money management, she should be the trustee. Term insurance is usually the only sensible way to get life insurance when cash flow is tight. Universal and whole life policies are really savings programs, and if you do have money to invest, there are more efficient ways to do it.

College

Many couples want to address the issue of paying for college for the children. If your children are approaching college age, this will be more urgent than if your children are younger. As mentioned, whether you have a legal obligation to contribute to your child's college expenses varies from state to state. Assuming that you want your children to attend college, how should you negotiate this with your wife? You do not want to leave it up in the air, but you also do not want to bind yourself to pay unlimited amounts for college. Although the majority of children attend college at state-supported institutions that cost from $10,000 to $15,000 per year, it is possible to spend upward of $40,000 a year at Duke, Columbia, or any Ivy League university.

Considering that this comes from after-tax dollars, there are few parents who can afford to give their children carte blanche to choose any school they want. I have seen couples impoverish themselves in order to send children to very expensive private colleges. I do not believe it is fair to the parents and do not believe it is at all wise to do. So there are a number of important things you may want to consider.

First, if you are going to commit to paying for college in your separation agreement, you should specify that the obligation is limited to the cost of room, board, and tuition at a state school for a state resident. A child who wants to attend a more expensive institution can take student loans, work, or negotiate other arrangements with the parents. Second, you can put aside money now or decide to manage it when the child goes to college. For most people, divorce stretches their cash flow so much that putting additional money away for savings while paying alimony or child support is unlikely to happen. If you and your wife have significant assets, you might decide to sequester some for college before dividing the assets between the two of you. This is ideal if you have the money. If not, you will have to agree to manage college when the need arises and agree that each of you will contribute relative to your ability to pay and to discuss the matter further when the child enters the junior year of high school. One final thought on college: If you are going to put money aside for college, think twice before putting it in the child's name. Having significant funds in the child's name, even in a custodial account, may preclude the child from obtaining financial aid. It is better to keep it in accounts in the parents' names and use it for college when the time comes.

The Psychology of Support

If you are in the majority of divorcing men who are paying child support to ex-wives, there are a number of things you may find troubling about child support. First is a feeling that you are paying money to your ex-wife rather than to your children. Some men want to spend the money directly, paying for clothing and other items, rather than through child support. But if the child is living principally with her mother and it is her mother who is directly administering the financial affairs of the child, having you pay bills introduces a level of complexity that will inevitably break down and cause trouble later. Simplicity is elegant and should be pursued. Your feeling that you have lost control because your ex does not have to provide you with an accounting is understandable on your part, but it is one for which there is no practical remedy. You need to get over it.

Another major problem that often arises in support discussions is the tendency of the mother to emerge as the economic bargaining agent for the children. This is most likely in traditional arrangements, in which the children live with her, you pay support, and she spends the money on the children. During support negotiations, there is usually spirited discussion about how much money is necessary for this and that. Invariably, we find the mother arguing in favor of additional spending on the child and the father, who is expected to pay, arguing for less spending. If you are not cautious, she slides into the role of the children's bargaining agent and you slide into the role of resentful provider. This is a bad psychological position for both of you because it positions her as the good guy and you as the bad guy.

The way to avoid this trap is to insist that the two of you follow a disciplined budgeting process. If the two of you have jointly calculated what the children cost, then any reductions in the children's budgets have to be decided on by both of you. And if there is a budget deficit, then any extra money to be spent on the children has to be balanced by specific reductions in the budgets of the parents. By making continual reference to the budgets, you insist on financial discipline for the whole family and stay out of the trap that arises when she gets to pose as the only parent dedicated to the children.

It is understandable that parents want to avoid depriving their children of the amenities of life. It is not unusual to find one or both parents arguing that the adults should do without whenever it is a question of reducing the standard of living for the children. The welfare of the children easily becomes a pious invocation of one or both parents, intended to embarrass the other parent into further concessions on behalf of the children. So people who cannot afford to keep their children in private school keep them there, even though it wrecks the overall family finances, because they feel too guilty to impose change on the children. I do not believe that you do your children any favors by casting the entire family into financial chaos because you do not have an adequate perspective on the situation. As I have noted so many times throughout this book, divorce is about change. All members of the family have to absorb their share of change and dislocation. All may have to tighten their belts for a while. For the parents to sacrifice their basic needs to preserve amenities for the children is shortsighted. Your children will thrive only to the extent that you and their mother thrive. You shortchange them if you render yourself or your wife perpetually broke for want of financial discipline applied to the children. Imagine that all needs could be ranked on a scale of 1 to 10. Having enough food to eat is a 10. But having lobster is a 1. Having proper clothing is a 10, but having a particular pair of designer jeans is a 1. In principle, no one in the family should get level 5 needs met until everyone else in the family has had level 4 needs satisfied. The family needs to share in good fortune and less fortune, more or less equally.

Rich House/Poor House

When couples agree on joint custody, with the children living half-time with each parent, child support discussions can easily bog down without careful consideration. Here is the problem. The father and mother each have to maintain a home fully equipped for the children. Each home needs a separate bedroom for each child, and each needs a full complement of computers, play stations, books, games, and other equipment that modern children demand. Consequently, the total costs for two completely equipped homes will exceed the total cost when one home is primary and the other is used by the children predominantly on weekends. Real joint custody is more expensive than joint legal custody. So when you budget you have to allow for this.

Joint custody does not work very well when there is a great disparity in the living standards of the two houses. The children quickly figure out where the goodies are, and their behavior will soon reflect that. Managing the consequential hard feelings of the parent in the "poor" home then becomes difficult. What this means is that your budgeting for joint custody will reflect higher costs, and the child support guidelines are a very poor guide for making joint custody work.

Alimony Defined

Alimony, also known as spousal maintenance, is support paid by one spouse to the other. I see one or two cases a year in which wives pay alimony to husbands, but it is clearly the exception. For the most part, husbands pay alimony to wives. Alimony differs from child support in that it is paid with pretax dollars. The payer gets to deduct alimony from gross income before calculating taxes. The recipient treats the alimony as taxable income. This may have some significant financial implications, as we shall see later.

When discussing alimony, we are concerned with three issues: whether alimony should be paid at all, how much alimony should be paid, and for how long it should be paid.

Should Alimony Be Paid?

Whether alimony should be paid generally depends on many factors. The two most important elements are need and capacity. First, alimony is not an issue if husband and wife both have the same income. So if you earn $75,000 a year and she earns $67,000 a year, this is not an alimony case. Alimony requires a significant disparity in income. There is no clear threshold of disparity that demarks the alimony case from the non-alimony case, but as a rule of thumb, I would suggest that unless your income is at least 50 percent greater than your wife's income, there is probably no alimony due. When there is significant disparity, alimony serves to reduce it. But there is no necessary premise that the two incomes be equalized. There are some conditions under which you want to consider the equalization of household incomes, but we will come to those later.

Types of Alimony

As mentioned in chapter 5, there are generally three types of alimony, each defined by how long alimony is to be paid and under what conditions it terminates. The first type is called rehabilitative alimony. This is alimony intended to support the spouse until she is able to support herself. It assumes that she is obligated to work for her own support and assumes that once she is employed, the alimony designated as rehabilitative will end.

Rehabilitative alimony is generally defined by how long it will take the wife to complete some educational, training, or other credentialing activity so she can qualify for employment at some defined level. There is a broad range of possible definitions here. A high school graduate who has been married 6 years might have rehabilitative alimony to qualify her for a year of training to become a secretary or a paralegal. Or a wife with a college degree might qualify for support through graduate school to get a law degree, an MSW, or another professional degree. It is a matter of what the couple agrees is a reasonable goal under the circumstances. Rehabilitative alimony can also be paid to supplement the salary of a woman who has been out of the paid workforce for some years and needs time to reestablish herself in a career for which she has the credentials but needs to rebuild her foothold in the industry.

When discussing rehabilitative alimony, we want to be able to specify the goals and objectives of the rehabilitation. We want to decide ahead of time the income level to which the wife is to be restored or the credential she will achieve before we regard her as economically rehabilitated and therefore ready for economic independence.

The second type of alimony, and the most traditional, is "permanent" alimony that is paid until the wife remarries or one of the parties dies. I put permanent in quotes because nothing is really permanent. It would be better to call it alimony of indeterminate duration, but the law calls it permanent or even lifetime alimony. This type of alimony recalls the days when women assumed a traditional homemaker role and did not assume an equal place in the workplace. Such alimony is paid until another man comes along to support the wife. In fault-based divorce, such alimony was paid only when there was a finding that the marital misconduct of the husband was the cause of the marital failure. If the wife was at fault, she received no alimony. Although permanent alimony was originally the creation of fault-based divorce, it has persisted under no-fault divorce.

The third type of alimony is alimony for a period of years, for a term either negotiated by the parties or imposed by judgment of the court. Alimony for a period of years is generally used as a compromise between permanent alimony and rehabilitative alimony. Whereas a long-term marriage would be expected to require permanent alimony and a short-term marriage would support only rehabilitative alimony, alimony for a period of years is designed to accommodate marriages of medium duration in which the courts are reluctant to impose an indeterminate alimony but are equally hesitant to limit alimony to rehabilitative support. Whereas there is an inherent logic to both permanent and rehabilitative alimony, there is no such logic that attaches to alimony for a period of years. We have no assurance that the wife will be able to support herself at the end of this period. If alimony is negotiated for 10 years, for example, it simply means that for the next 10 years, the wife will assume the risk that she will remarry or that she will be able to support herself at the standard of living that she seeks. Alimony for a fixed period is more about how risk is to be distributed than it is about anything else. Not all states have this type of alimony. All states will enforce a settlement agreement that specifies alimony for a period of years, but not all states will permit the court to impose such limits on alimony.

The Psychology of Alimony

The negotiation of alimony is the greatest challenge to most men when it comes to having a gentle divorce. If your wife is self-supporting, if the disparity between your incomes is not great, or if she is not seeking alimony, you will have a relatively simple and easy divorce. But when you have to cope with the feelings that often result from a demand that you continue to pay support to a woman with whom you no longer have a life, divorce is more difficult. And when your wife is the initiator and you don't want the divorce, her demand that you continue to support her can feel infuriating.

CASE STUDY: Marvin and Judy

Marvin and Judy are negotiating their separation agreement. Marvin is a physician and Judy has been a homemaker for 27 years, after an early career as a nurse. She never particularly liked being a nurse, and when

Marvin started to succeed in his practice, Judy was happy to give up nursing and devote herself to making a home for Marvin and their three children. Marvin is now 59 and Judy is 51. Their marriage has eroded for many years, and 6 months ago Judy told Marvin that she wanted a divorce. She had pleaded with him for years to devote more time to her and the family but felt that Marvin always put his practice first. Marvin resented Judy's critique because he believed that as an infectious disease specialist, he had no choice but to work the hours necessary to serve his patients. All successful physicians put in long hours, and Marvin believed that Judy was just unfair in her demands. The couple had never been able to resolve this issue, and Judy had gradually built a life for herself that had less and less to do with Marvin. She had made her own friends, become active in volunteer projects in the community and at their church, and devoted herself to supervising the three children, the youngest of whom was now in college.

When Judy told Marvin that she wanted a divorce, he was shocked at first. But as he thought about it he became angry with Judy. He had always worked as hard as he could to provide for his family. Now, when he was just approaching the time that he might slow down a little and be able to relax more often, here was Judy bailing out. It felt as if she had used him to get the kids raised and now that they were all off on their own she was done with him. Now she was going to go play and expect him to continue to work and support her. He felt used and abandoned by her.

Although they decided to try mediation, Marvin only agreed because he had heard how lawyers loved to litigate when doctors were involved, and he feared that legal costs would get out of hand if they did a litigated divorce. He was hoping to avoid an ugly fight but was nevertheless angry and indignant about the divorce.

Judy consulted with several lawyers. All the lawyers told her that because she was an economically dependent spouse, she was entitled to receive alimony from Marvin even though she was the one who wanted a divorce. Marvin earned about $300,000 a year and had the capacity to support her. They had been married for 27 years, and long-term marriages

*such as hers, she was told, justified permanent alimony—meaning that
Marvin would have to support her until she remarried, one of them died, or
the court allowed him to retire. Not only was she entitled to receive alimony, but under the laws of New Jersey, she was entitled to receive
enough alimony to allow her to live "in the manner to which she was accustomed," so long as Marvin earned enough income to afford that level of
support.*

*Marvin also consulted with lawyers and was told that indeed, he could
expect to pay alimony and that considering his income, the length of the
marriage, and the fact that Judy did not have a career, he could end up
paying as much as one-third of his income to Judy. "You mean to tell me
that I have to work 60 hours a week and she gets a third of my income for
doing nothing? How is that fair? She no longer has to do anything for me. I
lose the benefit of her services as a homemaker and companion, but she
gets to receive a big chunk of my income as long as she wants. That's
outrageous!"*

*His lawyer advised him that he could fight it in court but that it was
very unlikely that a judge would deny her alimony. They could struggle
in court to keep the alimony to a minimum, but the law in these cases
suggested that she would get substantial alimony. "Well, doesn't she
have any obligation to work? She is a trained nurse. I'm sure she would
need some retraining, but at most, she would need a year of training
and could easily earn $40,000 a year or more in any hospital around
here. Why is she able to retire and sit on her butt while I'm out busting
mine?"*

*Again the lawyer could only provide infuriatingly vague answers. "Well,
it would depend on what judge we got. Some judges might decide that she
had been a homemaker for so long that she didn't have to resume a career at 51, particularly one for which her skills were no longer current. We
might get a judge who expected her to earn something, and we might even
convince the judge to impute some income to her. That means that the
judge would assume that she was able to earn money and would reduce
the alimony to reflect that. But remember that the standard of living we're
talking about is based on what you earn, and even if the judge required*

her to work, the $30,000 or $40,000 she could earn would only reduce your obligation. She would never be expected to live on that salary. I hate to tell you, but you are swimming upstream on this one."

Marvin did not like what he was hearing. "But what about retirement? We had always talked about my retiring at 60, getting a smaller house on the water, and enjoying life before I got too old. What happens if I retire next year as I had planned?" Again the lawyer's answer was not comforting. "You can retire, but that does not mean that you would be excused from paying alimony. If she is able to earn enough income from her share of the assets to support herself, you might find a judge who would let you out. But remember that you are going to be talking to a judge who earns less than half of what you do and who can't retire until 65. In this state, a voluntary reduction of alimony does not usually support an application to reduce alimony. We do have some cases that suggest that if you retire at 65, the court will regard that as reasonable and reduce alimony. But there are no guarantees, even then." "So, let me get this straight," asked an incredulous Marvin, "I can't retire when we planned, but she can retire now. I have to work as hard as ever, but she doesn't have to do anything. She doesn't have to work, but I do. She doesn't have to do anything for me, but I have to support her. Tell me, where is the justice in this?" The lawyer could only shrug his shoulders.

Alimony and Anger

Marvin's sentiments are not unusual and reveal almost all the issues that arise in a negotiation about alimony.

Fault and Alimony

If she is leaving me, why do I have to support her? If I didn't do anything wrong, why do I get punished because she decides to dump the marriage? It is understandable that men experience the requirement of alimony as punishment. But punishment no longer has a place in the modern divorce.

With the shift to no-fault divorce, alimony can no longer be linked to misconduct but must be based on general concepts of equity and fairness. Marriage is a joint venture in which each spouse contributes and shares in the good and bad fortune of the marriage. Although husbands are more often than not the primary breadwinners, or at least earn more than their wives, the domestic contribution of the wife is her way of contributing to the welfare of the family.

Alimony has increasingly become more determined by general principles of contract in which the wife, having relied to her economic detriment on the economic contribution of the husband while she concentrated on homemaking and children, is entitled to continue to share in the benefits of the husband's career. It is now assumed that her contribution to the family has made it possible for him to leave the home every day and go to work. Without her contribution, he would have had to do both wage earning and homemaking and would not have been able to concentrate on career. If the wife failed to develop her own income-earning capacity because she had stayed home or worked part-time or gave up opportunities of self-advancement, it would be unfair to now tell her that she would have to unilaterally absorb the cost of that decision. So the needs of the wife seen in the context of the marital contract struck by the two parties has become the basis for considering alimony.

But the advent of no-fault divorce has not necessarily meant that divorcing people approach divorce form the psychological perspective of no-fault. When one of the spouses believes that the other has "caused" the divorce, it is not unnatural to believe that the other spouse should also absorb the consequences of the perceived bad behavior. The psychological stance of the noninitiator of the divorce is: "You want this and I don't. So you pay the price and leave me alone." "You want to leave me, so you go support yourself!" Or, "If you want to leave me, you'd better be prepared to support me anyhow!"

If She Can Work, Doesn't She Have to Do So?

As a general rule, your wife has an obligation to contribute to her own support if she is able to do so. If she has been employed throughout the marriage, she is expected to continue her employment and her income is applied to meet her needs before alimony is considered. The issue becomes more complex when she has not been employed throughout the marriage, if she gave up a career to devote herself to home and children, or if she has been employed only part time because she is caring for children at home.

Generally, your wife will seek to maintain the status quo. If the two of you had decided that she should stay home with the kids, don't be surprised that she wants to continue that way. If she has been a homemaker for 25 years and the kids are now out of the house, she will be reluctant—and perhaps frightened—to start a career in her late forties or fifties. And, depending on how much income you have, she may not have to go back to employment. It will depend on several factors. First, is there enough income that the two of you can maintain the status quo, more or less, without her resuming employment? If you are earning $65,000 a year as a teacher and the two of you have been struggling for many years to make it on that income, there will be more pressure on her to contribute financially. But if you are earning $165,000 as an executive and the two of you have not been struggling, there will be less pressure on her to begin a career.

Second, it also depends on how much she could earn. If she has a high school education and can earn $6 an hour, her contribution would be less significant than if she has an MBA and within a year can earn $50,000.

Third is the age and needs of your children. If your wife has been the primary caretaker for the kids and the cost of day care and after-school supervision would eat up most of her earnings, there is a less compelling argument for her returning to employment than if the youngest child is 16 and can take care of herself after school. So in the end, it comes to issues of need and capacity, and you will need to be pragmatic and reasonable in your approach. Your obligation to support her is derivative of the implicit marital contract by which you have lived, and you will have to engage her in a dialogue about that contract.

Why So Long?

Why does it have to go on for so long? Don't I have a right to a life, too?

The duration of alimony is generally determined by the length of the marriage and by whether it is realistic to expect that the wife will be able to earn enough income to support herself at a comparable level. All states provide that alimony ends upon the remarriage of the wife. We know that 75 percent of divorced women remarry within 5 years. This suggests that a majority of men who are paying alimony will not have to pay it for more than 5 years. On a statistical basis, there is only a one-in-five chance that you will have to pay alimony for longer than that. So what we are discussing when we talk about alimony that is long-term or "permanent" is the management of risk that your wife will not be married in 5 years and that she will not be able to support herself in an acceptable manner within 5 years.

The duration of the alimony obligation is thus related to the same historical facts as is the amount of alimony. Length of marriage, needs and capacity of each spouse, and the contract of the marriage still shape the outcome to this question.

How Much of My Income Is She Entitled To?

Several times, I have used the phrase "in the style to which she has become accustomed." To that we need to add some qualifiers. First is the question of whether you can afford it. In American society, there is no consensus about what people need. There are people who believe that a 2,000-square-foot house in a middle-class suburb is wonderful. And there are others who regard their 6,000-square-foot house as not grand enough. Most folks are happy with a Toyota, but others, who wear their cars like garments, feel deprived if they have to drive anything other than a luxury, high-status car. So what do we really need? The elaboration of need has been so extreme, particularly in the past 15 years, that once we get beyond basics, "need" becomes almost totally subjective. Alimony is supposed to address the subject of need, but we have no legislated or judicial consensus on just what people need.

So we again revert to history and contract. What you need is defined by what you are used to. If you have to do with less than you are accustomed to, that is defined as deprivation. So to have what you need, you seek to maintain the status quo, even if on a relative basis it seems like extreme luxury to others. The legal notion of "the style to which she is accustomed" is nothing more than a stated preference for the status quo. If the two of you have lived a Spartan existence, this will not be the time to ramp up to luxury. And if the two of you have had an elaborate lifestyle, the legal system will deprive either of you of it reluctantly.

If we assume that an important category in alimony negotiation is historical lifestyle, then the question arises how long people have to be married in order for the wife to acquire an entitlement to continue in that lifestyle. It is unclear just how long you have to be married for your wife's lifestyle to vest. Suppose that Marvin was already a millionaire as a result of smart investing in the stock market when he married Judy, a nurse with few assets. And suppose that they had lived together in his fancy mansion and that he had provided her with a fancy car and a luxurious way of life with fancy vacations, four-star restaurants, and shopping trips at elite stores. Suppose further that she had stopped working as a nurse to devote herself to being Marvin's companion. Let's also suppose that the couple did not have children.

How long does the marriage have to last for Judy to acquire the right to continuity of lifestyle if the marriage breaks up? Few would argue that Judy would have acquired much of an entitlement to alimony at any level if the marriage ends in 2 years. But what if the marriage ends in 7 years? What about 15 years? The longer the marriage lasts and the more Judy becomes accustomed to this way of life, the greater her claim. And if Judy has given up her career and become rusty in her skills, what is Marvin's responsibility to compensate for the loss of her career? As a nurse, Judy is in a field where knowledge changes rapidly. Someone out of nursing for 15 years has missed the whole revolution in computerized records, is way behind in knowledge of medications, and has missed great changes in medical technique. She may be able to requalify after a year of study, but she will now have to compete with others many years her junior. She has lost her seniority and forfeited many years of professional advancement. And no matter how many hours she works as a nurse, she can never earn enough to even approximate the standard of living to which she is now accustomed.

The question of fairness also arises here. Suppose that the reason the couple is getting divorced is that Marvin has grown bored with the relationship and after 15 years has found a younger woman. Does this mean anything, or is it just Judy's tough luck? Does she have to unilaterally absorb all the change that springs from Marvin's decision, or does she get protected in any way at all? Fault is not the issue. The issue is whether or not she has relied to her own detriment on Marvin's earlier assurance that they would be together permanently. And again, the questions are: What is her need? How is that need defined historically? What is her capacity to earn? What is your capacity to earn?

What Was Your Contract?

One of the things I encourage couples to do when negotiating alimony is to imagine that they were at the beginning of their marriage and were trying to decide how to allocate responsibility for earning money and domestic duties between them. You do not yet have children. You are each capable of earning a living, and you are each capable of developing a career. But when you decided to marry, you had both envisioned a traditional life with a home and children, and you want this for yourself.

So you want your wife to get pregnant and bear children. Childbearing and raising children will be large distractions from her career. She says that she is willing to take time off but is worried that her ability to earn will suffer. She quotes from a study that she read that said that women lose approximately 3 percent of their income capacity or income ceiling for each year they take off from their careers. She is willing to take a short maternity leave but will have to return to her career shortly after each child is born. In that event, she expects that you will take an equal role in caring for the child or children as they come along. You will be equally responsible for doctor visits, school issues, shopping expeditions, and the myriad tasks associated with raising children and running the house. You will stay home half the days that a child is home sick, and you will be equally responsible for transporting children to lessons, soccer games, and who knows what else.

You will arrange with your employer to be home for dinners with the children, and if your need to work shorter hours interferes with your own career development, you will cheerfully accept the consequences.

If you do all of these things, your wife will take responsibility for her own economic future. She will not subordinate her career to the family needs, and she will be as able as you are to put in the long hours necessary for promotion and advancement in the corporate and professional world. That is the alimony-free contract. To the extent that you deviate and your wife becomes dependent on your income for her future, you acquire an obligation to share the economic risk of your marriage proving unsuccessful because it would be unfair to simply shift all that risk to her.

I understand that it may be difficult for you to reconstruct the past as a hypothetical, but it is a useful exercise to cut through the fog of resentment you may feel when asked to part with a significant chunk of your future income to support an ex-wife. There has to be some commitment on your part to justice here, for if there is not, then your divorce will just play out as a battle of wills in a courtroom.

Some Principles for Thinking about Alimony

▶ The longer the marriage lasts, the greater the premise of parity in income.

▶ You both are obligated to contribute, but there has to be recognition of the impact of domesticity on income-producing capacity.

▶ There is economic value in staying home to attend to children. This applies to both past and future.

▶ In a long-term marriage, you have both acquired the right to maintain the status quo if you can afford it and to share in economic retrenchment if you cannot afford the status quo.

▶ Alimony is a pragmatic solution to a practical problem. It is not an appropriate vehicle of retribution or vindication.

Although this last point may seem obvious, it deserves special attention. As in most matters of divorce, your attitude will be reciprocated. If you approach alimony—or the withholding thereof—as a way to exact revenge on your wife for a failed relationship, your wife in turn will see alimony as a way to stick it to you. Remember: Alimony is a business transaction.

Thirteen

DIVIDING THE PROPERTY

KIRK AND KAREN ARE TRYING TO NEGOTIATE *how they are going to divide their property, and both are getting angrier by the minute. They married 20 years ago and have two children. Kirk is a police lieutenant and has only 2 years to go before he is eligible for retirement. The couple has owned a house for 18 years, which is now worth $220,000, with only a $47,000 mortgage balance left. They bought the house in 1985 using a $25,000 inheritance from Karen's grandfather as their down payment, but they own it jointly. They also have a 401(k) plan for Kirk with $67,000, an IRA of Karen's with $20,000, and some savings bonds inherited by Kirk from his mother valued at $18,000. Kirk has an antique car he owned before the marriage but restored during the marriage. He estimates it is worth $20,000. Finally, Karen has written and published two cookbooks during the marriage and last year received royalties of $6,000 from her publisher.*

Karen and Kirk have each been to see their lawyers in anticipation of discussing property division. Karen says that her lawyer told her that she was entitled to half of Kirk's police pension, half his 401(k) plan, and half the house plus repayment of the down payment that came from her grandfather's estate. She says that although she doesn't seek half of Kirk's savings bonds because they are inherited, she wants half the value of his antique car. She also says that she feels he is not entitled to any part of the value of her books, because she wrote them without any help from him, and in fact

in the face of a lot of discouragement from him. As Karen speaks, Kirk be-
comes red with anger. "You are so selfish. I've slaved over that house for 18
years. I paid the mortgage, built the deck, repainted the house, rehabilitated
the garage, and probably doubled its value with my hard work while you did
next to nothing, Where do you get off saying that you want the down pay-
ment back? That house should be more than half mine, and there is no way
you are getting more than half. You want your books because you wrote
them, but you want half my pension. What in hell did you do to earn that
pension? I worked nights, risked my life, and put up with 18 years of crap
from that department so I could retire early. You are not getting half my
pension, and I'll see you in court first. You're also not getting the car. I
owned it before we got married and I slaved to fix it up. It's mine, and you
can just forget about it!"

Kirk and Karen have some serious negotiating to do if they are going to
reach agreement. The division of marital property can be complicated, not
only because the law is complex, but also because the property can be-
come symbolic of all the struggles that caused the divorce. Before
watching this couple sort it out, let's look first at the law of equitable
distribution.

Overview of Equitable Distribution

Equitable distribution is notable for what it is not. Under rules of equitable
distribution, the divorce court is empowered to order property that is defined as marital to be transferred from one spouse to another without regard to the fact that title is in only one name. So having title to the property
does not mean that you get to keep it or that you don't get a share of it. But
equitable distribution is not community property. There is no legal assumption that the property is to be divided equally between the partners. So if it
doesn't belong to the person whose name is on it, and it doesn't get split
50-50, how is it supposed to be divided?

The law has provided a complex hodgepodge of principles that the judge
is supposed to apply. Although many of these principles fall away in practice, it is instructive to review them briefly. First, the marriage is to be seen
as an economic partnership in which each partner should, upon dissolution

of the partnership, be able to take those assets that he or she has produced. That is, if I created it, I ought to get it. If we created it together, it should be divided between us. But if you had nothing to do with creating it, you should not share in it. If this were the only principle applied, how would our couple, Kirk and Karen, fare in their divorce? Karen played no direct role in earning Kirk's pension and he played no direct role in writing her books, so shouldn't each keep the assets produced?

Equitable distribution law recognizes that the contributions of each spouse to any particular asset are not easy to discern. So the law states quite explicitly that the court, when deciding how to distribute the assets, must consider the noneconomic contribution of the non-employed spouse. In the case of a woman who stays home to manage the household and take care of the children, the court is to assume that her work at home made it possible for the husband to go to his job, earn money, and accumulate wealth. So even though Karen stayed home and Kirk went to work each week as a police officer, it is assumed that her job as manager of the home *made it possible* for him to go to work, and therefore she has earned a share of his pension. Similarly the fact that he supported her while she stayed home and wrote her books should entitle him to a share of the royalties earned by the book. But that does not necessarily mean that the asset should be divided equally between the two.

Having determined that the asset is marital property (we'll get to that in a minute), the court is supposed to apply several other criteria in a search for a just and equitable distribution. These criteria, depending on the state, include the following:

▶ The length of the marriage

▶ The needs of each party

▶ The age and credentials of each spouse

▶ The earning capacity of each spouse

▶ The amount of separate nondistributable property owned by each spouse

▶ The amount of debt of each spouse

▶ The age of each spouse

▶ The economic contribution of each spouse, except that in calculating the contribution of each spouse, appropriate recognition is to be given to the noneconomic domestic contribution of the nonemployed spouse

▶ The amount of property held separately by each spouse that is not subject to equitable distribution

▶ Other criteria that the court deems fair and just to consider

Among these criteria is not to be found the concept of fault, which except under the most egregious circumstances, is not to be applied. As a rule, division of property is no-fault.

Now you may ask, "With all these criteria, how do we know what a judge would order in any particular case? And if 99 percent of all divorces are settled by negotiation and a judge never actually hears the case, how do we know how to apply these principles?" It seems confusing because it is.

Before we sort it out, let's take a look at several other aspects of equitable distribution. The first question we ask when beginning to consider the subject in any divorce is: What property is marital and what property is subject to equitable distribution?

Separate Property

Any property that you owned before the marriage and that you still own in the same form you owned it before you married is separate property. It belongs to you alone, and the judge cannot give all or part of it to your wife. So the Rolex watch that you owned before the marriage that you still own is still yours. Any property given by a third party to you alone as a gift is your separate property. If your Uncle George gave you the Rolex as a present, it is yours alone. Finally, any property that you inherited during the marriage is yours alone. If during the marriage Uncle George died, leaving you the Rolex in his will, it is yours alone.

Most separate property is not as simple as Uncle George's Rolex watch. Kirk had an antique car before the marriage. Had he never fixed it, it would still be his alone. If you have separate property and it increases in value as a result of *passive market forces*, it is still yours and the increase in value is also yours alone. This applies to real estate, market accounts, stocks, bonds, and other securities as well. If the increase in value is the result of simple changes in the market and you did nothing to add to the value, it is still yours alone. But note the word *passive*. If the increase in value is the result of *active forces*, the application of marital energy or resources, then the increase in value is regarded as marital property.

Marital property is anything of value created or acquired or earned during the marriage. From the day you marry to the end of the marriage, all your earnings are marital property. So all of Kirk's earnings during the marriage and all the employee benefits such as his pension are marital property. If it was acquired during the marriage and it was not by gift or inheritance, it is, with a few exceptions, marital. So in the case of Kirk and Karen, his pension, his 401(k) plan, her IRA, and the royalties from the books she wrote are all marital property and subject to equitable distribution.

Commingled Assets

The tricky assets are those in which a separate asset has been mixed with a marital asset. Disputes over such assets send lawyers' children to college. Let's begin with Kirk's antique car. A year before they got married, he bought it for $1,000. It was a wreck, didn't run, and had problems throughout the body and engine. Had he left it sitting in the garage the past 20 years and it had increased in value to $10,000, it would still be all his. But during the marriage he restored the car to pristine condition. He rebuilt the engine. He haunted flea markets to find spare parts. He lovingly sanded down the body, fixed the rusted and dented parts, and gave it many coats of paint. With Karen's help, he reupholstered and completely reconditioned the interior. He spent thousands of hours and several thousand dollars restoring the car. In other words, he poured his energy and money into the car during the marriage. All of the value added by his effort and all the value added by the marital funds he spent on the car are now marital assets subject to equitable distribution between Kirk and Karen.

The house is another matter. Karen took $25,000 of inherited money and made the down payment on the marital home. Over the years, Kirk supported the house, making the mortgage payments and fixing it up. Moreover, the house was purchased in joint names, and both of them signed a large promissory note when they mortgaged the house. Signing a promissory note and incurring debt is the same as investing one's savings. The house is clearly a marital asset. Whether a judge, after a trial, might trace Karen's inheritance through the down payment and order it restored to her before the rest is divided is anyone's guess. The judge does not have to do so. All of the equity in that house is marital property.

Types of Property

Property is anything you own that has value now or in the future. When we think of property, we usually think of tangible assets such as real estate, bank accounts, brokerage accounts, jewelry, and other objects such as cars, motorcycles, or tools. But property goes far beyond that definition and in divorce sometimes stretches the definition of property beyond what we usually regard as reasonable. The most complicated types of property in divorce are those that have an intangible, future value. One example is anything in the category of intellectual property. Suppose that Kirk had spent some of his evenings working in his shop inventing a super duper widget and had finally succeeded in patenting the thing. Even though we have no way of knowing if anyone would ever want to buy such a device, the patent is marital property and any money that it may earn in the future is also marital property. The books that Karen wrote are another example. They may or may not sell in the future. But the possibility that they may have future value and generate a stream of cash in the future makes her copyright and royalty agreement with her publisher marital property.

Another category of intangible property is stock options. An employee is offered the right to purchase shares of her employer's stock at a preset price called the "strike price." The strike price is usually the price that the stock is trading on the day the option is issued. It has no value that day because buying at the strike price would not result in a profit. But if the stock increases in value, buying it at the lower strike price would produce a significant windfall profit. During the 1990s, when the stock market was very strong, many people made small fortunes exercising the options that had been granted to them by their employers. In today's market, stock options are less exciting. But in any event, they are subject to equitable distribution.

So any possible right to receive income in the future that is acquired during the marriage may be marital property. In some states, a professional license or even a professional degree may be regarded as marital property. Even though such property cannot be sold or transferred, it may be the subject of an appraisal that influences the distribution of other assets. Divorce economics is not always the same as real world economics. The right to sue someone for damages may be marital property. Kirk gets injured in an accident and loses 2 months at work. He sues the person who injured him for economic damages such as medical expenses and lost wages and also sues for compensation for pain and suffering. His suit, called a chose in action, is marital property. If he wins or settles his suit, some or all of the award may be regarded as marital. Most states treat recovery for pain and suffering as separate property, but treat any recovery of economic damages as marital.

The asset that generates the highest professional fees in divorce is a family-owned business or professional practice. Say John owns a dry-cleaning establishment acquired during the marriage. A business appraiser is engaged to determine the value of the business and conducts a study to see what similar businesses are selling for. Because such businesses are bought and sold, determining its value is not complicated. But if John has a law practice in which his greatest asset is his own skill and reputation, the problem of valuation is more difficult. Many states do not permit lawyers to sell their practices. Even where lawyers are so permitted, it is difficult to sell what is little more than your own reputation. Notwithstanding this obstacle, most states will treat the law practice as a going business on the premise that it would be unfair to the other spouse not to.

Business valuation values two parts of a business. The first is the tangible assets such as fixtures, inventory, machinery, equipment, furnishings, and accounts receivable. These hard assets are easy to value and present no controversy. The second part of a business is goodwill. Goodwill is the intangible aspect of a business that is essentially its reputation that keeps clients and customers coming back. Goodwill is the difference between a successful and a failing business. In a commercial establishment such as dry cleaning or manufacturing, there are broadly accepted principles for valuing goodwill that reflect the real market value of the business. But the valuation of goodwill in a personal services business or in a professional practice is much harder to understand and often makes men furious when they first learn about it.

Suppose Patrick has a law practice from which he earns $300,000 a year. Let us also suppose that he has worked 80-hour weeks for 20 years to build the practice and that he still works very long hours. Let us also suppose that if Patrick closed his practice and went to work for a large firm, his salary would be $200,000. In the jargon of divorce law, John's entrepreneurial income of $300,000 exceeds his salary income by $100,000. Equitable distribution valuation would assume that this excess income is the measure of goodwill in John's business. That excess income would be subjected to a capitalization ratio to determine the value of this cash stream. Typically, the capitalization ratio is between one and five times excess earnings, depending on the appraiser's methodology. So if the appraiser hired to appraise the value of Patrick's law practice chose a "cap" ratio of three, he would value the goodwill of the practice at $300,000. He would also add the value of the hard assets to get a total value of the practice. This is a routine occurrence whenever a spouse has his or her own professional practice. It also generates large fees and great bitterness. In conventional adversarial divorce, it is not uncommon for each lawyer to hire an appraiser and, lo and behold, each appraiser comes in with a valuation grossly distorted in the direction of the paying client's benefit. I recently mediated a case in which the physician-husband's accountant valued his medical practice at $200,000 and the wife's accountant valued the same practice at more than $2,000,000. Each appraiser had adopted those methodological assumptions that would influence the result in the desired direction. The challenge for you will be to find experts who will give objective and honest opinions of value. More on that later.

The three stages of equitable distribution are identifying marital assets, valuing the assets, and then distributing them. We have looked at identifying and valuing the assets. Now let's look at distribution.

Norms for Distribution of Assets

Here are two hypothetical scenarios to help you understand distribution.

Harris and Melinda are in the midst of their divorce and are beginning to wrestle with issues of equitable distribution. In particular, they are having difficulty agreeing on the distribution of the value of Harris's law practice.

Harris is a successful patent attorney. He went to law school after having completed a master's degree in mechanical engineering. Although the couple was married when he was attending law school, Harris maintained a part-time job throughout, and by taking some student loans had managed to support the family. Melinda became pregnant during Harris's first year of law school and gave up her nursing job when their daughter Lucy was born. By the time Harris graduated and passed the bar exam, their daughter was 3 years old and attending nursery school. As soon as he passed the bar, Harris opened his own law practice. Using the connections he acquired during his short engineering career, Harris quickly built a successful practice. During the divorce, the couple agreed on a forensic accountant to do an appraisal of the practice, and the accountant submitted a report in which he placed a value of $350,000 on Harris's practice. The couple owns a house that has been appraised at $450,000 and that has an outstanding mortgage balance of $100,000. Melinda has told Harris that she is willing to swap the house for the practice, with her receiving the house and Harris retaining his practice.

Scenario One

When Harris opened his practice, Melinda devoted herself to helping him succeed. To keep his overhead down, he brought all his secretarial work and bookkeeping home each night, and she would get it done the next day while Lucy was in nursery school. When he set up the office, she did all the shopping to acquire stylish furnishings at the lowest price. She spent endless hours encouraging him when he would come home discouraged because business had been slow that week. She also entertained frequently so that he could invite potential business contacts to their home for dinner. Throughout the early years of his practice, she was his ever-attentive partner in every way. It was only after Harris had been in practice for 5 years that Melinda was able to cut back her involvement. By then Harris was earning enough to afford full-time staff and also take enough income that the couple could live comfortably. But even then, Melinda continued to serve as his sounding board and to entertain clients. He always credited her with much of his success. "I could never have done it without Melinda," he would tell their friends.

Scenario Two

When Harris started his practice, Melinda was also trying to launch her own career as an artist. She had been an art major in college and had always wanted to become a serious professional painter. So she told Harris that although she was completely supportive of his endeavors, it would be unfair of him to expect her to do his secretarial work at the price of her own dreams and aspirations. So to save money, Harris would stay up late at night doing his own typing and bookkeeping. Because Melinda had no interest in cooking or entertaining, he could entertain clients only by taking them out to restaurants, and that was very expensive. Melinda seldom was willing to go along because she found his clients boring. And because she was so absorbed in her painting, she really did not take any interest when he wanted to talk about the problems he was having at work. Now, 10 years later, Harris feels that his success as a lawyer is due entirely to his own efforts. In the meantime, Melinda has filled their attic with completed canvases but, with the exception of the few paintings bought by sympathetic friends and relatives, has sold almost nothing.

If we are looking at scenario one, the division of the assets is probably quite easy. Melinda was a full life partner in the creation of Harris's law practice, and her suggestion of trading the house for the practice does not cause a problem for Harris.

When he consults his attorney, Harris is told that Melinda's contribution to his practice was substantial and therefore entitles her to a substantial share. The lawyer quotes the law of equitable distribution that cites the contribution of each partner to the economic value of the assets. So Harris agrees to Melinda's suggestion. The house and the practice have approximately the same value, and he regards each of them as entitled to half. The case settles easily.

The problem arises in scenario two.

Clearly, Melinda was no help to Harris. She let him struggle while she pursued her own career, a career that turned out to be completely unproductive. Harris tolerated Melinda's "career," but deep down always felt that she was really pretty self-indulgent in staying with a make-believe career long after it was evident to everyone that she had neither talent nor a knack for commercial success. He is also resentful of how Melinda spent the rest of her time and the money that he earned. When Melinda wasn't painting in her studio, she was most often at the gym or on the tennis court. As soon as he started to generate a good income, she hired a housekeeper to manage the domestic chores and justified it by saying it was necessary to her career. To Harris's way of thinking, Melissa was just spoiled and lazy and spent years playing at his expense. The idea that she would claim half the value of the practice he created without help from her was downright infuriating. And her blithe insistence that he pay her alimony on top of that was enough to send him into a rage.

When he consulted his attorney, he did not get the answers that he wanted. His attorney told him that in the state where they lived, there was a presumption that the assets would be split 50-50 between the spouses and that the burden of proof was on the one claiming more than half. It was true that the law spoke of who had contributed what to the marriage and that if they went to trial and got the right judge, one who was not too lazy, that judge might award him more than half, perhaps as much as two-thirds and maybe, if they put in a persuasive case, as much as three-quarters. The cost of carrying the litigation all the way to trial would be in the neighborhood of $50,000, according to the lawyer, and Harris, who has done considerable litigation in the patent field, fully understands how quickly and how high the bill can run up.

Sure enough, when Harris and Melinda talk, Melinda tells him that her lawyer has told her that she is entitled to half of everything. She says that she ran the household for all those years and that entitles her to half. And besides, she tells him, if her career had been successful he would have been entitled to half the value of her paintings. In fact, she was willing to give him half the paintings in the attic so that in case she became successful he could reap the benefit by selling the paintings. Harris is furious.

Cost-Benefit Analysis

Harris has a choice in scenario two. He can act on his indignation and accept the costs of the struggle, or he can pay Melinda more than he thinks she is entitled to. Let's look at the cost and benefits.

According to Harris's lawyer, his best-case possibility in court is three-quarters of the practice. Melinda seeks one-half of his practice or $175,000.

If he tries the case and wins, she gets only one-half of that, or $87,500. If it costs him $50,000 in legal fees, his best-case-scenario gain is $37,500, which is the difference between what he pays her and what the lawyer charges him. Note that this is his *best case* outcome. If he tries the case and the judge awards him 60 percent, he saves $35,000—the difference between 50 percent and 60 percent. But because it will still have cost him $50,000 in legal fees, he will have lost $15,000 even though he "won" on the issue.

But there are some other downside risks. First, he might not win, in which case he will have wasted $50,000. Second, the judge could direct Harris to pay Melinda's attorney fees which could be as high as his—another $50,000—or part thereof. Finally, the time it takes will cost Harris not only mental anguish but distract him from his practice. With discovery, depositions, and court appearances, the case could easily consume 200 hours of Harris's time. During that time, Harris might have earned $100,000. So the total downside risk for Harris if everything goes to hell is closer to $200,000 just to take a shot at saving $37,500. If you were to analyze this strictly as a business risk it would be a lousy deal.

On a strictly economic basis, it makes more sense for Harris to agree to Melinda's demand for half than it makes to fight her for three-quarters. But for a man—a MAN—that is a hard proposition to swallow. As men, we tend to get swept up in the principle of the thing. Why should she get something she isn't entitled to? Why should she be allowed to use the system to extort money from me? Am I a wimp or what? I can't just roll over and get rolled over. What kind of man am I? Lawyers love this reasoning because it guarantees large legal fees. But it is still pretty dumb in the final analysis.

Melinda's lawyer has also admonished her that she could lose in a trial. The judge could find that her contribution to the marriage did not earn her half of Harris's practice. And the judge could tell her to pay her own legal fees. So Melinda has her own cost-benefit problem. Melinda wants to get her life started as a single woman. She does not want this hanging over her for a year or two. And she doesn't want the divorce to be bitter, because she knows that would be bad for the children. So she has considerable motivation to negotiate and compromise. Were Harris to accept 55 percent of his practice, she could live with it. It would give him at least a symbolic victory, and he might go away feeling at least a little vindicated. For Harris, another 5 percent of his practice is worth $17,500 in his pocket at no cost. When you find yourself in such a situation, think in terms of symbolic resolution. In the long run, litigation in this type of issue is a sure loser.

The Power of 50-50

Even though equitable distribution laws have been designed to calibrate justice better than crude 50-50 formulas, the legal profession has nevertheless defaulted to 50-50. Lawyers don't get sued for malpractice settling for half the assets. To fully apply the law and come to agreement on all the factors that the judge is admonished to consider is an intellectual task worthy of a Talmudic scholar. If you have an unlimited budget, unlimited time, and the good fortune to draw a smart judge who is not overloaded with work, you may get the law applied in all its subtle elegance. But don't count on it. I often think that the public would be much better off if the property distribution laws simply required the equal distribution of marital property. Perhaps such a crude standard might result in an occasional injustice. But in the long run it would save divorcing people millions of dollars in legal fees.

Think about the logic of the demand for more than half the assets. When you propose that you deserve more, you are also proposing that she deserves less. It takes a strong personality not to experience such a suggestion as an attack on her value and self-worth. The statement, "I contributed more than you did" becomes a reprise of the struggles that led to the divorce originally. It is very unlikely that she can accept the proposition. Those are fighting words for sure. Think twice before you say them, because in most cases, the price that you are going to pay is not worth it.

The Psychology of Equitable Distribution

The issue that troubles Harris in our hypothetical case is not the only one that affects the way men feel about equitable distribution. Men often are troubled by the belief that their wives were lazy big spenders or that the divorce was her fault. This is particularly intense among men who are the noninitiators of the divorce. "I don't want this divorce. I didn't do anything wrong. Why does she get half my property?" It is also an issue when men think that their soon-to-be ex-wives have better economic prospects than they do. The wife may have a more dynamic career. She may anticipate a large inheritance. All of these issues generate a strong sense that justice requires that the man get more than half. But all run up against the same norm of 50-50 division.

The management of the issue when you negotiate with your wife is tricky. If it is your intention to get her to agree to take less than half of a particular asset or to take less than half of all the assets, you will need a more persuasive argument than "I deserve it and you do not." You may cite her greater prospects, your greater need, or some other reason that does not imply that she deserves less. Because as soon as you introduce that argument you will be met with stiff resistance and your wife's default to 50-50.

The reverse also happens frequently. Your wife cites your greater earning capacity as the reason that she should get more than half the assets. If you have already addressed that issue through the discussion of alimony, her argument will not be compelling. But if she is waiving alimony and you have significantly greater income or prospects for much higher income than she has, the court may find her argument compelling. In many cases you can concede a little more than half and defuse the issue. Or you may default to 50-50. It *is* a powerful position.

The Link between Equitable Distribution and Alimony

In most states, the statutes and cases on both alimony and equitable distribution instruct the judge to consider one when deciding the other. Alimony is supposed to be based on need. So if a wife is receiving millions of dollars in equitable distribution, her ability to generate investment income may be so great that it reduces or even obviates her need for alimony.

This may apply to you, but on a statistical basis, only a very small percent of couples have this level of wealth. If you are one of them, your wife's ability to generate income will become an important subject of discussion.

A common issue that arises here is how much income to attribute to the capital to be received by your wife. If she has a million dollars and we assume that she can earn 6 percent, then we are assuming investment income of $60,000, but only half of that if we assume an earnings rate of 3 percent. The discussion of imputed income quickly becomes a question of risk. The more aggressively invested, the more income or growth a portfolio will generate in the short run. But the more aggressively invested, the greater the risk of a calamitous decline in the capital in a falling market. During the 1990s, when the stock market appeared stuck in a rising mode, people felt comfortable assuming very high rates of return. After all, the Dow-Jones Index has averaged growth of 11 percent a year over the past 40 years. But the memory of the stock market crash of the last 5 years has dashed the optimism that prevailed for so long. So when I mediate with lawyers present today, it is not unusual to hear the wife's lawyer argue that we can assume income of only 2 percent, or 3 percent if the portfolio is invested wisely.

If you argue for a higher risk level, be careful that your argument does not backfire. To the extent that you impute income to your wife's capital, thus reducing her need for alimony, you also impute the same level of investment income to yourself, thus increasing your capacity to pay alimony. This becomes a thorny issue and needs to be approached with patience and prudence.

When discussing income imputed to investment as it relates to the need for alimony, the problem of savings also arises. Suppose the investment income imputed to your wife's capital is $60,000 a year and she claims a need for $100,000 a year of income. Does that mean that she needs only $40,000 a year from you in alimony? If the history of the marriage reflects a pattern of annual savings, you will be presented with the argument that she is not obliged to consume all of the investment income but is rather entitled to let it accrue so that her investment grows each year. So, for example, she may argue that she is entitled to accrue a percentage to account for inflation and another percentage to account for growth, leaving $20,000 toward her annual needs. Ergo, she argues, you should pay her $80,000. This can become very contentious.

Most people do not have enough capital that they have to worry much about investment income. Most middle-class couples have some equity in their house, one or two retirement plans, and maybe less than $100,000 in liquid assets. By the time you divide up the assets, you are each worth a few hundred thousand dollars at best, and imputed investment income is not an issue.

Discovery and the Myth of Hidden Assets

We have talked about the Greek Chorus phenomenon in which would-be experts try to advise you about your divorce and invariably counsel you that you are about to get taken. One of the favorite themes of the Greek Chorus is that your spouse must have hidden assets that only the most aggressive lawyer will be able to ferret out. Usually, this particular bit of advice is aimed at the wife, who is advised that she must be careful that her husband (you) may have secreted away a bundle of cash somewhere. When this kind of advice succeeds in kindling the fears of the wife, the only ones who profit are the lawyers.

The truth is at significant variance with the myth. Hidden assets are a problem in very few divorces. Very few people are in a position to hide assets successfully. First, you have to have a lot of assets to hide them. This rules out most people. Second, it is easy to trace most assets through a paper trail because very little income arrives in the form of cash. Those who are in cash businesses, such as restaurant owners and small retailers, may have access to significant amounts of cash. But remember that in order to hide cash from your spouse, you also have to hide it from the government. The successful hiding of assets requires tax evasion. In my experience, couples who have been taking "hot cash" are each knowledgeable about how much they have been taking, and both are aware that a stash may be hidden away in a safe deposit box. So the actual incidence of people hiding large amounts of money from each other is quite rare.

This does not necessarily mean that there are not hotly debated economic issues. In cases involving professional practices or small businesses, it is not uncommon for the spouse running the business to argue that business is down and that this reduces the value of the business for purposes of equitable distribution and reduces income for purposes of support discussions. Recent reductions in income give rise to much cynicism, and "RAIDS" or "recently acquired income deficiency" has become a cliché among lawyers. Most of these disputes center on accounting interpretations of expense reporting, in which the spouse operating the business defends the expenses listed as legitimate while the other spouse argues that expenses have been overstated to distort the true income of the business. These are legitimate issues about which people of goodwill can disagree. But these are not issues of hidden assets.

How to Avoid the Problem

The best way to avoid the problems of your wife's suspicions is not to create them in the first place. In large measure, how money gets discussed during the divorce will reflect how money was managed during the marriage. If one of you was secretive or duplicitous about money during the marriage, you can expect distrust and suspicion during the divorce. But if your financial dealings with your wife were open and honest during the marriage, and you don't do anything to mess it up during the divorce, you should be able to avoid suspicion and unnecessary discovery.

You avoid suspicion by disclosing information openly and willingly. It is in your interest that your wife be completely knowledgeable about the family finances. And you avoid suspicion by not engaging in power plays like shutting off credit cards or secretly transferring money from joint accounts. Trust takes time to build but only moments to destroy. And suspicion is like mold in that it grows best in dark places. Your strategy has to be to err on the side of disclosing too much information. Don't wait to be asked. In this chapter, I have provided a form for a certified statement of assets and liabilities. If you are in litigation, you will soon be required to provide something similar, so you might as well prepare one now and provide it to your wife.

STATEMENT OF ASSETS AND LIABILITIES

ASSETS:

Description	Value	Title (J,H,W)	Date of Statement or Appraisal	Exempt? Why?
REAL ESTATE				
BANK ACCOUNTS, MONEY MARKET ACCOUNTS, CERTIFICATES OF DEPOSIT				
LIFE INSURANCE (CASH SURRENDER VALUE)				
STOCKS AND BONDS				
RETIREMENT PLANS, PENSIONS, IRA'S, 401K'S, ETC.				
BUSINESSES OR PROFESSIONAL PRACTICES				
TANGIBLE PERSONAL PROPERTY AND VEHICLES				
OTHER (PLEASE SPECIFY)				

GROSS VALUE OF ALL ASSETS

LIABILITIES:

	Amount	Date of Statement
Mortgages on real estate		
Other long-term and short-term debts		
Credit card debts		

TOTAL LIABILITIES

NET WORTH (ASSETS - LIABILITIES)

All assets need to be disclosed whether or not you believe that they are your separate property. And the values given should be your best estimate based on whatever documentation you have. If you are estimating real estate values, say so. If you have appraisals, attach them. For each bank account or brokerage account, attach the most recent statements. Do the same with retirement accounts as well as all debts. The more supporting documents you provide without being asked, the more comfort you will induce in your wife. You also need to realize that your wife's lawyer is nervous about committing malpractice. Lawyers don't get sued for conducting too much discovery. They get sued for failure to conduct discovery. It is not unusual for lawyers to routinely demand that you produce every check and deposit slip going back 5 years. Lawyers make money when they bury themselves and you in paper. You have to assume that your wife's lawyer is counseling her to be exhaustive in her research about the family finances. If you want to minimize the time and money required by this, you do so by minimizing your wife's fear that you are playing games with the money. By providing information freely, you also let her lawyer relax. So disclose, disclose, and disclose.

Some Other Difficult Issues

Pensions

There are two types of pensions: defined contribution plans and defined benefits plans. A defined contribution plan, such as a 401(k) plan, is one in which you have deposited part of your earnings and your employer has deposited some matching amount. There are several variations of the 401(k) plan, but each is worth whatever is in it. They are defined by what has been contributed plus whatever growth (or loss) has accrued. Your Individual Retirement Account (IRA) is also a defined contribution plan. They are accounts that accept tax-deferred contributions and can earn money that is also not taxed until it is withdrawn, usually after you reach age 59½. If you withdraw money prematurely, the amount withdrawn is subject to taxes and penalties. Defined contribution plans do not present valuation problems because they are worth whatever the balance is at the time of distribution.

The type of pension plan that can become a headache is the defined benefits plan. These pension plans have no account balance. They are a contractual right you have acquired through your employment, in which your employer has promised to pay you a certain amount of money when you retire after reaching some particular age. Most defined benefits plans provide some formula based on the number of years of employment and the income you were earning when you retired. For example, a state teachers' plan may provide that you can retire at age 65 and after you have completed 20 years of service. In many plans, your retirement income is a percentage, for example one-half, of the average income you had in your last 3 years of employment. So if you were earning an average of $80,000 in your last 3 years, your pension would be $40,000 a year. Pension plans vary considerably, with some more generous than others. Some plans, such as police and firefighters' 1's plans, allow retirement after 20 years of service, no matter how old you are. This can make them very valuable because if you retire at age 40 and you have a life expectancy of 85, you will collect the pension for 45 years. This could amount to several million dollars by the time you die. Some pensions are indexed for inflation, which means that the amount of the pension will increase each year to keep pace with inflation. There are many different types of plans and if you have such a pension plan, you will need to obtain a copy of the plan so you know what it is worth.

The problem with defined benefit plans in divorce rests in the manner in which they are distributed. There are two ways to distribute them, one of which is easy and one of which is difficult. The easy way is deferred distribution. The pension is divided when it goes into pay status. Using a document called a Qualified Domestic Relations Order, the judge directs the pension plan administrator to sequester some portion of the pension acquired during the marriage and to pay the appropriate portion to the spouse when the employed spouse begins to receive it. So assume a marriage of 15 years with a police officer who was employed as an officer for 5 years before he married. If he is getting divorced, three-quarters of the pension rights he has acquired is regarded as marital because the portion acquired before the marriage is not marital and whatever rights he acquires after the divorce is not marital. If he is projected to retire at 20 years of service, one-half of three-quarters, or three-eighths, of his pension will be subject to distribution, and if he and his wife agree to a 50-50 division, she will receive approximately three-eighths of his pension check when he begins to collect it. In deferred distribution, there are no complex calculations on which the spouses have to agree.

The more difficult form of distribution is called an offset method. A pension is similar to an annuity. You can go to an insurance company and tell them that you want to buy an annuity that pays you $1,000 a month starting at age 60 and continuing until you die. They will calculate what that would cost them, assuming that you live to some actuarially assumed age, calculate projected interest rates, and add a profit. Then they will tell you that they will agree to your request if you pay them $80,000. What they have done is converted the future stream of cash payments to you to a present value in which they assume that the money you pay them will generate enough income to cover their payments to you as well as earn a profit for them.

Any future cash stream can be reduced to a present value.

The difficulty arises when we try to establish the present value of the pension. The calculation of present value is based on a number of actuarial assumptions, including prevailing interest rates, the age at which the employee is assumed to retire, and whether or not the pension is indexed for inflation. The bottom line here is that, depending on the assumptions made by the actuary doing the calculation, the present value of a particular pension can vary greatly. One actuary might calculate the value of a pension at $100,000 while another calculates it at $300,000. As with many other expert witnesses that service the divorce industry, actuarial science has its share of actuaries who tilt their findings in the direction of the client footing the bill. So one problem in settling is the inconsistency of findings in actuarial reports.

A second problem arises when we try to distribute the assets. Suppose that the pension valuation is $300,000. And suppose that there is a house with equity of $200,000 as well as various savings totaling $100,000. Suppose further that the husband, who is the one with the pension, is 50 years old and, given the fact that he has to pay alimony and child support, cannot retire until he is 65. Finally, assume that the couple agrees that all property will be divided 50-50. If we do an offset in which the husband keeps his pension, the wife must get everything else. Although the husband can look forward to his full pension in 15 years, he ends up with access to no assets and no savings for those 15 years. It would make much more sense for this couple to do a deferred distribution in which the wife gets her share of the pension when it goes into pay status in 15 years, and for the couple to divide the other $300,000 between them. Now they would each have access to $150,000 in capital with which to rebuild their lives.

Offset distribution makes sense only when the present value of the pension is small or when there are a lot of other assets so that the husband still has some liquid assets even though he retains the entire pension.

If you are going to have a present value analysis performed, discuss the choice of actuary carefully so that you get one who understands what is required of a neutral party. It is not a good idea to get two expert reports because the predictable variation in the reports will simply cause cynicism and bitterness.

The Marital Home

Many couples have most of their equity in their house. At least one of you has to move out and establish another household. Let's assume that you are the prototypical couple in which your wife will be the parent of primary residence for your two children, ages 9 and 14, and the children will spend alternate weekends and at least one night during the week with you. What should happen to the ownership of the marital home? Your wife wants to stay in the house as long as possible. She is attached to the house. It is not just a house to her; it is home. Moreover, she is worried about the children, and she has read that the best thing for kids is to have as little disruption as possible. So she is very resistant to any scenario that requires her to sell the house. Whether there are practical options to selling the house depends on many other factors.

First, do you have the cash flow to keep the house? Many couples have bought a more expensive house than they can really afford. In these families, we usually find that both spouses are employed and that the entire salary of one of them is dedicated to paying the mortgage and taxes on the house. In such a case, the wife's household, if she stays in the house, could claim 80 percent of the family income so that you do not have enough income left, after paying support, to live a middle-class life. Not only do you have insufficient income, but because all your savings are tied up in the house until your equity is liquidated, you cannot consider owning a home of your own. You can live with such a situation for a year or two, and then you become resentful. So if your wife staying in the house means that you have to regress to living like an undergraduate student, you are correct to push for other options.

Second, what other assets do you have? The ideal scenario, if your wife is to stay in the house, is for her to buy your interest using other assets so she owns the house outright. If you have enough assets so that she can keep the house and have at least some cushion of cash, and if the cost to support the house is realistic relative to reasonable support payments from you, this may work well. She may be willing to live "rent poor," and that is a decision for her to make.

The least desirable option is for you to continue to own the house with her. It is difficult to agree on managing repairs and maintenance. It keeps your capital tied up and also keeps you tied to each other economically when you are trying to adjust to lives apart. Finally, most such arrangements provide that the house will be sold at some future date, most typically at the time the youngest child graduates high school. So while it postpones the inevitable, it still means that she will have to move. This often engenders continued resentment on her part. You should explore any amicable way to avoid this. As this book is being written, mortgage rates are at their lowest in 30 years. It may be possible to refinance with enough equity drawn out to buy you out, yet keep the house affordable.

Throughout these discussions, it is important that you recognize how emotional this issue can be for both of you and that you retain your patience and sensitivity.

Stock Options

In the 1990s, it was common for companies to use stock options as part of employees' compensation packages. During the wild stock market of that time, many employees became rich from their stock options. Consequently, stock options continue to fuel fantasies of wealth, even though the stock market is not so exciting anymore. Your stock options are a potentially troublesome issue because they might not be worth anything now. The strike price—the price at which they can be exercised—may be way above the current market price. Nevertheless, your wife will seek her part of the options because they represent potential wealth. If the options are vested, they are clearly marital and must be shared. But what if they have not vested yet? What if they vest only if you stay employed another 2 years? It has been argued that because you will be earning them, at least in part, after the marriage that they should not be treated as a marital asset. Courts have decided the issue both ways, and there is not a judicial consensus. So when I am working with a couple and there are unvested stock options, I counsel the couple to negotiate a compromise in which the nonemployee spouse gets some options, but not as many as she would if they were vested. The compromise usually resolves the matter, and I recommend it to you.

Debt

Debt is an offset against assets. Just as you subtract your mortgage from the value of your house to determine your equity, you generally subtract the value of all your debts to determine your net worth. Debt acquired during the marriage is marital debt, just as assets acquired during the marriage are marital assets. And as with assets, it does not matter whose name is on the debt. If it is acquired during the marriage, it is marital. Some debts cause more problems than others. When debt was incurred over the objection of one spouse, it tends to generate resentment when the objecting spouse is held equally responsible for the debt. I frequently see couples who have run up a lot of credit card debt in the period immediately before the separation. Short-term debt often reflects the disarray that accompanies divorce. Couples who are already incurring deficits incur more as they separate and begin supporting two households before coming to grips with needed budget cuts. So $10,000 or $20,000 of credit card debt can be accumulated rapidly. The biggest problem with credit card debt is that the interest charged is usually so ferocious that the minimum monthly payments become a large part of the monthly budget, thus requiring more and more use of credit cards. If that describes you and your wife, it will require immediate attention before it becomes too big to handle without a bankruptcy.

I counsel people to approach debt with the same pragmatism that I encourage throughout the separation. Incurring debt is the same as spending assets. If you have spent it, it is gone, and it does not matter that you should have, would have, or could have done something else had you been wiser at the time. Debt has to be paid off. Short-term debt should be paid off first. Because it is so costly, short-term debt such as credit card debt should be retired using any liquid assets available. If you have a house that still has equity, a second mortgage or a refinanced first mortgage may be a workable solution to retiring the credit card debt. It is all right if modest amounts of such debt remain for each of you to pay off in the future, but not more than a few thousand dollars each. And you need agreement that neither of you will continue to run up further credit card debt. Credit card debt is a measure of disarray, so you need to recognize that it reveals underlying emotional agendas that should be approached with sensitivity and gentleness. If you are the primary wage earner, you have to assume that your wife feels frightened and vulnerable facing the divorce. If you feel that she is using her credit cards too much, it is tempting just to cut them off, but this temptation must be resisted. Your unilateral move here will be interpreted as a crude exercise of power that will just frighten her into litigation. You must build cooperation around this issue.

One issue that often becomes a problem involves debt to one of your parents. Suppose your wife's parents loaned you $30,000 for the down payment on your house 10 years ago. When they loaned you the money, they did not specify a repayment date, did not require you to pay interest, and simply said to pay it back someday when you could afford it. Now you are getting divorced, and your wife claims that the two of you have to pay back her parents. You think that the money was really a gift and don't see why you should have to pay it back now after all these years. In some states the absence of a promissory note, a history of interest payments, or other indication of debt might allow you to escape without repayment. In others, a judge might or might not recognize the debt or might conclude that it was a gift to the two of you and therefore is marital property. This is a situation in which you can try to take advantage of the situation but sow long-term seeds of discord and resentment. At the least, it is clear that your wife's parents did not intend to make a gift to you to be carried away by you after a divorce. If you take the money that they believe you are not entitled to, you will destroy the chance of continuing goodwill from them. It is a genuine loss from the perspective of your children. The money, in some way, should revert to their family. This is where you get to act like a gentleman.

One final note about debt. About two or three times a year I see a couple that, through bad management or financial misfortune, have accumulated so much debt that it is strangling them. They will not be able to pay it off in the reasonable future, and their attempt to pay it off preempts their ability to thrive. For such couples I counsel bankruptcy. Bankruptcy, though regarded by many as too humiliating to consider, is actually the product of historical reform. It grew as a reform to the days of debtors' prisons, and it is designed to give people overwhelmed by bad fortune a clean start in life. You and your wife each have an absolute right to go bankrupt. If you file for bankruptcy, you can discharge all the debt in your name, including debt for which both of you are liable. Just because you are married does not mean that each of you is responsible for the other's debts. If her name is not on a loan that you have incurred and if you discharge it in bankruptcy, your creditors cannot seek repayment from your spouse. But if it is a joint debt and you discharge it, they can seek payment from her. So if most of your debts are joint and you are overwhelmed by debt, it is important that you declare bankruptcy together. If this is something you should consider, a consultation with a bankruptcy lawyer is appropriate. No one likes to think about bankruptcy, but if it the difference between your family being able to thrive or not, you should consider it carefully. (As this book is being written, Congress—primarily as a result of large campaign contributions and ferocious lobbying from the banking industry—is about to pass a bill that will make it much harder for middle-class people to declare bankruptcy. If you need to declare bankruptcy, you should be aware that time may be short.)

Cutoff Date

Assets acquired during the marriage are subject to equitable distribution. The marriage begins on the day you get married. But when it ends is a little more complicated. In most states the official cutoff date for equitable distribution is the day one of you files for divorce. The cutoff date is significant because anything you acquire after that date is not marital property. So if the day after the divorce complaint is filed, you buy a lottery ticket and win, you are under no obligation to share your winnings with your spouse. For most people, the cutoff date is not quite so dramatic because in the few months it is going to take to get things resolved, you are unlikely to receive a big windfall. But there are some routine acquisitions that may be affected. If your employer makes contributions to your pension plan on a routine basis, the contributions that occur after the cutoff are yours alone. If you get a bonus after the date, it may be all yours. If the bonus is a reward for work performed before the cutoff date, that part of the compensation would be regarded as marital. But if the cutoff date was a year ago and you get a bonus for work done since that date, then it is yours alone.

The date the divorce complaint is filed is an absolute cutoff date. Most states provide that the cutoff date is the day the marriage ended. However, this can be difficult to establish. If your wife tells you that she wants a divorce on January 1, it could be claimed that this is the day the marriage ended. But if you convince her to try marital counseling and you try that for 3 months unsuccessfully, when did the marriage end? Certainly the date of separation is a good indicator. But what happens if the two of you continue to have sex after you have separated? Is the marriage truly at an end upon the separation? The issue can get tricky when one of you wants to establish an earlier date than the other because to do so helps one or the other. This can become contentious. If the two of you have decided to mediate, you will probably conclude negotiations in a few months, during which time it is not likely to matter. But if you contemplate a long process or you contemplate a long period of separation before generating a document, it is a good idea for the two of you to agree on a cutoff date and to memorialize it in a memo signed by both of you. Your lawyer or mediator should raise this with you, but if one of them does not, you should raise the issue.

Preparing to Negotiate

In preparation for negotiation with your wife, you should develop your proposals together with the reasoning behind the division of each asset. The result should be a table showing all assets and liabilities that would belong to each of you if your wife were to agree to your proposal. Let's return to Kirk and Karen, whom we met at the beginning of the chapter.

Kirk has prepared a table showing his proposed distribution of assets between him and Karen.

Asset	Value	Karen	Kirk
House	$173,000	$173,000	—
Karen's IRA	$20,000	$20,000	—
Projected value of Karen's book royalties	$30,000	$30,000	—
Antique MG	$20,000	—	$20,000
Kirk's Police Pension	$350,000	—	$350,000
Kirk's Savings Bonds (exempt) not included in total	$18,000		
Kirk's 401(k)	$67,000	$50,000	$17,000
Joint Savings Account	$16,000	$12,000	$4,000
Karen's 2002 Jeep	$18,000	$18,000	—
Kirk's 1997 Honda	$4,000	—	$4,000
Household Furnishings	$30,000	$30,000	—
TOTALS	**$728,000**	**$333,000**	**$395,000**

Even though the totals look like Kirk has more than Karen, in reality he does not. First, his pension was valued on the assumption that he would retire at age 50 because that is when he is eligible. But with his alimony and child support obligations, he can't retire until he is 60 at the earliest. So the real value of the pension to him is less than the appraised value.

Second, the pension is all tax deferred. It will all be taxed as collected. Almost all of Karen's assets are free of tax. She keeps the entire house and has no tax when she sells it. She also has most of the liquid assets. Kirk can't get anything out of the pension until he is 60.

The pension is the most important asset to Kirk. If Karen wants part of the pension, then they should sell the house and divide the equity equally.

Karen reviewed Kirk's proposal with her lawyer. He told her that at trial she would probably get half of everything but that much of Kirk's argument had merit. A perfect 50-50 division would have each of them getting $364,000 at face value, $31,000 more than in Kirk's proposal. With the tax benefits she was getting in the house, she probably had at least half of the net tax value already. Karen thought about it and agreed to the proposal.

Kirk has made a reasoned proposal in which he has taken both his own and Karen's interests into account, and it has been accepted. Karen might have held out for a few more dollars, and he probably would have conceded. But the way this developed was quite realistic. For a small percentage of divorcing couples, the division of assets may be more complicated than that of this couple. But for most, the division will be close to 50-50 and will not be the most difficult issue.

"And this is Helen, my wife by a previous marriage."

Fourteen

NEW RELATIONSHIPS AND DIVORCE

AN OLDER WOMAN AT A COCKTAIL PARTY strikes up a conversation with a man.

She: So, what do you do?
He: I'm unemployed.
She: Well, what were you doing before you were unemployed?
He: I just got out of prison where I spent 20 years for murdering my wife.
She: Oh, so you're single?

As mentioned in chapter 1, divorce is a process with a beginning, middle, and end. Part of the end has to do with reestablishing yourself in the social world and perhaps building a new relationship with someone who might someday become your mate. Starting to date again is surely one of the rites of passage for newly separated and divorced men.

As I have pointed out before, within 2 years of divorce, 80 percent of men remarry. I'm not sure whether this is good news or not because I have seen too many men remarry too fast and for the wrong reasons.

Are You Ready?

Just because you are single does not mean you are ready to date. Where are you in the continuum of adjustment to the divorce? If you were the initiator, you are more likely to be ready than if you were the noninitiator. It is the latter who has spent less time coming to grips with the divorce and what it means. If you are still bleeding from the rejection and are acutely needy, you are not ready to date. For starters, you are not emotionally available to someone else—something that will become readily apparent to her in a short time. The last thing you need now is a series of new rejections.

How do you know if you are ready? In large part, it depends on what you want to talk about on a date. If you are still having trouble getting used to living alone, if you are still embroiled in a struggle over the divorce, or if you have not yet made peace with the divorce, you are not ready because what you want to talk about—the divorce—is not what she wants to hear. Your divorce, its aftermath, and its struggles may be exciting to you, but it is tedious to everyone else. And if you go out on a date with a woman who spends the evening complaining to you about her divorce, run away as fast as you can. She is not ready to date, either. People are not ready for new relationships until they are emotionally finished with their last one. They do not have enough emotional energy and are too needy to become anything but a drain on you. If you have a powerful impulse to rescue such a damsel in distress, check it out with a shrink before you get too involved.

I think that too many men underestimate how much time it takes to recover from a divorce and how much time you need by yourself to calm down. It is a mistake to assume that the first thing you have to do is get as many women into your bed as you can. Many divorced people tend toward promiscuity in the first months of availability, just to reassure themselves that they are still attractive. But after a while, it gets to feel tawdry and undignified. Slow down and take it easy.

Some men have an easier time than others. I have met many men who essentially moved from their mother's house to their wife's house. They have never lived alone, have never created or maintained a household of their own, and haven't a clue how to go about it. Some of them panic because they don't know what to do. Some move back to their mother's house and resume their adolescence. Others live in squalor or in Spartan apartments in which the television is the central piece of furniture. These are the men who are most desperate to get married again, just so they have someone to take care of them. Because they are also likely to settle for anyone who will take care of them, they are off to a troubled second marriage. If this profile even vaguely describes you, then you have a lot of work to do before you consider a relationship.

Acquire Competence

Unless a woman is desperate for any man who will have her, helpless men who live like they did when they were undergraduates turn her off. Women are attracted to men who will not be a burden, who can pull their own weight, and who can manage—or at least contribute to the running of—a household. If you don't know how to take care of yourself, now is the time to learn. You need to set up a real home, not what we used to call a crash pad. A tidy, reasonably well-decorated apartment, a reasonably equipped kitchen, and your ability to put an attractive meal on the table indicate a man who has pulled himself together and has something to offer. If you don't know how to do these things, take some lessons. Secure the assistance of some friend who has reasonable taste and furnish your home. If you need to hire a designer, tell him your budget up front. Have someone help you equip your kitchen and stock it properly so it looks like someone competent lives there. At all costs, keep it clean. If you can't pay someone to clean and do the laundry, learn to do it for yourself. Attending a cooking class is a great way to meet other people while you learn a new, useful skill. Going to a self-service laundry and seeking advice from an attractive woman on how to use fabric softener may get you more than clean clothes. Helplessness is your enemy. Competence is the aphrodisiac for the modern woman. A good pot roast is more likely to get you laid than a new sports car.

Even if it doesn't help you with women right away, your new competence will go far toward reassuring your children that you are squared away and can take care of them when they are with you.

Loneliness

For many newly separated people, loneliness is a painful part of adjustment. When you are used to living in a bustling household with children underfoot, living by yourself can, in the beginning, produce an aching sense of loneliness. Don't try to fill the void prematurely with another woman. This is the time for hanging out with friends. If you don't have enough friends to hang out with, now is a good time to ask yourself why not. Is it simply that you never spent the time to cultivate relationships with others? Many men don't. They rely on the incidental companionship they find at work and also rely on their wives to manage their social lives. It is not unusual to find couples in which the wife is the social secretary of the couple. She remembers the birthdays of friends and relatives, arranges the dates with other couples, and generally manages the emotional life of the family. Look hard at your history because if that picture fits your marriage and you feel lonely, it may be because you allowed your own social management skills to atrophy or just never developed them in the first place. So again, it's time for you to learn some new tricks.

Don't be afraid to call on friends and family. There is nothing wrong with telling people you are close with that you have too much unstructured time on your hands and that this would be a good time to invite you to dinner. If you crave more human contact, join something. Political campaigns, volunteer work, hiking clubs, or anything else that is meaningful to you will offer numerous opportunities to join with others, even though it may take some initiative to research the possibilities. This country has an incredible number of organizations built around every conceivable interest; you should be able to find several that intrigue you. Doing these things gets you out of the house and also gets you out of your head. While it's useful to reflect on your life, it is also useful to live it fully.

You should also consider therapy. Psychotherapy is not just for the seriously deranged. Find a competent shrink who can help you explore the feelings that go with building a new life alone. Your divorce lawyer or mediator should be able to help you find one. Therapy does not have to be long term to support you through the transition. Many men do not have friends with whom they can have intimate discussions, and many are reluctant to burden their buddies with a lot of personal stuff for fear of being seen as a wienie. And even if you do have friends you are comfortable with in this kind of discussion, their tolerance is not unlimited, and after a session or two they are ready for you to get over it and move along. So the therapist who is paid to listen to you recount your feelings and problems and is paid to help you work them through may save a lot of wear and tear on your friendships.

Another vehicle, unfortunately not popular with men, is a support group. Support groups come as coed and as men only. There is something to be said for joining a coed group because chances are good that you will be the only man among a dozen women—not a bad place to be. Support groups generally do not have open enrollment and do not take new members once the group has gotten under way. You may have to research and wait until a group near you is starting up. Churches are often a good source of such groups, and you usually do not have to belong to that congregation to join a singles or support group.

Although I don't believe it is good to overfill your life with a frenetic social schedule, there is no reason to spend much time feeling lonely. Of course, if you are one of those persons who never likes to be alone, maybe now is the time to figure out why you have never discovered the pleasure of your own company. It is good to learn to go to the movies or to attend social events and performances by yourself. Eating alone in restaurants is hard for many people, but having a nice meal accompanied by a good book can be a great pleasure.

The Discomfort of Dating

I received a call one evening not long ago from a friend who had been through a long, drawn-out divorce. "I have a date tonight. It will be the first time I have been on a date in 25 years. What do I do? What do I wear? Where should we go? Should I pay or should we share the check?" When you step back and look at it, dating is sort of an awful experience. Two people who have not met, or who have met but don't know much about each other, get together to see if they will like each other's company. They don't know enough about each other to be comfortable, and the sense of being on display and on the spot is acute. Both may be uncomfortable and fear disapproval and rejection. Although having a date is supposedly a good thing when you are single, many people I talk to, particularly people who have been out of the singles scene for a long time, are very ambivalent about dating. Sometimes it goes well, and other times it goes poorly.

If you are comfortable in situations with new people, dating will be easy for you. But if you are like most men, dating may initially be less than comfortable. I suggest that you keep it as low-key as possible. Trying to wow and impress a woman on a first date adds too much tension to the endeavor. If the two of you are going to like each other, it's easier to find out if the event isn't too much of a production. Meeting for coffee and an afternoon walk in the park may be much easier on both of you than dinner and dancing at a fancy club. If it's a performance for you, it's also a performance for her, and it may be a burden on both of you. Take it easy.

Actually, I am not convinced that dating a lot is really necessary. It's much easier to get to know people through common activities where you already have something to talk about and can get a sense of each other over time in a natural setting. Working on a political campaign, serving on the board of a nonprofit organization, or helping with charity fundraisers may do a lot more for you socially than blind dates. It's also easier to have friends introduce you to another person at a small gathering where there are other people to carry the conversation while you get to know each other. So when it comes to dating, there is nothing wrong with staying within your comfort zone rather than making a frantic dash to make sure you have a "date" every Saturday night.

Some Dos and Don'ts of Dating

DON'T GO ON AND ON ABOUT YOUR MARRIAGE AND DIVORCE. Keep the discussion of your divorce to an absolute minimum. You can report in a matter-of-fact way that you are still working out your settlement or that you have resolved the settlement and are waiting for the divorce to become final. But whatever you do, do not go into gory detail about the struggles you are having. Never use a date as an opportunity to unload about your divorce or your ex. It makes you very unattractive to a woman. Nor do you want to tell her how you are disillusioned with marriage. Women want to know that you are emotionally available, and a man still embroiled in a struggle with his wife is clearly not available. Wounded people still wearing their hearts on their sleeves are too tedious to bear. I would also suggest that if she starts doing something similar, she is not ready for a relationship with anyone. People in need of rescue are trouble, and your impulse to rescue needs to be suppressed.

DON'T GO ON AND ON ABOUT YOUR KIDS. Another thing not to do with people who are new to you is to talk a lot about your kids. Yes, they are the joy of your life, and every one of them is a future Pulitzer Prize winner or Olympic champion. But don't carry on. And don't get into your frustrations about visitation or the difficulties you are having working out your parenting arrangement with your ex-wife. No one wants to get involved with someone who is having custody and visitation struggles. It marks you as a bad candidate for a relationship because it spells nothing but trouble, with stepfamily issues in the future. (And, of course, if she is so embroiled, run away quickly.) When meeting someone new, carry your baggage lightly. In fact, your ability to do this without faking it too much is a good indicator of whether you are ready to be dating anyone. You don't want to appear needy. To the contrary, you want to present the appearance of someone whose life is in order and who has something to offer to others.

DON'T SUGGEST GETTING YOUR KIDS TOGETHER WITH HER KIDS. This raises something we have discussed before in the chapter on children. When you are dating someone new, the kids are a liability—not an asset. Do not bring your children together with a new date until you know her well and think that the relationship may blossom into something robust. It is hard enough to build a relationship with someone new without requiring that she also establish one or two additional relationships with your children. And if she has kids of her own and you want her kids to meet your kids, you are creating a very complicated social system. A group of six people involves at least thirteen relationships. It is much too much stress on a new relationship to manage such a complex social group. The expectations and fears carried in by the various members of the group create so much confusion and tension that the friendship can be sunk well before it's launched. Be very circumspect about including children until there is a substantial relationship in place.

DON'T TRY TO IMPRESS. Too many men are tempted to use a first meeting as an opportunity to parade their resume and impress the other person with how important they are. It is a big turnoff for most women. Your achievements, your possessions, and your accomplishments should be revealed slowly. If you are a high flyer, let her pull it out of you over several meetings. Let her keep discovering new, interesting things about you. Let her observe that you are modest and reluctant to brag about yourself. Women detect phonies quickly. If you are playing a role, it will show, and she will wonder why you are so insecure. Relax and be yourself. There is no need to sell yourself on a first meeting. If you have enough to offer to warrant another meeting, it will be evident. The two of you are just there to see if you want to get together again.

DO LISTEN MUCH MORE THAN YOU TALK. Women want men who will not only share their own feelings, but who will listen to women talk about theirs. As a general rule, in any situation when there are two of you and you are doing more than half the talking, you are talking too much. Just so you have a reliable benchmark, I suggest that you aim at doing one-third of the talking and let her do two-thirds. As she starts to tell you about herself, do not interrupt her with information about yourself. Ask her for more details. "And then what happened?" "How did you feel when that happened?" Active listening requires that you listen not only for the content of what is said, but also that you acknowledge the degree of emotion with which it is said. This is how women talk to each other. If she feels that you can talk to her as well as her girlfriend can, she will be very impressed and will want more. But don't press her for intimate details of her life. Let her disclose information as it is comfortable for her. Be interested, but do not pry. At the end of the meeting, you want her to feel that she had a good time just being with you and that it was comfortable. Then you will find her amenable to further dates.

How to Meet New People

There are so many single people that a giant industry has been spawned to help you find someone to be with. More recently, online dating services have become mainstream, where only a few years ago they were suspect. Many people I know have met significant others this way, and you will want to check out whether this is comfortable for you. How you go about finding people to date will depend on your social and personal resources. If you have polished social skills, a gift for gab, and self-confidence, you can meet women almost anywhere. Do what makes you comfortable and resist pressure to go where you are not comfortable. Older traditional ways to meet people through common activities and introductions by people who know you both are still the most dignified and, I think in the long run, the most effective. Many churches sponsor singles groups and Sunday school classes for singles that provide a structured, secure environment for meeting other singles. There are ample resources to help you find your way, but you have to choose the ones that are right for you.

If you are awkward when it comes to meeting new people and you feel really out of your depth, there are resources that can help. There is an entire new industry of "personal coaches," people with various types of credentials and competence who may be able to teach you how to manage a date. There are women who serve as "date coaches," who will give you feedback and help you through the awkward early stages of meeting someone.

The Danger of Rebounding

As you reenter the singles world, you are thrown in with the newly single, the never married, and some who have been single a long time. The range of need on the part of the women you will meet will be broad. Many women are just looking to meet someone and are quite relaxed about whether a relationship develops. These women like to date and to be involved and are patient in whatever search they are conducting. Others are not patient and are very eager to be married. So if you are needy and you meet someone needy, the two of you may move much faster than you should to an intimate relationship with expectations of permanence. These are the couples that remarry too quickly before they really know each other (or themselves) well enough to make wise judgments about marriage.

Rebound marriages are the product of hasty decisions and needy people. They get you in trouble because they put you in a relationship for which you are not ready. You have not yet thought through a perspective on your prior marriage and have not yet put it emotionally behind you. Your kids have not yet had time to settle down and get used to their new situation. If you start living with someone new before everyone has settled down, you introduce a level of new disruption that may be unbearable. One problem that arises is the resentment of your ex-wife. Even women who initiate a divorce may resent it when they feel that they have been replaced too quickly. If she has not yet disconnected from you, her jealousy—as unreasonable as it may seem—will be played out through your children. In order to build a successful new life, you need the goodwill and best wishes of your former spouse, if possible. You need her to accept your new partner as a good person and a good influence on your children. Bad timing interferes with this. And if the new woman in your life has children of her own and is also a victim of bad timing, you can assume that the rivalry between her kids and your kids will be a mess.

Although there are no hard-and-fast rules, let me suggest some timing guidelines. It takes about a year for most couples to adjust to a separation and to let go of each other. It takes a year or two to meet and get to know one or two new women. Some people are lucky and find great chemistry with the first woman they date. But most men need a period of experimentation and need to meet more than a few women before they identify someone with whom they would want to pursue a serious relationship. Once you have identified such a person, it probably takes 2 or 3 years before you know that person well enough to contemplate marriage. So I would expect that if you have given yourself and your children enough time and have maintained reasonable caution in deciding to remarry, that 5 or 6 years from time of separation to remarriage will not seem like a long time. Of course you may well do it in a much shorter period, but I think that taking it slowly increases the probability that your subsequent marriage will be successful.

Dating Your Ex

You have separated and done it well. You have worked out a fair agreement and a cooperative parenting relationship so the children are adjusting well. Somehow you have managed to preserve a sense of mutual affection and goodwill and still regard each other as friends. You are also each a little lonely and unsure about making your way in the world socially. What could feel more natural that hanging out together, going out to dinner, coming over for dinner, and even spending the night. It's understandable, but not a good idea. The two of you have endured great pain to create the degree of separation that now exists. At least one of you—and possibly both of you— probably went through years of deliberation and ambivalence and examined your relationship from every conceivable angle before coming reluctantly to the conclusion that it couldn't work. What was that all about? Although it may be temporarily comfortable to slip back into old patterns, it just sets you up for miscues, new rejections, and hurt feelings. You may think it's just a date. She may think it's a reconciliation between you two and that you seek to renew the relationship. Then when you don't call for 3 days, she feels rejected again. And when she hears you were seen at the movies with a date, now she is really angry. Were you just leading her on? Was this your twisted sense of humor?

Reconciliation rarely succeeds because the separation itself and all the negotiation that went into it have further damaged and eroded an already damaged relationship. If you and your ex are lonely, it is better to figure out how to go make it in the world than to slide back together. It's too confusing for you, for your family, and for the friends around you. It is also very unlikely to end well.

Age Appropriateness

It is a cliché that older men want to date younger women. Perhaps it is just an ego booster when a 50-year-old man dates a 29-year-old woman. It reassures you that you are still sexy and attractive, that you still have what it takes. It is also not a great idea. I have come to believe that as you get beyond a 10-year age difference, you assume ever-greater risks in a relationship. More than a generation's difference, particularly in such a youth-oriented culture, is simply an unnecessary risk factor. A fling or two, fine. But the pursuit of a long-term serious relationship spells trouble on many levels. I recall vividly a client I represented many years ago who was 62 by the time he was divorced. He started dating a 32-year-old woman and quickly got serious. He enjoyed the envy of other men when he appeared

with this great-looking younger woman and also enjoyed the adoring defer-
ence he showed her. He was a successful physician with plenty of money,
and he enjoyed treating her lavishly. For her part, she had never enjoyed the
kind of power and freedom that came with being adored by this older, mas-
terful, and wealthy man. So they decided to live together and then get married.

But not all was wonderful for him. He had a large circle of friends made
up of people he and his first wife had known for many years. But the
women in these couples rejected his new wife. They were not about to accept as an equal a woman young enough to be their daughter and young
enough to evoke wistful longings in their own middle-age husbands. So he
stopped being invited to events and soon found himself with a shrinking social circle. His new wife had girlfriends, but he had nothing in common
with their husbands, so social evenings with these couples didn't work well.
Even his own children avoided him socially, because it made them uncomfortable to be with their father and a wife who was their own age peer. They
were also afraid that it would somehow betray their own mother to embrace
his new wife.

Then there was the issue of children. His new wife wanted children and
he didn't. After all, he had been a parent for 35 years, had raised three children of his own, and now had two grandchildren. But the new wife pre-
vailed. How could he deny her something so central to the identity and life
of a woman? He hoped that he would be lucky and that she wouldn't get
pregnant, but 1 year after the wedding, she announced that she was pregnant and gave birth 8 months later, just before his sixty-fourth birthday.
Now he would have an adolescent child just as he started pushing 80, and
he could not imagine how he would manage that. Five years later they divorced. Life hadn't been easy for a man in his mid-sixties trying to live
with a small child. This couple had never been able to come to terms on
how to allocate the duties of parenthood. He resented that she was no
longer available to dote on him, and she resented his refusal to join in any
preschool conferences and other activities with the child. The divorce was
not at all surprising; they should never have married. Age differences are a
risk factor, and the bigger the difference, the bigger the risk. Your needs are
too different, your energy levels are too different, and even your values are

too different. Save yourself the trouble and date women who are at approximately the same stage in life that you are and who have as much experience and life sophistication as you have. It may save you a lot of grief later.

Conclusion

When you emerge from an unsuccessful marriage, it is natural and logical to look for someone new. And it will be a measure of a successful divorce if about 5 years later you have built a successful new relationship with a compatible woman. But the goal is not remarriage. Remarriage to the right person is but a reflection of the goal that is to live a rich and robust life after your divorce. You will not do this successfully unless you are genuinely finished with your divorce and until you and your children have settled down to new lives.

If you have sorted out your own feelings, have come to understand what you contributed to your divorce, and have emerged as a mature and interesting person, you do not have to worry about meeting women; they will come looking for you.

Index

A

Acknowledging convergent interests,
 165–66
Adultery. *See* Affairs
Advice
  about moving out, 178–79
  from friends
    case study: bad divorce, 17–18
    case study: good divorce, 27–29
    Greek Chorus Phenomenon, 49–51
  from lawyers, 113–18
    case studies, 18–19, 27–28, 110–18
    on family dynamics, 116–18
    legal, speculative nature of, 113–14
    maintaining skepticism about, 118
    on negotiation strategy, 114
    not to move, 179–80
    philosophical, 115–16
  from parents, 50–51
Affairs
  case studies, 60–61, 62, 63–65
  continuing marriage after, 59

  damage control after exposure,
   62–63
  as grounds for divorce, 85
  impact on divorce, 60–62
  by initiator, 59–60
  long standing, 58–59
  no-fault divorce and, 86–87
  settlements and, 61–62, 65
  as symptoms of marital problems, 59
  by wife, 63–65
  by you, 62–63
Affirming conciliatory gestures, 163
Age
  alimony and children's, 268
  appropriateness, dating and, 315–17
  emancipation (end of child support),
   92–93, 250
Agreements
  about children before moving out,
   184
  contracts vs., 157–58
  separation, 39, 93, 158, 184, 258

Alimony
  age of children and, 268
  anger about
    amount, 269–71
    duration, 269
    fault and, 266–67
    wife's unemployment, 267–68
  case study, 263–66
  court's interest in, 88
  defined, 261
  as difficult issue, 93–94
  equitable distribution of property and,
    288–90
  gender neutrality of statutes for, 93
  income disparity and, 261
  investment income and, 288–90
  lawyers' advice about, 111, 115–16
  length of marriage and, 270, 272
  marital contract and, 267, 268, 270,
    271–72
  permanent, 78, 94, 262
  prevalence of, 93
  principles for thinking about, 272–73
  psychology of, 263
  reasonable objectives for, 78
  redistributive, 95
  rehabilitative, 94–95, 261–62
  savings patterns and, 289–90
  settlement norms, 150
  taxes and, 95–96, 261
  for a term of years, 95, 262–63
  women's movement and, 93–94
Analyzing the issues before negotiating,
  168–69
Anger
  about alimony, 266–71
    amount, 269–71
    duration, 269
    fault and, 266–67
    wife's unemployment and,
      267–68
  affair seen as justification for, 61, 62,
    65
  attacking problems, not people,
    170–71
  avoiding blame through, 56
  death spiral of relationships and,
    52–54
  from divorce process vs. marriage
    failure, 1–2
  emotional divorce and, 33–34
  impact on legal process of divorce,
    9, 11
  in initiator, 45
  keeping disputes within mediation,
    147–48
  management needed in divorce, 11
  mediation and management of,
    144–45
  in noninitiator, 45, 47, 49, 54, 56
  reducing the scope of disagreement,
    143–44
  reframing hostile statements, 142–43,
    147
  self-defeating behavior and, 159–60
  Western culture and, 11
Assets. *See also* Division of marital
    property
  commingled, 279–80
  cutoff date for distribution, 300–301
  debt offset against, 298–99
  disclosing information about, 291,
    293
  hidden, myth of, 290–91
  marriage as economic partnership
    and, 276–77
  statement of liabilities and, 292
Attacks
  defending against, avoiding, 164–65
  discussing moving out and, 183–84
  feelings vs. behavior, 76, 157, 158–59
  on initiator of divorce, 45–46
  mediator's role in anger management,
    144–45
  neutral language instead of, 44, 46,
    169

on problems, not people, 170–71
reducing the scope of disagreement,
143–44
reframing, 142–43, 147
as self-defeating behavior, 160
tone of voice and, 163–64
unequal division of property seen as,
287
Attorneys. *See* Lawyers

B

Bankruptcy, 300
Beginning phase of divorce. *See also*
Decision to divorce
affairs, challenge of, 58–65
case study: husband as initiator,
42–44
common problems
death spiral of relationships,
52–54
Greek Chorus Phenomenon, 49–51
impulse to reconcile, 51–52
temptation of temporary
separation, 54–55
villain and victim roles, 55–58
defined, 12
if you are the initiator, 44–47
if you are the noninitiator, 47–49
Behavior. *See also* Attacks
feelings vs., 76, 157, 158–59
neutral language about, 169
self-defeating, avoiding, 159–60
success-promoting, for negotiations,
160–69
Birth control, marriage changed by, 5
Blame. *See also* Attacks; Punishment
avoiding for oneself through anger, 56
freedom from, in the future, 77
one-sided, unusualness of, 61
self-defeating behavior and, 159–60
talk about, avoiding, 76
victim role and, 56–58, 61–62
Bonuses (income), 236–37

Budgets
actual costs vs. estimates, 227, 230
allocating for children, 242–47
analyzing the issues before
negotiation, 168–69
bonus income and, 236–37
case study, 230–47
child support based on, 253, 259
discretionary expenses, 230, 239
form
allocating for children, 242–47
blank, 228–29
case study: Liz, 232–33
case study: Will, 234–35
comprehensiveness of, 226
overview, 227
good faith in preparing, 225–26
importance in negotiations, 225
increasing income, 241
as preparation for mediation, 148
preparing, 227, 230
reducing spending, 237–41
refinance debt, 238
rounds of reductions, 240–41
summary of savings, 240
total vs. take-home pay, 236–37
Businesses, family-owned
division of property and, 281–87
recent reductions in income and,
291
valuation of, 281–82, 286–87
Business model for divorcee
relationships, 71–72
Buying a house vs. renting, 190–91

C

Car expenses, reducing, 240
Case studies
advice from lawyers, 18–19, 27–28,
110–18
affair's impact on divorce, 60–61, 62,
63–65
alimony, 263–65

Case studies (*cont.*)
  bad divorce, 15–24
    adversarial litigation, 19–21
    advice from friends and lawyers,
      17–19
    children's comfort, 38
    cooperation as parents, 37–38
    decision to divorce, 16
    emotional divorce, 34
    fairness, 37
    initial situation, 15
    rebuilding lives after, 36
    resolution of later disputes, 39
    3 years later, 23–24
    trial scheduling and settlement,
      21–23
  budgeting, 228–45
    allocating for children, 242–47
    analyzing discretionary spending,
      239
    bonus income and, 236–37
    budget form for Liz, 232–33
    budget form for Will, 234–35
    increasing income, 241
    overview, 227, 230
    possible reductions, 239–40
    refinance debt, 238
    rounds of reductions, 240–41
    summary of savings, 240
    total vs. take-home pay, 236–37
  child support, 253–56
  custody
    children's needs, 210–11
    equality issues, 214–15
    household rules issues, 217–18,
      219–20
    medical treatment issues, 221
    overview, 205–8
    parenting schedule issues, 212,
      213
    risk tolerance issues, 222
  division of marital property, 275–76,
    283–85, 302

  good divorce, 25–33
    advice from friends and lawyers,
      27–29
    children's comfort, 38
    cooperation as parents, 37–38
    decision to divorce, 26–27
    emotional divorce, 34
    fairness, 37
    5 years later, 32–33
    initial situation, 25–26
    mediation, 29–32
    rebuilding lives after, 36
    resolution of later disputes, 39
    settlement, 32
  initiator for divorce, 42–44
  negotiations, 155–56
Cash flow, selling the house and,
    185–86, 296–97
Certification of mediators, 135–36
Change, as necessity in adaptation to
    divorce, 43
Characteristics of good divorce
  children comfortable in each
    household, 3, 38
  cooperation as parents, 3, 37–38
  emotional divorce, 2, 33–34
  later disputes can be resolved, 3,
    38–39
  mutual agreement on fairness, 3,
    36–37
  overview, 2–3, 33–39
  rebuilding lives after, 3, 34–36
Children. *See also* Child support;
    Custody; Parenting; Visitation
    rights
  age appropriateness of dates and, 316
  agreements about, before moving out,
    184
  alternating living in the house with,
    196–97
  budget allocation for, 242–47
  comfort in each household after
    divorce, 3, 38

custody and needs of, 210–11
custody preferences of, 90–91
dating and, 36, 311, 316
expenses in budget, 227
hiring a lawyer and, 122–23
household rules for, 217–19
informing about divorce, 74
legal process management and, 8–9
medical treatment for, 220–21
moving sooner vs. later and, 181
objectives for, 78
real home needed for, 191–92
relocation area and, 188–90
risk tolerance issues, 222–23
schoolwork and parenting schedules,
    212–14
selling vs. not selling the house and,
    185, 187–88
time off from needed, 209–10
victim role and, 57, 58
Child support
    amount of, 92, 250–52
    budget-based, 253, 259
    case study, 253–55
    changing over time, 92–93
    college expenses and, 257–58
    costs with pro-rata allocation, 254
    costs with pro-rata allocation based
        on income, 255–56
    court's interest in, 87–88
    defined, 249
    end of (emancipation age), 92–93, 250
    federal requirements for, 92, 250
    financial chaos from overconcern
        about, 259–60
    health insurance issues, 256–57
    legal formulas complicated for, 251
    life insurance issues, 257
    linking to time spent with child, 251,
        252
    mediation clauses for, 93
    mother as bargaining agent for
        children, 259

    parents' needs and, 259–60
    psychology of, 258–60
    state guidelines for, 92, 249, 250–52,
        254
    taxes and, 261
    who pays, 91–92, 249–50
Choosing a mediator, 135–39, 161
Church membership, divorce and, 35
Coaches for dating, 313
Collaboration. *See* Proposing the
    collaboration
College, child support and expenses for,
    257–58
Comfort
    of children in each household, 3, 38
    dating and, 309–10, 313
    dating your ex and, 315
Commingling of assets, 279–80
Community property, equitable
    distribution vs., 276
Commute, relocation decision and, 188,
    189
Competence, acquiring, 192, 307
Complaint for divorce, 98–99
Concessions. *See also* Negotiations
    affirming, 163
    not moving out and, 179
Conciliation, affirming, 163
Contracts
    agreements vs., 157–58
    enforcing using litigation, 158
    marital, alimony and, 267, 268, 270,
        271–72
Convergence, acknowledging, 165–66
Cooking, learning, 192, 307
Cost-benefit analysis, 286–87
Counseling. *See also* Psychotherapy
    after an affair, 59, 64
    agreeing to, when initiating divorce,
        47
    asking for, when not initiating
        divorce, 49
    divorce vs. marital, 72–73

Counseling (*cont.*)
informing children about divorce and, 74
overview, 72–73
reconciliation sought through, 51–52
during temporary separation, 55
Counselors, mediator referrals from, 161
Custody, 87–92. *See also* Parenting; Visitation rights
case study
children's needs and, 210–11
equality issues, 215–17
household rules issues, 217–18, 219–20
medical treatment issues, 221
overview, 205–8
parenting schedule issues, 212, 213
risk tolerance issues, 222
changing parenting arrangements later, 91
children's needs and, 210–11
children's preferences and, 90–91
court's interest in, 87–88
disparity in living standards and, 260
by father
communicating about, 195–96
increase in, 178
fears of fathers about, 202–3
gender and family roles, 204–5
guardianship issue, 89, 201–2
historical perspective on, 200–201
household rules, 217–20
joint, 90, 201
joint legal, 90, 201, 202, 211–17, 260
law of, 200–202
lawyers' advice about, 113, 114–15, 117
legal fights as uncommon for, 199–200
media sensationalism about, 199
mediation about, 141
medical treatment for children and, 220–21
nurturance issue, 89, 201–2

parenting schedules and joint custody, 211–17
parent of primary residence, 90, 201
parents' needs and, 209–10
as poisoned concept, 88, 200
punishment and, 89
residence issue, 88–89
risk tolerance issues, 222–23
shared parental responsibility, 90
sole, 89–90, 202, 203
Cutting off communication, 160

D

Damage control after affair exposure, 62–63
Dates. *See* Time
Dating
age appropriateness and, 315–17
alternating living in the house and, 196
avoiding talk about divorce, 310–11
children and, 36, 311
coaches for, 313
collaboration period and, 75
discomfort of, 309–10, 313
guidelines, 310–12
insecurity about, 35
learning to fend for yourself first, 307
listening more than talking, 312
loneliness and, 308
meeting new people, 310, 312–13
neediness and, 313
noninitiator of divorce and, 74
parenting schedules and, 211
promiscuous, 306
readiness for, 305–7
rebounding danger and, 313–14
recovery time from divorce and, 306, 314
relocation area and, 189
temporary separation and, 55
trying to impress, 311–12
while still living with wife, 53, 75
your ex, 314–15

Death spiral of relationships, 52–54

Debt. *See also* Budgets
  bankruptcy and, 300
  credit card, 298, 299
  division of marital property and,
    298–300
  divorce complicated by, 226
  to a parent, 299–300
  paying off short term, 299
  refinance, 238
  statement of assets and liabilities,
    292

Decision to divorce. *See also* Initiator of
    divorce
  as beginning phase of divorce, 12
  case study: bad divorce, 16
  case study: good divorce, 26–27
  changes in institution of marriage
    and, 4–5
  characteristics of good divorce
    children comfortable in each
      household, 3, 38
    cooperation as parents, 3, 37–38
    emotional divorce, 2, 33–34
    later disputes can be resolved, 3,
      38–39
    mutual agreement on fairness, 3,
      36–37
    overview, 2–3, 33–39
    rebuilding lives after, 3, 34–36
  conviction needed for, 45–46
  difficulty of, 1
  emotional vs. legal processes, 8–9
  initiator for, 6–7, 41–49
  legal changes and, 5–6
  living in the same house after, 52–54,
    71–75, 177–78, 180–81
  role confusion after, 52
  socializing after, 53
  streams of events triggered by, 1
  woman as initiator, 6–7

Defending against attacks, avoiding,
    164–66

Deferred pension distribution, 294–95,
    296

Defining problems by defining interests,
    171–72

Depositions, 101–2

Desertion, as grounds for divorce, 85

Despair
  deadlocked disputes and, 148, 161–62
  impasse in negotiations, 175

Dining out alone, 309

Discomfort of dating, 309–10, 313

Discovery, 99–102
  as basis for negotiations, 102
  depositions, 101–2
  of hidden assets, 290–91
  interrogatories, 101
  mediation and, 102
  overview, 99–100
  production of documents, 100–101

Disputes after divorce, good vs. bad
    divorce and, 3, 38–39

Division of marital property
  case studies, 275–76, 283–85, 302
  commingled assets, 279–80
  complexity of laws about, 96, 97
  court's interest in, 88
  cutoff date for, 300–301
  debt and, 298–300
  disclosing information about assets,
    291–93
  discovery, 99–102, 290–91
  equitable distribution
    alimony and, 288–90
    community property vs., 276
    cost-benefit analysis for, 286–87
    criteria for, 277–78
    cutoff date for, 300–301
    defined, 96–97
    equal distribution vs., 96–97, 276
    family-owned businesses or
      practices and, 281–87, 291
    increase in value during marriage
      and, 279

Division of marital property (*cont.*)
  equitable distribution (*cont.*)
    inheritance and, 279–80
    noneconomic contributions and, 277
    norms for, 283–85
    overview, 276–78
    psychology of, 288
    recent reductions in income and, 291
    stages of, 282
    symbolic resolution, 287
    title in one name and, 276
  50-50 formulas, 276, 287, 288
  future income, right to receive, 281
  hidden assets, myth of, 290–91
  lawsuits as marital property, 281
  negotiation needed for, 276
  norms for
    initial situation, 283
    scenario one, 283–84
    scenario two, 284–85
  pensions, 293–96, 301, 302–3
  preparing to negotiate, 301–3
  property defined, 280
  recent reductions in income and, 291
  selling vs. not selling the house and,
    296–97
  separate property, 278–79
  statement of assets and liabilities, 292
  stock options, 280–81, 297–98
  symbolic resolution, 287
  types of property, 280–82
Divorce, bad (case study), 15–24
  adversarial litigation, 19–21
  advice from friends and lawyers, 17–19
  children's comfort, 38
  cooperation as parents, 37–38
  decision to divorce, 16
  emotional divorce, 34
  fairness, 37
  rebuilding lives after, 36
  resolution of later disputes, 39
  3 years later, 23–24
  trial scheduling and settlement, 21–23

Divorce, good
  case study, 25–33
    advice from friends and lawyers,
      27–29
    children's comfort, 38
    cooperation as parents, 37–38
    decision to divorce, 26–27
    emotional divorce, 34
    fairness, 37
    5 years later, 32–33
    initial situation, 25–26
    mediation, 29–32
    rebuilding lives after, 36
    resolution of later disputes, 39
    settlement, 32
  characteristics, 2–3, 33–39
    children comfortable in each
      household, 3, 38
    cooperation as parents, 3, 37–38
    emotional divorce, 2, 33–34
    later disputes can be resolved, 3,
      38–39
    mutual agreement on fairness, 3,
      36–37
    rebuilding lives after, 3, 34–36
  measures of, 24–25
  moving sooner vs. later and, 180–81
  paradoxical method of achieving, 4
  possibility of, 2, 10–11
  premises of this book, 2
  proposing to seek, 68
Divorce law. *See* Law of divorce
Documents. *See also* Budgets
  preparing for mediation, 148–49,
    167–68
  production of, in discovery, 100–101
  statement of assets and liabilities, 292

E

Emotions. *See also* Attacks; *specific
    emotions*
  adult conduct in divorce, 12–13
  affair's impact on, 60

behavior vs., 76, 157, 158–59

cooperation of divorced parents and, 37–38

death spiral of relationships, 52–54

difference between initiator and noninitiator, 42

emotional divorce, 2, 33–34

gender and, 7, 10–11, 204

"happy marriage" definition and, 4, 5, 7

importance of understanding, 41

initiation of divorce by women and, 6–7

legal vs. emotional processes of divorce, 8–9

loneliness, 35, 307–9

negative attribution, 53

in negotiations, not acting out, 157, 158–59

in noninitiator, 47

self-defeating behaviors and, 159–60

tasks for collaboration, 75–79

End phase of divorce, 12. *See also* Dating; Rebuilding lives after divorce; Separation agreement

Equality, as custody issue, 214–17

Equitable distribution of property. *See also* Division of marital property

alimony and, 288–90

community property vs., 276

cost-benefit analysis for, 286–87

criteria for, 277–78

cutoff date for, 300–301

defined, 96–97

equal distribution vs., 96–97, 276

family-owned businesses or practices and, 281–87, 291

increase in value during marriage and, 279

inheritance and, 279–80

noneconomic contributions and, 277

norms for, 283–85

overview, 276–78

property defined, 280

psychology of, 288

recent reductions in income and, 291

stages of, 282

symbolic resolution, 287

title in one name and, 276

Equity, selling the house or not and, 184–85, 297

Expenses. *See* Budgets; Finances

F

Fairness

importance in negotiations, 154–55

mutual agreement on, in good divorce, 3, 11–12, 36–37

proposing the collaboration and, 68–69

pro-rata allocation of child support and, 255–56

working for a mutually acceptable solution, 174–75

Fault-based divorce. *See also* Grounds for divorce

alimony as punishment and, 266

change to no-fault divorce, 5–6, 86

grounds for divorce, 85–86

no-fault divorce vs., 86–87

Fears

about moving out, 178–80, 183

of fathers about custody, 202–3

Features of good divorce. *See* Characteristics of good divorce

Federal guidelines for child support, 92

Feelings. *See* Emotions

Feminism. *See* Liberation of women

Fending for yourself, 192, 307

Finances. *See also* Alimony; Budgets; Child support; Division of marital property

affairs and mistrust about, 58

bankruptcy, 300

cost-benefit analysis, 286–87

debt, 226, 238, 298–300

Finances (*cont.*)
  defining problems by defining
      interests, 171–72
  developing all options, 172–74
  discovery, 99–102
  discretionary expenses, 230, 239
  dividing moving costs, 193–94
  if she is moving out, 194–95
  implications of separation, 182, 183,
      184–87, 193–94
  managing, while still living together,
      73–74
  as mediation priority, 140–41
  objectives for, 78–79
  overspending and divorce difficulties,
      226
  pensions, 293–96, 301, 302–3
  preparing documentation for
      mediation, 148–49, 167–68
  production of documents, 100–101
  selling vs. not selling the house,
      184–87, 296–97
  during temporary separation, 55
  types of middle-class families and,
      226
  unilateral actions, avoiding, 74–75,
      119–20, 299
  valuation of businesses, 281–82,
      286–87
Freedom from blame, 77
Friends
  advice from
      case study: bad divorce, 17–19
      case study: good divorce, 27–29
      Greek Chorus Phenomenon,
          49–51
  age appropriateness of dates and, 316
  introductions to women from, 310
  loneliness and, 308
  loss after divorce, 35
  moving sooner vs. later and, 180
  socializing after the decision to
      divorce, 53

Friendship with ex, expectations for, 33,
      71–72
Future
  choosing objectives, 77–79
  developing a vision, 76–77
  differing visions of, 177–78
  divorce negotiations affected by,
      154–55
  income, division of property and, 281
  negotiations and, 166–67
  shift from past to, 146–47, 166–67

G

Gender. *See also* Liberation of women
  alimony and, 93–94
  emotions and, 7, 10–11, 204
  family roles and, 204–5
  hiring a lawyer and, 128
  initiation of divorce and, 6–7
  negotiation models and, 153–54
Gifts
  equitable distribution and, 278
  viewing loans from parent as, 299–300
Goals and objectives
  for alimony, reasonable, 78
  for children, 78
  choosing for the future, 77–79
  common, collaboration and, 67–68
  financial, 78–79
  remarriage, 317
  vision of the future, 76–77
  for your children, 78
Good divorce. *See* Divorce, good
Goodwill, maintaining in good divorce,
      2, 9
Greek Chorus Phenomenon, 49–51
Grounds for divorce
  change from fault-based to no-fault,
      5–6, 86
  fault-based, 85–86
  irreconcilable differences, 86
  as legal requirement, 84
  no-fault vs. fault-based, 86–87

separation as, 86
unimportance of, 85, 86–87
Guardianship, as custody issue, 89, 201–2
Guidelines and rules
    dating, 310–12, 314
    hiring a lawyer, 121–29
    household rules for parenting, 217–20
    for initiator of divorce, 46–47
    for managing (while still living
        together)
        day-to-day interactions, 71–73
        finances, 73–74
        new social lives, 75
        news of your breakup, 74–75
        parenting issues, 74
    mediator qualities to seek, 137
    for negotiation
        self-defeating behaviors to avoid,
           159–60
        strategic elements, 170–75
        success-promoting behaviors,
           160–69
    for noninitiator of divorce, 48–49
    proposing the collaboration
        emotional tasks to complete, 75–79
        key talking points, 68–70
    for temporary separation, 55

H

Happiness, grounds for divorce and, 85,
    86
Health insurance, child support and,
    256–57
Helplessness, self-defeating behavior
    and, 160
Hiring a lawyer, criteria for, 122–29
    assertive vs. aggressive personality,
        124
    calm and pragmatic approach, 123–24
    caseload allows time for you, 128–29
    children's needs understood, 124–25
    dirty tactics not used, 126
    fees reasonable, 126–28

gender, 128
    legal knowledge and experience, 123
    mediation supported, 125–26
    small vs. large law firms, 123
    star lawyers, 129
Hiring a mediator, 135–39, 161
Homemaking skills, learning, 192, 307
Household rules for parenting, 217–20
Housing. *See also* Finances; Selling the
    house; Separation
    alternating living in the house,
        196–97
    budgeting for, 227
    buying vs. renting, 190–91
    children's comfort in each household,
        3, 38
    co-ownership problems, 186, 196–97
    deciding where to relocate, 188–90
    developing all options, 172–74
    disparity in living standards and, 260
    dividing moving costs, 193–94
    division of property and, 279–80,
        296–97
    fears about moving out, 178–80, 183
    learning homemaking skills, 192, 307
    living in the same house temporarily,
        52–54, 71–75, 177–78, 180–81
    moving sooner vs. later, 180–81
    need for a real home, 191–92
    refinance debt, 238
    second mortgage for paying off debt,
        299
    selling vs. not selling the house,
        184–88, 296–97
    setting up a home, 192, 193
    working for a mutually acceptable
        solution, 174–75

I

Impasse in negotiations, 175
Income. *See also* Budgets
    bonuses, 236–37
    disparity in, alimony and, 261

Income (*cont.*)
future, division of property and, 281
increasing, 241
investment, alimony and, 288–90
pro-rata allocation of child support
based on, 255–56
recent reductions in, 291
Incompatibility, as grounds for divorce,
86
Indifference, as opposite of love, 34
Infidelity. *See* Affairs
Initiator of divorce, 41–47. *See also*
Decision to divorce; Noninitiator
of divorce
advantage for, 41–42
affair by, 59–60
anger in, 45
case study, 42–44
conviction needed by, 45–46
giving your wife time, 46
guidelines, 46–47
moving out and, 181
proposing the collaboration, 68, 70
psychological differences for
noninitiator, 42, 43–44
readiness for dating and, 305–6
refusing reconciliation attempts, 52
refusing to fight, 45–46, 47, 54
telling your wife, 44–47
using "I" statements, 44, 46
using neutral, non-blaming language,
44, 46
villain role, 55–56
Insecurity about dating, 35
Insurance
child support and, 256–57
reducing spending on, 239
Interests
acknowledging convergence, 165–66
defining problems by defining, 171–72
good postdivorce relationship and, 171
long view of, 173
Interrogatories, 101

Intimacy, cooperation of divorced
parents and, 37
Intimidation, as self-defeating behavior,
160
Investment income, alimony and,
288–90
Inviting negotiation through mediation,
160–61
Issues of divorce (legal). *See also*
specific issues
alimony, 93–96
child support, 92–93
court's interest in, 87–88
custody, 88–92
division of marital property, 96–97
out-of-state property and, 85
resolution as legal requirement, 84,
87–88
"I" statements, using, 44, 46, 182

J

Joint custody, 90, 201
Joint legal custody. *See also* Custody
consensual decision-making in, 202
defined, 90, 201
disparity in living standards and, 260
parenting schedules and, 211–17
Judges
legal rights interpreted by, 113–14
myth of protection by court and,
120–21
time pressures on, 120
variation in quality of, 120
Jurisdiction of the divorce court, 84–85
Justice, lawyers' concerns other than,
105–6, 107–8

L

Language
"I" statements, 44, 46, 182
neutral for
discussing moving out, 182, 183
discussing selling the house, 187

initiating divorce, 44, 46
  negotiations, 169
  tone of voice and, 163–64
Laundry, learning to do, 192, 307
Law firms, small vs. large, 123
Law of custody, 200–202
Law of divorce. *See also* Judges;
  Litigation
  changes in grounds for divorce, 5–6
  court-mandated mediation, 134–35
  emotional vs. legal processes, 8–9
  equitable distribution overview, 276–78
  grounds for divorce, 5–6, 84, 85–87
  issues of divorce, 87–97
    alimony, 93–96
    child support, 92–93
    court's interest in, 87–88
    custody, 88–92
    division of marital property, 96–97
    out-of-state property and, 85
    resolution as legal requirement, 84,
      87–88
  jurisdiction of the court, 84–85
  legal advice from lawyers, 113–14
  legal requirements for divorce, 84
  legal rights uncertain under, 113–14
  myth of protection by the court,
    120–21
  "nonrational" factors, 113–14
  overview of legal procedure
    discovery, 99–102
    motion practice, 102–3
    need for understanding, 97
    negotiation and, 97
    pleadings, 98–99
    trial, 103
  state as *parens patrie* (parent of last
    resort), 87
  as state matter, 83–84
Lawyers. *See also* Hiring a lawyer,
  criteria for; Litigation
  adversarial attitude of, 18–19, 27–28,
    105–6, 108–9, 153–54

advice from, 113–18
  about negotiation strategy, 114–15
  case studies, 18–19, 27–28, 110–18
  on family dynamics, 116–18
  legal, speculative nature of, 114
  maintaining skepticism about, 118
  not to move, 179–80
  philosophical, 115–16
as advocates, 105–6, 107–8
  aggressive, 119, 124
  analytic skills of, 107
  assertive vs. aggressive, 124
  "conflicted out", 126
  control of divorce process and, 18–19,
    29
  cultural handicaps of, 115
  dirty tactics counseled by, 126
  divorce process complicated by,
    109–10
  emotional reactions to, 25
  fees and billing, 123, 126–27
  50-50 division of property favored by,
    287
  hiring, 122–29
  letting them do the talking, 120–21,
    160
  limiting the role of, 122
  managing, 118, 122
  mediation resisted by, 132–33
  mediators trained as, 136–37
  myths about, 119–22
  negotiation missing from education
    of, 106–7
  persuasive skills of, 107
  proposing careful use of, 69
  psychological understanding
    inadequate in, 116–18, 179–80
  reality check provided by, 149–50
  "reasonable" financial objectives and,
    78
  role in mediation, 131–34
  star, 129
  striking the first blow, 119–20

Lawyers (*cont.*)
  thinking like, 107–8
  tough negotiations favored by, 153–54
  truth and justice not concerns of, 105–6, 107–8
Learning to fend for yourself, 192, 307
Liabilities. *See* Debt
Liberation of women
  alimony and, 93–94
  divorce law changed by, 5–6
  marriage changed by, 4–5
Life insurance
  child support and, 257
  reducing spending on, 239
Listening
  active, 162
  on dates, 312
  in negotiations, 161–62
Litigation. *See also* Judges; Law of divorce; Lawyers
  adversarial system of, 11, 29–30, 105–7, 108–9
  agreements vs. contracts and, 157–58
  changes in the last century, 106
  chronic, 34
  complaint for divorce, 98–99
  custody fights as uncommon, 199–200
  depositions, 101–2
  discovery, 99–102, 290–91
  emotional vs. legal processes, 8–9
  enforcing contracts using, 158
  interrogatories, 101
  lawsuits as marital property, 281
  motion practice, 102–3
  negotiation before vs. after, 97
  overview of legal procedure, 97–103
  pleadings, 98–99
  prayer for relief, 98
  production of documents, 100–101
  slowing down the process through, 175
  trial, 21–23, 103

  typical courtroom ending, 81–83
  urge to punish and, 57
Living in the same house temporarily
  death spiral of relationships and, 52–54
  difficulties of, 178–78, 180–81
  managing
    day-to-day interactions, 71–73
    finances, 73–74
    new social lives, 75
    news of your breakup, 74–75
    parenting issues, 74
Loneliness, 35, 307–9
Love
  indifference as opposite of, 34
  popularization of romantic, 5, 86

M

Marriage. *See also* Remarriage
  changes in institution of, 4–5
  continuing after affairs, 59
  legal definition of, 83
  rebound, 313–14
Media, sensationalism about custody in, 199
Mediation. *See also* Mediators
  asking for, when not initiating divorce, 49
  case study: good divorce, 29–32
  clause in separation agreement, 39, 93
  court-mandated, 134–35
  defined, 131–32
  discovery and, 102
  endorsement by mental health professionals, 133
  initiator vs. noninitiator and, 70
  inviting negotiation through, 160–61
  keeping disputes within, 147–48
  lawyers' role in, 133–34
  lawyers' support for, 125–26
  legal profession's resistance to, 132–33
  movement, 132–33

need for, 150–51
as no-risk proposition, 133
preparing documentation for, 148–49,
    167–68
as problem-solving approach, 145–46
proposing the collaboration and, 69
skepticism about, on wife's part, 161
styles of, 138–39
Mediators. *See also* Mediation
agenda set by, 140–41
anger management and, 144–45
boring dialogue promoted by, 147
choosing, 135–39, 161
discussion management by, 141–48
experience needed by, 136
immediate concerns of, 140–41
impasse in negotiations and, 175
lawyer consultation recommended by,
    149–50
legal knowledge needed by, 136–37
need for, 150–51
options explored with, 145–46
personal attacks and, 144–45, 165
preparing documentation for, 148–49,
    167–68
reframing by, 142–43, 147
role of, 131–32, 141–42
scope of disagreement reduced by,
    143–44
shift from past to future encouraged
    by, 146–47
styles of mediation, 138–39
tone of voice in negotiations and, 164
training and certification for, 135–36
using, 139–42
Medical insurance, reducing spending
    on, 239
Medical treatment for children, 220–21
Meeting new people, 310, 312–13
Middle phase of divorce, 12. *See also*
    Children; Finances; Housing;
    Separation
Minimizing differences, 165–66

Money. *See* Finances
Motion practice, 102–3
Moving out. *See also* Housing;
    Separation
advice about, 178–79
agreements about children before,
    184
buying vs. renting, 190–91
children's comfort in each household,
    3, 38
deciding where to relocate, 188–90
deciding who leaves, 178–80
developing all options, 172–74
dividing moving costs, 183–84
fears about, 178–80, 183
initiator and, 181
learning to fend for yourself, 192, 307
letter acknowledging reasons for,
    178–79
loneliness after, 35, 307–9
need for a real home, 191–92
neutral language about, 182, 183
proposing the collaboration and,
    182–84
refusing, and concessions hoped for,
    179
selling vs. not selling the house,
    184–88, 296–97
setting up a home, 192, 193
sooner rather than later, 180–81
by wife, 195–96
Myths
about lawyers, 119–22
hidden assets, 290–91

N
Negative attribution, 53
Negotiations. *See also* Alimony; Child
    support; Division of marital
    property; Mediation; Proposing
    the collaboration
acknowledging convergent interests,
    165–66

Negotiations (*cont.*)
   active listening in, 162
   affirming conciliatory gestures in,
      163
   before vs. after litigation, 97
   agreements vs. contracts, 157–58
   analyzing the issues before, 168–69
   attacking problems, not people,
      170–71
   behavior vs. feelings in, 157, 158–59
   business vs. divorce, 154
   case study, 155–56
   commitment to staying in, 69–70
   common goals and, 67–68
   consensual decision-making for, 153
   defining problems by defining
      interests, 171–72
   developing all options, 172–74
   discovery as basis for, 102
   future affected by, 154–55
   future vs. past and, 166–67
   if she is moving out, 195–96
   impasse in, 175
   increase in negotiated settlements,
      106
   inviting, through mediation, 160–61
   lawyer bills and, 127
   lawyers' advice about, 114
   lawyers not educated for, 106–7
   listening more than talking, 161–62
   marital problems replayed in, 156–57
   minimizing differences, 165–66
   models, men's vs. women's, 153–54
   needed for settlements, 36–37
   neutral language for, 169
   not taking the bait, 164–65
   parenting and, 155
   planning and preparing for, 167–69,
      301–3
   self-defeating behaviors to avoid,
      159–60
   selling the house and, 187
   of separation, 181–84
   strategic elements of, 170–75
   success-promoting behaviors, 160–69
   summarizing what you've heard in,
      162
   support, budgets and, 225
   tone of voice in, 163–64
   working for a mutually acceptable
      solution, 174–75
No-fault divorce. *See also* Grounds for
      divorce
   alimony and, 267
   change from fault-based divorce to,
      5–6, 86
   fault-based divorce vs., 86–87
Noninitiator of divorce, 47–49. *See also*
      Initiator of divorce
   anger in, 45, 47, 49, 54, 56
   case study, 42–44
   dating and, 74
   in divorce counseling, 73
   finding help, 48
   guidelines, 48–49
   moving out and, 181
   proposing the collaboration, 68, 70
   psychological differences for initiator,
      42
   readiness for dating and, 305–6
   reconciliation sought by, 51–52
   taking time to gain perspective, 48
   victim role, 56–58, 61–62
   what to ask of your wife, 48–49
Norms for division of marital property
   initial situation, 283
   scenario one, 283–84
   scenario two, 284–85
Nurturance, as custody issue, 89,
      201–2

O

Objectives. *See* Goals and objectives
Offset method of pension distribution,
      295–96
Online dating services, 312–13

Options
  developing all, 172–74
  searching for, 145–46

P

Parens patrie (parent of last resort), 87
Parenting. *See also* Child support;
    Children; Custody; Visitation
    rights
  budget form preparation and, 227
  cooperation in good divorce, 3,
    37–38, 72
  custody and parents' needs, 209–10
  defining problems by defining
    interests, 171–72
  gender and family roles, 204–5
  household rules, 217–20
  managing issues while still living
    together, 74
  as mediation priority, 140
  medical treatment for children and,
    220–21
  mother as primary residential parent,
    178
  need for time off from children,
    209–10
  negotiations' importance for, 155
  risk tolerance issues, 222–23
  schedules and joint custody, 211–17
    consecutive nights, 214
    equality issue, 214–17
    long weekends, 214
    weekends, 211
    weeknights, 212–14
  state as *parens patrie* (parent of last
    resort), 87
  victim role and, 57
Parents, advice from, 50–51
Passivity, as self-defeating behavior,
  160
Past
  coming to terms with, 75–76
  negotiations and, 166–67

punishing wife for, 76
  shift to future from, 146–47,
    166–67
Pensions
  cutoff date for distribution and, 301
  deferred distribution, 294–95, 296
  defined benefits plans, 294–96
  defined contribution plans, 293
  division of property and, 293–96, 301,
    302–3
  offset method of distribution,
    295–96
  taxes and, 302
Permanent alimony, 78, 94, 262
Phases of divorce, 12
Planning for negotiations, 167–69
Pleadings, 98–99
Prayer for relief, 98
Preparing for negotiations, 167–69,
    301–3. *See also* Budgets
Pretrial motions, 102–3
Production of documents, 100–101
Promiscuity, 306
Property. *See* Division of marital
    property
Property, defined, 280
Proposing the collaboration, 67–79
  common goals and, 67–68
  emotional tasks to complete
    choosing objectives, 77–79
    coming to terms with the past,
      75–76
    developing a vision of the future,
      76–77
  guidelines for relating to your wife
    about
    day-to-day interactions, 71–73
    finances, 73–74
    managing news of your breakup,
      74–75
    new social lives, 75
    parenting issues, 74
  initiator vs. noninitiator and, 68, 70

Proposing the collaboration (*cont.*)
  key talking points
    commitment to resolve all issues, 69–70
    desire for fair results, 68–69
    seeking a decent divorce, 68
    using a mediator, 69
    using lawyers carefully, 69
  moving out and, 182–84
  positive stance for, 70
Provocations. *See* Attacks
Psychology of divorce issues
  alimony, 263
  child support, 258–60
  equitable distribution of property, 288
  initiator vs. noninitiator, 42, 43–44
Psychotherapy. *See also* Counseling
  for noninitiator, 48
  rebuilding a life and, 308–9
  therapists as mediators, 139
Punishment
  alimony and, 265–67, 273
  custody and, 89
  early divorce law and, 109
  grounds for divorce and, 87
  for infidelity, 61, 65
  litigation as, 57
  for the past, 76

Q
"Quickie" divorces, 84–85

R
Readiness for dating, 305–7
Rebounding, danger of, 313–14
Rebuilding lives after divorce. *See also* Dating
  case study: bad divorce, 23–24, 36
  case study: good divorce, 32–33, 36
  as characteristic of good divorce, 3, 34–36
  developing a vision of the future, 76–77

as measure of good divorce, 24–25, 34–35
  moving sooner vs. later and, 180–81
  as purpose of divorce, 1
  success and divorce process, 1–2, 3, 25
Reconciliation
  dating your ex, 314–15
  impulse to, 51–52
Recovery time for divorce, 306, 314
Redistributive alimony, 95
Reframing
  attacking problems, not people, 170–71
  by mediators, 142–43, 147
Rehabilitative alimony, 94–95, 261–62
Rejection
  feelings of, in noninitiator, 47
  managing anger from, 56
  victim role and, 56, 58
Relationships, new. *See* Dating
Remarriage. *See also* Marriage
  divorce rate for, 35
  goal of, 317
  percent of divorced population remarrying, 1, 4, 35, 77
  rebound, 313–14
Renting vs. buying a house, 190–91
Residency
  as custody issue, 88–89
  jurisdiction of the divorce court and, 84–85
Resolution
  of later disputes, 3, 38–39
  required for issues of divorce, 84, 87–88
  symbolic, 287
Risk tolerance, as parenting issue, 222–23
Roles
  confusion after decision to divorce, 52
  family, gender and, 204–5

of lawyers in mediation, 133–34
mediator, 131–32, 141–42
victim, affairs and, 61–62
victim, noninitiator as, 56–58
villain, initiator as, 55–56
Rules. *See* Guidelines and rules

S

Savings patterns, alimony and, 289–90
Schedules and joint custody, 211–17
    consecutive nights, 214
    equality issue, 214–16
    long weekends, 214
    weekends, 211
    weeknights, 212–14
Self-determination, mediation styles
        and, 138
Self-discipline, required for good
        divorce, 12–13
Selling the house
    cash flow issue for, 185–86, 296–97
    children's welfare and, 185, 187–88
    delaying for a year or two, 188
    equity issue for, 186–87, 297
    house vs. home and, 184–85
Separation
    alternating living in the house,
        196–97
    buying vs. renting a house, 190–91
    dating your ex, 314–15
    deciding where to relocate, 188–90
    deciding who leaves, 178–80
    differing visions of the future and,
        177–78
    dividing moving costs, 193–94
    fears about moving out, 178–80, 183
    financial implications of, 182, 183,
        184–87, 193–94
    as grounds for divorce, 86
    if she is moving out, 194–96
    learning to fend for yourself, 192, 307
    letter acknowledging reasons for
        move, 178–79

loneliness after, 35, 307–9
moving sooner vs. later, 180–81
need for, 177
need for a real home, 191–92
negotiating, 181–83
property rights and, 179
rules for temporary, 55
setting up a home, 192, 193
temporary, temptation of, 54–55
Separation agreement. *See also*
        Alimony; Child support
    attempting to enforce in court, 158
    children and, 184
    college expenses in, 258
    mediation clause in, 39, 93
Settlements. *See also* Alimony; Child
        support; Custody; Division of
        marital property; Negotiations
    affairs and, 61–62, 65
    case study: bad divorce, 21–23,
        36–37
    case study: good divorce, 32, 37
    failure rate of, 36
    increase in negotiated settlements,
        108
    mediation clauses in, 39
    mutual fairness in good divorce, 3,
        11–12, 36–37
    negotiation needed for, 36–37
Shaming. *See* Attacks; Blame
Shared parental responsibility (legal
        term), 90
Sole custody, 89–90, 202, 203
Spending. *See* Budgets; Finances
Spousal maintenance. *See* Alimony
State guidelines for child support, 92,
        249, 250–52, 254
Stock options, division of property and,
        280–81, 297–98
Styles of mediation, 138–39
Summarizing what you've heard, 162
Support. *See* Alimony; Child support
Support groups, 309

T

Taxes
  alimony and, 95–96, 261
  child support and, 261
  pensions and, 302
Telling others about the divorce. *See also* Friends, advice from
  children, 74
  custody by father and, 195–96
  on dates, avoiding, 310–11
  friends and relatives, 74–75
  reasonable time before, 48
Threatening, as self-defeating behavior, 160
Time. *See also* Future; Past
  alimony for a term of years, 95, 262–63
  child support linked to time with child, 251, 252
  cutoff date for equitable distribution, 300–301
  dating guidelines for timing, 314
  end of child support, 92–93, 250
  for recovery from divorce, 306, 314
Title to property, equitable distribution and, 276
Tone of voice in negotiations, 163–64
Training of mediators, 135–36
Trials
  case study: bad divorce, 21–23
  decrease in, 108
  depositions of witnesses, 101–2
  expert witnesses, 101–2
  fears about moving out and, 178–79
  overview, 103
Trust
  affairs and mistrust about finances, 58
  destroyed by lawyers, 120
Truth, lawyers' concerns other than, 107–8, 109–10
Tuition, child support and, 257–58
Tutoring, reducing spending on, 240

U

Unhappiness, as grounds for divorce, 85, 86

V

Valuation of businesses, 281–82, 286–87
Victim role
  affairs and, 61–62
  in noninitiator, 56–58
Villain role, 55–56
Visitation rights. *See also* Custody; Parenting
  court's interest in, 87–88
  as integral to custody issues, 89
  mediation about, 141

W

Web sites, mediation-related, 161
Weekends
  long, 214
  parenting schedules for, 211, 214
Weeknights
  consecutive, 214
  parenting schedules for, 212–14
Witnesses
  deposition of, 101
  expert, 101–2
Women's movement. *See* Liberation of women
World Wars I and II, marriage changed by, 4–5